BOWLFOOD

C·O·O·K·B·O·O·K

BOWLFOOD

C·O·O·K·B·O·O·K

LYNNE ARONSON
&
ELIZABETH SIMON

Illustrations by Laurie LaFrance

WORKMAN PUBLISHING · NEW YORK

Library of Congress Cataloging-in Publication Data
Aronson, Lynne.
Bowlfood cookbook/by Lynne Aronson and Elizabeth Simon:
Illustrations by Laurie LaFrance.
p. cm.
Includes index.
ISBN 0-7611-0002-4 (pbk.)—ISBN 0-7611-1457-2 (hc.)
1. Cookery. I. Simon, Elizabeth (Elizabeth F.) II. Title.
TX 714.A757 1999   641.5—dc21
99-17895   CIP

Cover and book design by Janet Vicario
Front cover photograph by Louis Wallach / Back cover photos by Sara Matthews

Workman books are available at special discounts when purchased in bulk for premiums and sales
promotions as well as for fund-raising or educational use. Special editions or book excerpts can be
created to specification. For details, contact the Special Sales Director at the address below.

WORKMAN PUBLISHING COMPANY, INC.
708 Broadway
New York, NY 10003-9555

First printing April 1999
10 9 8 7 6 5 4 3 2 1

To the ones who show us every day the simple,
true pleasure of eating bowl food:
Jasper, Chet, Bean Boy and Wei-wei Dyl,
Ezra Spoon and Ping

THANKS TO

Peter Workman and Suzanne Rafer for enjoying their lunch so much at Lola Bowla that they invited us to write this book • Tom Odeen for generously accommodating us with the time and place to carry out our mission • Charly Uman for always helping no matter what it takes • Mr. Chen a.k.a. Chen Bao-ping, master chef and helping hands, xie-xie • Molly Aronson for her ability to "telebake" and her delicious pastries • Charles Webb for his refined pastry know-how • Coo-Coo a.k.a. Jose Espana for lunch after lunch after lunch • Marcy Singer for her good humor and judgment while helping us test recipes • Peter Parker for his bar humor and palate • Adam Barnett for his undying spirit • Mille Simon for her hours of devoted searching and tagging, love you Mom • Vickie Tillman for her eternal support • Toni Donofrio for her friendship • Tina Thompson for her consistent professionalism • Evie Righter for her seeing it our way • Lizzy for her hours of digging • Victor for his honesty while tasting all of our recipes • Pearl Aronson for her lovingly made bowls of soup, thanks Mom • Gayle Simon for her support and puddy trick at Lola • The entire staff of both Lola and Lola Bowla for their upbeat spirit and support • The amazing team of professionals at Workman, without whom this book would not have been possible • Our dads and da kids, Rachel "Bagel," Brian "Binky," Traci "Garrett," Zac "Noodlehead," and Noah "Peanut."

Contents

Chapter 1

Get a soup or stew or sauce off right—with a great stock or broth. Ours are easy to prepare, and their intriguing flavors will dazzle you. There are fragrant stocks for Asian-based bowls and for Mediterranean bowls. They open the door to endless possibilities.

Chapter 2

Light and brothy or hearty and filling, soup is natural bowlfood. Ladle out and enjoy Corn Soup with Ricotta and Spinach Dumplings, Hot-and-Sour Chowder, Lamb with Orzo and Curry Broth, and Green Thumb Gazpacho, to name just a few.

Chapter 3

These are luscious dishes with richly satisfying aromas and deep, flavorful tastes. Mojo-Marinated Chicken, Roasted Pork Loin with Honey-Hoisin Marinade, and Chili-Roasted Vegetables all make for delectably big bowls.

Chapter 4

A little touch of the East, a little touch of the West, and a lot of good slurping and supping. Nutty Rice Noodles with Tangy Beef and Watercress, Pearl Pasta with Fresh Peas and Gorgonzola, Mango and Coconut Rice, and Thai Paella—all delicious in a bowl.

Chapter 5
DUMPLINGS AND DOODADS

The irresistible little snacks and go-withs that are found in just about every culture are often more fun to eat than the main dish. Crab Empanadas, Mango and Rum-Cured Salmon Rolls, Chickpea Fritters, Asian Baby Back Ribs, and Mashed Potatoes—of course—are just a few favorites.

Chapter 6
SALAD BOWLS

Spinach Salad with Warm Pecan-Garlic Vinaigrette, Seafood-by-the-Sea Salad, Grilled Ratatouille Salad with Sherry-Shallot Vinaigrette, Warm Potato and Wild Mushroom Salad—tantalizing compositions that prove there's no limit to how far you can go when it comes to devising a great salad.

Chapter 7
GREAT LITTLE BOWLS OF FIRE & SPICE

Here's the pizzazz: Spicy combinations from a range of ethnic traditions to use as rubs, glazes, marinades, dips, and dollops. Porcini Garlic Paste, Horseradish Rouille, Tomato Soy Sauce, Avocado Wasabi, Apricot and Apple Chutney: They may be small of bowl, but they're big in flavor.

Chapter 8

SWEET BOWLS & A FEW SIPS

Bowlfuls of Chocolate Bread Pudding, Raspberry Ice Cream, Pineapple Upside-Down Cake with Tangy Vanilla Sauce, Baked Apples with Ricotta and Maple Syrup. Easy, sophisticated, and the bowlfood way to end a meal.

BOWLED OVER

BowlFood is comfort food. Food served in bowls is unintimidating and homey, inviting and ready to be consumed. Everything in the bowl is conveniently chopped, minced, or sliced into bite-size morsels, with the exception of noodles, and they're so much fun to eat, who cares if they need to be twirled and slurped? Bowls are eater-friendly, they say, "Good stuff inside, sit down and enjoy."

Both of us have known this for some time now. We have been exchanging ideas about foods, their cultural heritage, and their presentation for quite a while. We first met as cooks at the Union Square Café, and it was in that kitchen, home to so much talent, that we realized we had a mutual take on what goes into making a dish successful. We're both deeply fascinated by the proper balance of flavors and feel that great food is, in part, the result of this balance—salty and sweet, sweet and tart, and so on.

When Lynne decided to open a café next to Lola, her popular Manhattan restaurant, she had the idea to serve her food in bowls. Called Lola Bowla, this casual lunchtime spot invites diners to enjoy their meals—based on favorite ethnic Asian and Mediterranean cuisines—in bowls of all sorts. Some are deep enough to hold luscious soups and stews, some small for side dips and sauces, some shallow and wide for dumplings and stuffed foods. Some are beautiful, some amusing. All hold food that tastes delicious. And that's what this book is all about—delicious bowlfuls.

BowlFood Cookbook is a perfect balance of our talents—Lynn is a professional chef who is also an artist, and Elizabeth is a writer and adventuresome cook who travels extensively. Together we have created enticing recipes—eclectic, fragrant, pleasurable—that will give you many bowls' worth of good eating. Some have been enjoyed at Lola Bowla, some are brand new. There are main bowls to fill you up, including Mojo-Marinated Chicken, Seafood Stew in Tamarind Broth, and Roasted Pork Loin with Honey-Hoisin Marinade. There are small bowls to serve in tandem—don't miss Three-Onion Potato Cakes, Chicken Pot Stickers, and Shrimp and Yuca Fritters. There are soup bowls, salad bowls, and bowls of dumplings and other doodads to serve however you please. All great bowl meals should come to a sweet end, and that's where dessert bowls come in—wait till you try our Pineapple Upside-Down Cake with Tangy Vanilla Sauce.

We hope you have as much fun reading and cooking our recipes as we did creating them. Won't you join us in a tempting bowl?

—Lynne Aronson and Elizabeth Simon

A Word About Side Bowls

Most of our recipes come with a suggestion or two for a side bowl. Basically anything can be a side bowl, an accessory to the main event. Sometimes they're condiments—dipping sauces and broths, chopped herbs and relishes. Sometimes they're full-blown side servings, an eclectic accompaniment to an entrée. And sometimes they're really entrées, but served out in smaller portions just right to round out a meal.

We offer our side bowl lists as suggestions, as go-withs that appeal to us. But don't feel locked into them. The book is filled with possibilities and we invite you to mix and match to suit your own palate. One other thing—when we can't decide between three or four side bowls to prepare, sometimes we make them all and call it a meal. What could be better?

Chapter 1

BUILDING BLOCKS

STOCKS AND BROTHS

You probably already know that a good stock makes a great soup. But we've taken that basic culinary premise a few steps further. Our philosophy: A good stock leads to a better bowl of broth, to a still-better bowl of soup, to an even more intriguing bowl of stew, and it certainly leads to a richer sauce. Stock, to our way of cooking, is a strategic, magnificent building block. Who knows where, in what fantastic bowl, it will end? But it all begins with something fresh-cooked and shimmering, whether it is chicken, vegetable, or shellfish. A good-quality stock that's tailored to the flavors you like makes all the difference between another hunger-abating meal and one that goes beyond function to truly inspired cooking.

Making stock is easy and stock freezes beautifully, enabling you to quicken the pace of making a meal later—both reasons to go ahead and prepare a big batch. But there is the time factor. Making stock requires time, and because not everyone has enough of it, we've included short-cut ways to flavor store-bought broths as substitutes. Although the short-cut recipes may make it easier for you to savor the many flavors and textures in other chapters, at some point, we hope, you'll make our stocks from scratch.

In this chapter we include two basic stocks for chicken and two for vegetable. We season our stocks with spice bundles to impart an Asian or Western influence. The nuances kaffir lime leaves and curry leaves lend to an Eastern-inspired dish, bay leaves and rosemary lend to a Western one. What ginger contributes in one stockpot, garlic will contribute in another. Two spice bundles, two basic stocks, but four building block recipes: Chicken Stock for Asian Bowls and Chicken Stock for Mediterranean Bowls; Vegetable Stock for Asian Bowls and Vegetable Stock for Mediterranean Bowls. We've also included two terrific shellfish stocks for the more adventurous to choose from.

With stock on hand, you are only a step or so away from our wonderful broths, which are really little more than stocks that have been enriched with the addition of vegetables, herbs, spice blends, pastes, or even another stock. Customize a stock to meet your own personal tastes. Divide it in half and enrich each batch differently. With a little extra effort you can turn one stock into two very distinctive broths, say, Hot-and-Sour Broth and Ginger's Hot Broth. Then go one step further: Try dazzling a bowl of one of our broths with Shrimp and Yuca Fritters, or if you prefer, add thin Chinese egg noodles, or maybe a sprinkling of chopped scallions, or maybe nothing at all. As we said before, one bowl leads to another. It is a movable, improvisational feast, and once you get the feel for it the possibilities are endless.

CHICKEN STOCK FOR ASIAN BOWLS

This stock serves as the base or as a major enhancement to almost all the Asian-inspired bowl recipes in this book. An Asian Spice Bundle plus fresh cilantro and Kaffir lime leaves infuse the stock with authentic Far Eastern flavors.

- 1 **Asian Spice Bundle (recipe follows)**
- 5 **pounds chicken backs, wings, and necks, rinsed**
- 5 **ribs celery, chopped**
- 2 **large onions, chopped**
- 2 **carrots, chopped**
- 1 **bunch scallions, white and green parts, chopped**
- 1 **bunch fresh cilantro, chopped**
- 1 **head garlic, unpeeled but halved and crushed**
- 1 **cup chopped unpeeled fresh ginger**
- 5 **fresh Kaffir lime leaves**
- 2 **tablespoons grated lime zest**
- ½ **cup soy sauce**
- 4 **quarts cold water**

1. Combine all the ingredients in a large stockpot and bring to a boil over high heat. After 5 minutes of boiling, skim off any foam on the surface. Reduce the heat to low and simmer, covered, for 2 hours, skimming off any residue that forms on the surface.

2. Remove the pot from the heat and let the stock cool, then strain it through a fine sieve set over a large bowl. Press the solids with the back of a spoon to extract as much liquid as possible. Discard the solids.

Simmer, Don't Boil

A basic principle applies to making all stocks and broths—they should never be boiled to quicken the cooking process or for speedy reduction. This will definitely change the flavor and texture. The fats will combine with the liquid, the flavor will not be as clean, and the texture will be oily. Instead, while your stock or broth is simmering, carefully skim off the residue from time to time, gently simmering until the finish. If you find that your stock or broth is cloudier than you would like, strain it through a fine mesh sieve or one lined with cheesecloth.

5

Shortcut Stocks

There will be times when there just isn't time to make one of our longer-cooking basic building block stocks. That should not stop you from using our recipes, though. When time is short, take advantage of this quick version. In addition to needing virtually no cooking time (as opposed to over 3 hours for the original), it is good-tasting and serviceable. Like our originals, it freezes well, too.

> *4 cans (14 ½ ounces each) low-salt chicken broth*
>
> *1 spice bundle, Asian (this page) or Mediterranean (page 21)*

1. Combine the broth and spice bundle in a stockpot and bring to a boil over high heat. Reduce the heat to a simmer and cook, uncovered, for about 15 minutes.

2. Remove and discard the spice bundle. Use the stock immediately.

Makes about 8 cups

3. Return the strained stock to the pot and bring back to a simmer. Simmer, uncovered, until the liquid is reduced by half, about 1 hour.

4. Cool thoroughly in the refrigerator. When the stock is cold, remove the layer of fat that has formed on the surface. Use immediately, or transfer the stock to airtight containers and refrigerate for up to 1 week or freeze for up to 1 month.

Makes about 8 cups

ASIAN SPICE BUNDLE

Little bundles of spice (and herbs) hold the key to flavoring your stocks. We rely on two, in particular: the Asian Spice Bundle that follows and the Mediterranean Spice Bundle on page 21.

> **½ cup fermented black beans, rinsed**
> **2 tablespoons coriander seeds**
> **4 or 5 star anise**

Rinse a piece of cheesecloth under cold water and squeeze it dry. Place all the ingredients in the center of the cheesecloth, pull the ends up together, and tie with a piece of string. Discard the bundle after using.

A SMALL ASIAN PANTRY

CILANTRO, known also as Chinese parsley, is the most widely used fresh herb in the world. It has a distinct "green," almost "grassy" flavor and is indispensable in many Thai recipes. When the plant goes to seed, it is known as coriander and imparts a mild fragrance with a flavor reminiscent of lemon, sage, and caraway. Cilantro is available in supermarkets and is best stored with its stems in a jar of water. Cover the leaves loosely with plastic wrap or a plastic bag and refrigerate.

KAFFIR LIME, unlike the common lime, is used in cooking for its zest and leaf rather than its juice. Though not meant to be eaten, the leaf is an aromatic ingredient, used extensively throughout Southeast Asia to impart a flowerlike citrus fragrance and taste. The leaves are available both fresh and dried. Look for them fresh in the refrigerator case in Asian markets or dried in jars on the spice shelf.

FERMENTED BLACK BEANS, also called Chinese black beans, are black soybeans that have been preserved in salt. They are said to be the oldest recorded soy food in history, predating miso and soy sauce in daily use. They are sharp, savory, and salty in flavor and must be rinsed before using. Chop and use as a seasoning; you will only need a small amount. If sealed tightly in a container and stored in the refrigerator or a cool, dry place, they will hold for up to a year, if not indefinitely. They are available in plastic bags in Chinese and Asian markets and are sometimes also labeled "salted black beans."

STAR ANISE, a spice whose name directly translates from the Chinese as "eight points," is native to Southwest China. The hard brown pointed pods impart a licorice-like flavor and aroma but should not be eaten. They are available in jars in Chinese and Asian markets.

Rimless bowls, like these featuring a traditional blue willow pattern, are perfect for serving light broths.

CHA-CHA CHILI BROTH

Not Your Ordinary Grass

We're talking lemongrass, the potent, lemony-flavored stalks that can be added to stocks, stews, and broths to intensify and round out flavor, and add the aroma of freshly cut grass as well as the refreshing scent of zested lemon peel. You can coarsely chop whole stalks and add them to any stock that later will be strained. Or peel, trim, and chop the stalks before use—remove the outer sheath, cut and discard the green tops, trim off the root bottoms, and finely chop or grind.

Native to Asia, lemongrass can be found in most Asian markets. If you can't find it, substitute 1 teaspoon grated lemon zest for each teaspoon of minced fresh lemongrass. Don't be afraid to buy more than you need; wrapped airtight in plastic it freezes well.

This light, packed-with-flavor, vibrantly colored red-orange broth is great for building bowls of grilled seafood and vegetables or potatoes. Try it poured over Cellophane Noodles with Cracker-Crusted Mustard-Fried Bass (page 113) for a real treat. For a quick vegetarian version, substitute water for the chicken stock. Serve the broth with bowls of warm couscous.

I large red bell pepper, stemmed, seeded,
   and chopped
2 chipotle peppers, chopped
I fresh poblano chili, seeded and chopped
I red onion, coarsely chopped
2 ribs celery, chopped
2 carrots, peeled and chopped
I small fennel bulb, trimmed and chopped
2 stalks lemongrass (both tops and bottoms)
   finely chopped
¼ cup finely chopped peeled fresh ginger
2 fresh Kaffir lime leaves, or ½ teaspoon lime zest
¼ cup tomato paste
8 cups Chicken Stock for Asian Bowls
   (page 5)
2 cups water
¼ cup fresh lime juice
Salt, to taste

1. Combine the red bell pepper, chipotle peppers, poblano, onion, celery, carrots, fennel, lemongrass, and ginger in a food processor or blender and pulse until coarsely chopped.

2. Transfer the vegetable mixture to a stockpot or large saucepan, add the lime leaves and tomato paste, and stir to combine. Cook, stirring occasionally, over medium heat for about 5 minutes.

3. Add the chicken stock and water. Bring to a boil over medium heat, then reduce the heat to low and simmer, uncovered, for about 1 hour.

4. Remove the broth from the heat and strain through a fine sieve set over a medium heatproof bowl. Press the solids with the back of a spoon to extract as much liquid as possible. Add the lime juice and season with salt. Use immediately, or cool, transfer to airtight containers, and refrigerate for up to 1 week or freeze for up to 1 month.

Makes about 4 cups

SHRIMP AND YUCA FRITTERS
(page 184)

SHRIMP POT STICKERS
(page 162)

CHICKEN POT STICKERS
(page 160)

CURRY BROTH

By blending your own curry powder, as we do, you'll be able to adjust the flavor of this broth to suit your individual taste. If you are hungry for a spicy broth, just add a bit more cayenne pepper. Or, for a more unusual taste, try adding an untraditional spice, like star anise. The appeal of this broth is its vibrant yellow color and exotic flavor. It adds an exceptional finishing touch to both shellfish and poultry. It also makes a great sauce for Ricotta and Spinach Dumplings (page 163) or stuffed cabbage, a.k.a. The Gift of Cabbage (page 168).

- **3 pounds whole button mushrooms, cleaned**
- **1 pound carrots, coarsely chopped**
- **5 ribs celery, coarsely chopped**
- **2 medium onions, coarsely chopped**
- **4 tablespoons (½ stick) unsalted butter, in pieces**
- **¼ cup curry powder, preferably homemade (recipe follows)**
- **8 cups Chicken Stock for Asian Bowls (page 5)**
- **2 cups dry white wine**
- **Salt and freshly ground black pepper, to taste**

1. Working in batches, combine the mushrooms, carrots, celery, and onions in a food processor. Process until all the vegetables are chopped in small pieces. Set aside.

2. Melt the butter in a stockpot over medium heat. Add the curry powder and stir well to blend. Reduce the heat to low and cook for 1 minute, stirring constantly and being careful not to let the mixture burn.

3. Add the chopped vegetables and stir to coat well. Cover and cook over low heat for 30 minutes, stirring often to avoid burning or sticking.

4. Add the chicken stock and wine, increase the heat to high, and bring the liquid to a boil. Reduce the heat to low and simmer, uncovered, for about 45 minutes.

5. Remove the pot from the heat and strain the broth through a fine sieve set over a large heatproof bowl. Press the solids with the back of a spoon to extract as much liquid as possible. Season the broth with salt and pepper. Use immediately, or cool, transfer to airtight containers, and refrigerate for up to 1 week or freeze for up to 1 month.

Makes about 6 cups

Assorted teacups and saucers make unexpected, attractive broth bowls.

CURRY POWDER

Since curry powders quickly lose their punch, they should be ground the traditional way, that is, as needed. The possibilities for blending spices, seeds, and herbs into curry powders are infinite, and most cooks, regardless of their cultural heritage and training, have their own interpretations. Some blends are ground dried, while others are compounded into pastes, and each imparts a different flavor.

This homemade curry powder blend is our basic variation on an endless theme. Although the cayenne gives it some heat, to us it seems tame. Once you've tried it, experiment by altering the amounts as suits your palate or your cooking needs. Be sure to keep notes on the blends you create. You'll want to be able to reproduce the ones that work well.

  3 tablespoons cumin seeds
  2 tablespoons fenugreek seeds
  2 tablespoons coriander seeds
  2 tablespoons ground turmeric
  1 tablespoon cayenne pepper
  1 tablespoon ground cardamom
  ½ teaspoon ground cinnamon

1. Combine the cumin, fenugreek, and coriander seeds in a dry medium-size skillet over medium heat. Shaking the pan continuously to prevent burning, heat until the seeds are fragrant and just beginning to smoke, 1 to 2 minutes.

2. Transfer the seeds to a small bowl to cool, then grind to a powder in a spice grinder.

3. Return the mixture to the bowl and add the remaining spices. Stir to mix and place in an airtight container. Store in a cool, dry place.

Makes about ½ cup

GINGER'S HOT BROTH

An essential ingredient in the richly flavored Risotto with Braised Duck and Spicy Ginger Broth (page 138), this broth can also stand on its own as an appealing steaming bowl with nothing more than noodles or sautéed squid or both added. The broth benefits greatly from the medium-hot flavor of jalapeño peppers, so do use the full amount suggested.

3 tablespoons olive oil

6 ribs celery, chopped

3 large carrots, peeled and chopped

2 medium onions, chopped

1 head garlic, unpeeled but halved and crushed

½ cup finely chopped peeled fresh ginger

4 jalapeño peppers, stemmed and chopped
  with seeds

¼ cup ketchup

¾ cup dry white wine

8 cups Chicken Stock for Asian Bowls
  (page 5)

1 bunch fresh cilantro

¼ cup fresh lime juice

Salt and freshly ground black pepper, to taste

1. Heat the olive oil in a stockpot over low heat. Add the celery, carrots, onions, garlic, ginger, and jalapeños. Cook, stirring, until the onions are transparent, 5 to 8 minutes.

2. Stir in the ketchup, then add the white wine, chicken stock, and cilantro. Bring to a boil over high heat, then reduce the heat to low and simmer, uncovered, for 1 hour.

3. Remove the broth from the heat and strain through a fine sieve set over a medium heatproof bowl. Press the solids with the back of a spoon to extract as much liquid as possible. Add the lime juice and season with salt and pepper. Use immediately, or cool, transfer to airtight containers, and refrigerate for up to 1 week or freeze for 1 month.

Makes about 6 cups

A stack of small bowls placed in the center of the table next to a tureen of steaming hot broth makes an informal presentation.

CHILI PEPPERS:
FRESH AND DRIED, HOT AND NOT

When it comes to chili peppers, bigger is not necessarily better, but smaller is definitely hotter. The seeds and ribs—where most of the heat comes from—are more densely concentrated in little peppers because of the pods' tiny architecture. These are the chilies from which you will want to remove the seeds and ribs before using. But be careful: Wear rubber gloves and avoid touching your eyes while you work. And wash your hands thoroughly when you are finished.

There are some two hundred varieties of chilies, each different, each offering its own characteristics to a dish, whether in flavor, color, or intensity. Here are a few of our favorites; all are available year-round.

JALAPEÑOS: The most popular chili, the green jalapeño, is medium-small in size, with rich, abundant flesh. It gives a real kick to just about anything you want to spice up. The red jalapeño is simply the green pepper that has ripened. It has a sweet flavor. Dried and smoked jalapeños, called *chipotles,* are coffee-brown in color, sweet and smoky in flavor, and delicious in soups and sauces, to mention only two possibilities. Chipotles are available canned either in vinegar or in adobo, a spicy tomato-based sauce.

SERRANOS: Bright green and hot when not ripe, red, sweet, and hot when mature, the fresh serrano chili adds savory excitement to salsas and curries. Dried and sometimes powdered, it is known as *chile seco.*

POBLANOS: The long, dark green (almost purplish-black), thick-fleshed poblano is never eaten raw. Great for stuffing, when cooked it is full flavored and smoky-tasting. When dried, the poblano turns a deep red-mahogany and is known as an *ancho.* Ancho chilies can be purchased whole or ground. Whole, they are available either loose or in bags in most better-stocked supermarkets,

SCOTCH BONNETS: One of the hottest chilies is the Scotch bonnet, which adds a fiery intensity to any recipe. Use whole or diced, with or without seeds. They are available in the produce section of most large supermarkets.

HOT-AND-SOUR BROTH

Nam Pla

Called *nam pla* in Thai and Laotian, *nuoc mam* in Vietnamese, *tuk trey* in Cambodian, this sauce of cured, small, protein-rich fish (most often anchovies) is used as commonly in Southeast Asia as salt is used in the Western world.

Although there are some differences among brands—particularly with intensity of flavor—you can control the punch *nam pla* adds. Always taste, every step of the way, adding a dab at a time until you've pumped up the overall flavor of the recipe to suit your taste.

Available in Asian markets, *nam pla* once opened should be stored in the refrigerator in an airtight container, where it will keep for up to 1 year.

The addition of vinegar to this broth unites the individual flavors of pineapple, ginger, and *nam pla* (Asian fish sauce), creating a bracing combination. When this is used as a base for Hot-and-Sour Chowder (page 53), the heat factor doubles, resulting in fiery satisfaction.

> 2 cups pineapple juice
> ¼ cup cider vinegar
> ¼ cup finely chopped peeled fresh ginger
> 3 tablespoons (packed) light brown sugar
> 2 teaspoons chili paste
> 3 stalks lemongrass, chopped
> 8 cups Chicken Stock for Asian Bowls (page 5)
> ½ cup rice wine or dry sherry
> ¼ cup ketchup
> ¼ cup nam pla (Asian fish sauce)
> ¼ cup fresh lime juice
> Salt and freshly ground black pepper, to taste

1. Combine the pineapple juice, vinegar, ginger, brown sugar, chili paste, and lemongrass in a medium nonreactive saucepan and bring to a boil over medium-high heat. Cook, uncovered, until the liquid is reduced by half, 5 to 10 minutes.

2. Add the chicken stock, rice wine, and ketchup and bring to a boil. Reduce the heat to low and simmer, uncovered, for about 30 minutes.

3. Remove from the heat and stir in the *nam pla* and lime juice. Season with salt and pepper. Strain the broth through a fine sieve set over a large heatproof bowl. Use immediately, or cool, transfer to airtight containers, and refrigerate for up to 1 week or freeze for 1 month.

Makes about 9 cups

SWEET-AND-SOUR RED PEPPER BROTH

When you have a great broth like this one—balanced with sweet and sour flavors and an aromatic infusion of ginger—all you need to do is float several savory ingredients on top and you have an attractive, luscious soup bowl. Try shrimp, scallions, sprouts, herbs, or greens.

> **4 cups Chicken Stock for Asian Bowls (page 5)**
> **I cup Sweet-and-Sour Red Pepper Drizzle (page 119)**
> **I medium onion, chopped**
> **¼ cup chopped peeled fresh ginger**
> **¼ cup fresh lime juice**

I. Combine the chicken stock, red pepper drizzle, onion, and ginger in a medium saucepan and bring to a boil over medium heat. Reduce the heat to low and simmer, uncovered, for 30 minutes.

2. Remove the pan from the heat and strain the broth through a fine sieve set over a medium heatproof bowl. Stir in the lime juice. Use immediately, or cool, transfer to airtight containers, and refrigerate for up to 1 week or freeze for 1 month.

Makes about 4 cups

CURRIED CORN BROTH

By combining the freshest corn available with water and a fragrant seasoning, you can produce a light, flavorful broth that is great as a tasty, soupy sauce for grilled fish, seared scallops, or steamed red snapper. (This broth makes a superb corn chowder, too.)

6 cups fresh corn kernels (10 to 12 ears),
   the freshest available
1 tablespoon curry powder, preferably homemade
   (page 10)
½ teaspoon ground turmeric
10 cups cold water
Salt and freshly ground white pepper, to taste

1. Combine the corn kernels, curry powder, and turmeric in a large saucepan and cover with the water. Bring to a boil, then reduce the heat to low and simmer, uncovered, for 45 minutes.

2. Remove the broth from the heat and strain through a fine sieve set over a large heatproof bowl. Return to the pan, bring to a boil, and simmer for 15 minutes. Season with salt and white pepper. Use immediately, or cool, transfer to airtight containers, and refrigerate for up to 1 week or freeze for up to 1 month.

Makes about 4 cups

CURRIED CORN AND ROASTED PEPPER BROTH

Sometimes a day in the kitchen can be likened to a day in the lab, with you playing the role of scientist. By experimenting with different combinations of broths, it is always possible to invent a new taste sensation. By adding an herb or vegetable purée, you can also change the texture of a broth to create a sauce. For starters, try reducing the broth by one half, then blend in ¼ cup of Basil Paste (page 131) and serve this full-flavored herb, spice, and vegetable sauce with grilled fish.

5 cups Chicken Stock for Asian Bowls (page 5)

3 cups Curried Corn Broth (page 15)

4 cups fresh corn kernels (7 to 8 ears)

2 cups chopped, roasted and peeled red bell peppers
    (see box, page 18)

2 large beets, roasted, peeled, and chopped
    (page 23)

2 large carrots, chopped

1 fresh Scotch bonnet pepper or serrano chili,
    stemmed, halved, and seeded

2 tablespoons tomato paste

¼ cup rice vinegar

2 tablespoons fresh lime juice

Salt and freshly ground black pepper, to taste

1. Combine the chicken stock, corn broth, corn kernels, roasted peppers and beets, carrots, Scotch bonnet pepper, and tomato paste in a medium saucepan. Bring to a boil over high heat, then reduce the heat to low and simmer, uncovered, until the broth is red in color, about 45 minutes.

2. Remove the broth from the heat. Stir in the vinegar, lime juice, and salt and pepper.

3. Strain the broth through a fine sieve set over a medium heatproof bowl. Press the solids with the back of a spoon to extract as much liquid as possible. Use immediately, or cool, transfer to airtight containers, and refrigerate for up to 1 week or freeze for 1 month.

Makes about 4 cups

*The deeper the bowl,
the hotter the broth will stay.*

To Roast and Peel Bell Peppers

Sweet, smoky roasted fresh red or yellow peppers dramatically enhance even the most basic salad, sandwich, soup, or pasta. There are several ways to roast peppers, our favorite being over a wood-burning grill. The smooth, earthy flavor this method imparts is so fabulous that you'll want simply to toss the roasted peppers in a bowl with some crisp greens, goat cheese, and Shallot-Parsley Vinaigrette (page 224) and eat them with a hearty herb bread. If you do not have access to a grill, a gas burner works just fine, too.

1. If using a grill, preheat to high. If using burners on a gas stove, place a small roasting rack directly over each burner.

2. Put the bell peppers on the rack (either grill or stovetop) and char, turning gradually with tongs, until evenly blackened all over, 8 to 10 minutes.

3. Transfer the peppers to a bowl and cover tightly with plastic wrap. Let stand about 15 minutes.

4. With your fingers, remove the charred skin of the peppers. Don't wash the peppers or you will sacrifice the flavor.

5. Stem the peppers, halve, and discard the seeds inside. Use immediately or store in an airtight container in the refrigerator for up to 1 week.

TAMARIND BROTH

Tamarind

You've probably tasted tamarind and didn't even realize it, as it's a main ingredient in such bottled condiments as Worcestershire and Pick-a-Pepper sauces. Tamarind is the sour, tart, citrusy-flavored fruit of trees that grow wild throughout the wet tropics of Asia, Africa, and Latin America. It is ▶

Here's a tangy, sweet-and-sour broth with a distinctive balance of flavors. The citruslike character of tamarind is sugar sweetened and spiced up with ginger and lemongrass for added depth. Add noodles and chopped scallions to give this broth a wonderful raison d'être.

8 cups Chicken Stock for Asian Bowls (page 5)

6 scallions, chopped

½ cup tamarind concentrate

½ cup chopped peeled fresh ginger

½ cup soy sauce

¼ cup sugar

3 tablespoons rice vinegar

2 stalks lemongrass, chopped

2 star anise

1 fresh serrano chili, stemmed, halved, and chopped with seeds

1. Combine all the ingredients in a stockpot and bring to a boil over medium heat. Reduce the heat to low and simmer, uncovered, for 30 minutes.

2. Remove the broth from the heat and strain through a fine sieve into a medium heatproof bowl. Press the solids with the back of a spoon to extract as much liquid as possible. Use immediately, or cool, transfer to airtight containers, and refrigerate for up to 1 week or freeze for 1 month.

Makes about 6 cups

ASIAN CHICKEN STOCK ROUNDUP

To say that we use our six building block stocks frequently is an understatement. In addition to the broths in this chapter, here is a listing of other recipes that call for Chicken Stock for Asian Bowls in this book (please check the Index for page numbers).

- Carrot Cardamom Soup
- Corn Soup with Ricotta and Spinach Dumplings
- Dal Soup
- Golden Delicious Egg Drop Soup with Crabmeat Dumplings
- Latin Chicken Soup with Noodles
- African Chicken and Peanut Stew
- African White Fish Stew
- Spicy Peanut Sauce
- Rice Noodles with Chicken, Shrimp, and Spicy Peanut Sauce
- Sesame Sauce
- Pan-Seared Scallops with Egg Noodles and Sweet-and-Sour Red Pepper Drizzle
- Spicy Stir-Fried Squid with Orange Segments and Egg Noodles
- Fiery Red Curry Sauce
- Not-So-Fried Rice
- Risotto with Braised Duck and Spicy Ginger Broth

---

also harvested on plantations in India.

Tamarind pulp is found in long lumpy brown pods that are filled with seeds. The pulp must first be extracted, then macerated. Fortunately, tamarind is available commercially in two different forms: as concentrated liquid or as paste. The bricks of paste must be soaked, then pushed through a sieve to remove the seeds. Either form of tamarind can be found in many specialty food markets.

If you cannot find tamarind concentrate or paste, improvise by combining 1 tablespoon finely chopped pitted prunes with 1 tablespoon fresh lemon or lime juice for each tablespoon of tamarind. Tightly covered, tamarind keeps in the refrigerator for months.

CHICKEN STOCK FOR MEDITERRANEAN BOWLS

A sister to Chicken Stock for Asian Bowls, this stock features the flavors of the Mediterranean—fennel, oregano, and basil. Serve this as a delicate stand-alone or use it as a building block stock.

Sweet with a mild anise flavor, fennel is considered a digestive. Hence, this simple chicken stock can be considered good for what ails you. Oregano, used extensively with tomato-based dishes, here lends a touch of Provence, and beautiful basil, though most seductive when used fresh, helps bond the flavors of the other ingredients.

> **5 pounds chicken backs, wings, and necks, rinsed**
> **4 ribs celery, chopped**
> **2 large onions, chopped**
> **2 carrots, chopped**
> **2 bunches fresh Italian (flat-leaf) parsley, chopped**
> **I head garlic, unpeeled but halved and crushed**
> **I large fennel bulb, trimmed and chopped, or**
> > **I tablespoon whole fennel seed**
> **I small turnip, chopped**
> **I tablespoon dried oregano**
> **I cup (loosely packed) fresh basil leaves, chopped**
> **I cup canned tomatoes, drained, seeded, and**
> > **chopped**
> **I Mediterranean Spice Bundle (recipe follows)**
> **4 quarts cold water**

I. Combine all the ingredients in a large stockpot and bring to a boil over high heat. After 5 minutes of boiling, skim off any foam on the surface. Reduce the heat to low and simmer, covered, for 2 hours, skimming off any foam that forms on the surface.

2. Remove the pot from the heat and let the stock cool, then strain it through a fine sieve set over a large bowl. Press on the solids with the back of a spoon to extract as much liquid as possible. Discard the solids.

3. Return the strained stock to the pot and bring back to a simmer. Simmer until the liquid is reduced by half, about 1 hour.

4. Cool thoroughly in the refrigerator. When the stock is cold, remove the layer of fat that has formed on the surface. Use immediately, or transfer the stock to airtight containers and refrigerate for up to 1 week or freeze for up to 1 month.

Makes about 8 cups

Mediterranean Spice Bundle

This little bundle imparts an almost mintlike, mild lemony fla-vor and aroma to the stock. We prefer to use dried imported bay leaves, which are commonly available in supermarkets, because fresh leaves can sometimes make a stock taste bitter.

> **I bunch fresh thyme sprigs**
> **4 bay leaves**
> **2 tablespoons black peppercorns**

Rinse a piece of cheesecloth under cold water and squeeze it dry. Place all the ingredients in the center of the cheesecloth, pull the ends up together, and tie with a piece of string. Discard the bundle after using.

Serve a savory broth in a bowl with a Mediterranean motif as an accompaniment for fluffy couscous.

BEET AND ORANGE BROTH

Whttps en winter settles in as it does over most of this country, fresh produce markets are often limited in their offerings. Oranges, available everywhere year round, can enliven even the coldest and bleakest days. Here they add not only flavor but zing to a colorful broth.

> 2 medium oranges with unblemished skins
> ⅛ cup olive oil
> ½ teaspoon curry powder, preferably homemade
>   (page 10)
> ¼ teaspoon ground cinnamon
> 2 large carrots, cut into 1-inch dice
> 1 large red onion, cut into 1-inch dice
> 2 cups canned whole tomatoes, drained
> 2 cups diced, roasted and peeled beets (see box, facing page)
> 4 cups Chicken Stock for Mediterranean Bowls (page 20)
> 2 cups dry white wine
> Salt and freshly ground black pepper, to taste

1. With a paring knife or citrus zester, peel away just the zest of the orange, leaving the white pith behind. Finely chop the zest and set aside. Reserve the oranges for another use.

2. Heat the olive oil in a large stockpot over medium heat. Add the curry powder and cinnamon and cook, stirring constantly, for 30 seconds. Add the carrots, onions, tomatoes, beets, and orange zest. Cover and cook over medium heat until the vegetables are softened, about 10 minutes.

3. Add the chicken stock and wine and bring to a boil. Reduce the heat to low and simmer, uncovered, until all of the vegetables are very tender, about 30 minutes.

4. Remove from the heat and strain the broth through a fine sieve set over a medium heatproof bowl. Press the solids with the back of a spoon to extract as much liquid as possible. Season with salt and pepper. Use immediately, or cool, transfer to airtight containers, and refrigerate for up to 1 week or freeze for up to 1 month.

Makes about 5 cups

To Roast Beets

Given the option to either boil or roast fresh beets, the choice should be simple: Roast them, of course! Boiled beets lose much of their flavor and their color; slow-roasted beets produce a sweet, earthy flavor and a brilliant red juice. Here's how to do it:

1. Preheat the oven to 400°F.

2. Trim off the beet tops, leaving about 1 inch of stem. Scrub the beets thoroughly.

3. Roast the beets on a baking sheet until they can be easily pierced with the tip of a knife. Depending on the size of the beets, this will take at least 1 hour. Remove the beets from the oven and cool for about 30 minutes.

4. Cut off the tops and bottoms with a paring knife and peel the beets. Use as directed in individual recipes.

Lids help keep side bowls of broth warm throughout the meal.

ROASTED RED PEPPER BROTH

Wait until you taste this crisp, clear, red broth. Gently spiced, it is excellent ladled over hot couscous with cooked fresh corn off the cob and seared or grilled scallops added. It is also simple to prepare.

> 2 tablespoons olive oil
> 4 carrots, chopped
> 2 cups chopped, roasted and peeled red bell peppers
>   (see box, page 18)
> 2 red onions, chopped
> 1 whole fresh Scotch bonnet pepper or serrano chili
> ½ cup tomato paste
> 8 cups Chicken Stock for Mediterranean Bowls
>   (page 20)

1. Heat the olive oil in a stockpot over medium heat. Add the carrots, roasted red peppers, onions, Scotch bonnet pepper, and tomato paste and cook, stirring, until the vegetables are softened and fully coated with tomato paste, 5 to 8 minutes.

2. Add the chicken stock and bring to a boil. Reduce the heat to low and simmer, uncovered, for 30 minutes.

3. Remove the pot from the heat and strain the broth through a fine sieve set over a large heatproof bowl. Press the solids with the back of a spoon to extract as much liquid as possible. Use immediately, or cool, transfer to airtight containers, and refrigerate for up to 1 week or freeze for 1 month.

Makes about 6 cups

You-Can-Kiss-Me Roasted Garlic Broth

Even with the amount of garlic called for here, this broth is mild and sweet in flavor; not a trace of the garlic's pungency lingers. Once you fall in love with the taste of roasted garlic, you will want to substitute this broth for other chicken stocks in such recipes as Latin Chicken Soup with Noodles (page 54) or Onion Soup with Stilton Cheese (page 58). With the addition of cooked white beans, roasted tomatoes, and shredded cooked chicken, it can easily be transformed into a delicious and hearty meal-in-a-bowl.

> **2 large onions, unpeeled, chopped into 1-inch pieces**
>
> **3 heads garlic, unpeeled, quartered and crushed**
>
> **¼ cup olive oil**
>
> **4 ribs celery, chopped into 1-inch pieces**
>
> **8 cups Chicken Stock for Mediterranean Bowls (page 20)**
>
> **¼ cup soy sauce**
>
> **2 sprigs fresh thyme**
>
> **2 bay leaves**
>
> **Coarse (kosher) salt and pepper, to taste**

1. Preheat the oven to 400°F.

2. Combine the onions and garlic in a roasting pan and toss with the olive oil. Roast, stirring occasionally for even browning, for 35 minutes. Cool slightly.

3. Chop the celery and roasted onions and garlic together by hand or pulse briefly in a food processor. Transfer the chopped vegetables to a large stockpot and add the stock, soy sauce, thyme, and bay leaves. Bring to a boil, uncovered, over high heat, then reduce the heat to low and simmer, still uncovered, until reduced by half, about 1 hour.

Each time you raise the lid on a covered bowl, you get a steamy whiff of a broth's inviting aroma.

4. Remove the pot from the heat and strain the broth through a fine sieve set over a large heatproof bowl. Press the solids with the back of a spoon to extract as much liquid as possible. Use immediately, or cool, transfer to airtight containers, and refrigerate for up to 1 week or freeze for 1 month.

Makes about 1 quart

Keep chunky ceramic bowls in all colors; they come in handy for serving everything from sauces to broths.

MEDITERRANEAN CHICKEN STOCK ROUNDUP

In addition to the broths that are based on Chicken Stock for Mediterranean Bowls, here's where you can find all the other places we use it (please check the Index for page numbers).

- Cool Hand Cuke Soup
- Onion Soup with Stilton Cheese
- Lentil Soup with Roasted Garlic and Herbs
- White Bean and Mushroom Soup with Chickpea Fritters
- Stewed Short Ribs
- Mustard-Rubbed Chicken Thighs and Yellow Split Pea Stew

- No Choke Artichoke Stew
- Capellini with Manila Clams, Lobster, and Asparagus in Lobster Broth
- Tagliatelle with Fresh Corn and Lump Crab
- Pearl Pasta with Fresh Peas and Gorgonzola
- Simmer My Juices and Give Me a Little Couscous

VEGETABLE STOCK FOR ASIAN BOWLS

Get in the habit of saving vegetable scraps, such as mushroom stems, tomato tops, onion peelings, and herbs that have seen better days. Dedicate part of your freezer space to storing them, then make sure to remember to add them to the stockpot. This Asian-flavored vegetarian combination would be a good place to start.

½ cup finely chopped lemongrass (both tops and bottoms)
5 ribs celery, chopped
4 carrots, chopped
2 large onions, chopped
1 red bell pepper, stemmed, seeded, and chopped
1 bunch fresh cilantro, chopped
1 head garlic, unpeeled but halved and crushed
¼ cup chopped peeled fresh ginger
1 cup chopped fresh tomatoes, or canned, drained
2 fresh jalapeño peppers, stemmed, seeded, and chopped
1 Asian Spice Bundle (page 6)
4 quarts cold water

1. Combine all the ingredients in a large stockpot and bring to a boil over high heat. Reduce the heat to low and simmer, uncovered, for about 1 hour.

2. Remove the pot from the heat and cool the stock. When cool, strain through a fine sieve set over a large bowl. Press the solids with the back of a spoon to extract as much liquid as possible. Use immediately, or transfer the stock to airtight containers and refrigerate for up to 1 week or freeze for 1 month.

Makes about 3½ quarts

Quick Vegetable Stock

You can easily jump-start a vegetable stock. Begin with canned vegetable broth, which is widely available in supermarkets, but freshen up its flavor by adding either an Asian or Mediterranean Spice Bundle and as many of the vegetables you have on hand that we call for in the respectively flavored building block stock recipe. It's probably best to halve our original recipe, which means you will need 4 cans broth (14½ ounces each), and simmer the vegetables in it for about 15 minutes. Strain and use. That said, and all convenience aside, there is still nothing like one of our vegetable stocks made from scratch!

BLOND MISO BROTH

Aso, Miso!

Miso, or fermented soy-bean paste, is packed with protein and has been one of Japan's culinary staples for centuries. In fact, its aroma and taste are so appealing that it is eaten for breakfast, lunch, or dinner in the form of *miso shiru*, or miso broth. We love it because it's healthful, flavorful, and easy to use. Typically you should be able to find two different kinds—yellow and red—in Asian markets and natural foods stores. Miso paste is made from soybeans that have had either a wheat, rice, or barley mold added. The most common miso paste is yellow, or blond, and is fairly salty and tart. Red miso comes two ways, either sweet or salty.

Store in airtight containers in the refrigerator for up to 1 year.

Blond miso paste is responsible for the appealing earthy, yellow-ocher color of this broth. Serve it alone, or use it to steam open clams or mussels.

> **4 cups Vegetable Stock for Asian Bowls (page 27)**
> **½ cup mirin, sweet sherry, or sweet vermouth**
> **½ cup blond miso paste**
> **¼ cup dried shrimp, rinsed**
> **1 ounce dried bonito flakes**
> **2 tablespoons finely chopped peeled fresh ginger**
> **1 strip (10 to 12 inches long) of konbu (dried seaweed)**
> **Chopped fresh chives or cilantro leaves, for garnish**

1. Combine all the ingredients in a medium nonreactive saucepan and bring to a boil over high heat. Reduce the heat to low, cover, and simmer, for 30 minutes.

2. Remove the pan from the heat and strain the broth through a fine sieve set over a large heatproof bowl. Press the solids with the back of a spoon to extract as much liquid as possible. Use immediately, or cool, transfer to airtight containers, and refrigerate for up to 1 week or freeze for 1 month.

Makes about 4 cups

ASIAN VEGETABLE STOCK ROUNDUP

Look for Vegetable Stock for Asian Bowls in the following recipes (please check the Index for page numbers).

- Chilled Bell Pepper and Beet Soup with Lemongrass
- Roasted Garlic and Boniato Soup with Crispy Thai Mushroom Roll

ALL DRIED UP BUT READY TO GO

Dried shrimp are some of the stinkiest culinary delicacies you'll come across. Having said that, you're probably wondering why we use them. Well, here's why: It's for their unmistakable tangy concentrated shrimp flavor. You're likely to love them, hate them, or grow to appreciate them. Whichever the case, use them sparingly, as a seasoning in dry-fried dishes.

You can buy dried shrimp in Asian markets, either loose or in plastic bags. Choose the largest and pinkest for the best flavor. Although some people recommend soaking them, dried shrimp never do become tender. A good rinsing does, however, remove any bits of unwanted shell remaining but leaves much of the salty flavor intact.

FOR BLOND MISO BROTH:

MUSTARD OIL

MUSTARD SEEDS

VEGETABLE STOCK FOR MEDITERRANEAN BOWLS

When you aren't sure of your guests' dietary restrictions or preferences, turn to this easy, flavorful stock that can be used as a vegetarian base for soups, like Carrot Cardamom Soup (page 46), or for your own noodle or pasta bowl concoctions.

1 pound button mushrooms, wiped clean and chopped

7 ribs celery, chopped

2 large onions, chopped

2 red bell peppers, stemmed, seeded, and chopped

2 parsnips, chopped

2 fennel bulbs, trimmed and chopped

2 heads garlic, unpeeled but halved and crushed

2 cups chopped fresh tomatoes, or canned, drained

1 cup (loosely packed) chopped fresh Italian (flat-leaf) parsley

1 Mediterranean Spice Bundle (page 21)

4 quarts cold water

1. Combine all the ingredients in a large stockpot and bring to a boil over high heat. Reduce the heat to low and simmer, uncovered, for about 1 hour.

2. Remove the pot from the heat and cool the stock. When cool, strain through a fine sieve set over a large bowl. Press the solids with the back of a spoon to extract as much liquid as possible.

3. Return the strained stock to the pot, bring to a simmer, and simmer, uncovered, until the liquid is reduced by half. Cool, transfer to airtight containers, and refrigerate for up to 1 week or freeze for 1 month.

Makes about 8 cups

MEDITERRANEAN VEGETABLE STOCK ROUNDUP

Look for Vegetable Stock for Mediterranean Bowls in the following recipes (please check the Index for page numbers).

- Porcini Vinaigrette
- Shallot-Parsley Vinaigrette

Don't just use these Japanese bowls for light soups. They're also good for brothy noodle and rice dishes.

TOMATO HORSERADISH BROTH

This bright-tasting broth is light yet hearty enough to stand up to a dish like charred beef. It is equally magnificent when partnered, as a soup, with poached flaked salmon and boiled new potatoes.

- 1 pound fresh horseradish root or 1 cup prepared horseradish, drained
- 4 pounds ripe tomatoes, chopped
- 4 ribs celery, chopped
- 3 large carrots, finely chopped
- 2 large onions, finely chopped
- 1 turnip, chopped
- 8 cups Vegetable Stock for Asian Bowls (page 27)
- 4 cups dry white wine
- 1 cup tomato paste
- Salt and freshly ground black pepper, to taste
- A Pinch for All Seasons (page 246), to taste

Fill earthy-looking terra-cotta tureens with an earthy-tasting broth. Each complements the other nicely.

1. Scrub the horseradish root thoroughly, if using, leaving the skin intact. Chop into small pieces. Combine the fresh or prepared horseradish with the tomatoes, celery, carrots, onions, and turnip in a large stockpot. Add the water, wine, and tomato paste and bring to a boil. Reduce the heat to low and simmer, uncovered, for 1 hour.

2. Remove the pot from the heat and strain the broth through a fine sieve set over a large heatproof bowl. Press the solids with the back of a spoon to extract as much liquid as possible. Return the broth to the pot, bring to a simmer, and simmer until reduced by half, about 30 minutes. Season with salt and pepper and A Pinch for All Seasons. Use immediately, or cool, transfer to airtight containers, and refrigerate for 1 week or freeze up to 1 month.

Makes about 6 cups

LOBSTER STOCK

Summertime Lobster

If you live in an area where fresh whole lobsters are readily available, don't just grill or boil them—although they are pretty terrific both those ways.

Go a step further and turn the tail and claw meat into Seafood-by-the-Sea Salad (page 200), Farfalle and Lobster with Ramps and Spicy Bread Crumbs (page 116), or Thai-Style Summer Lobster and Noodle Salad (page 205). You'll be glad you did.

We are fortunate to spend some of the year in New England, where, during the summer months, lobster is in season and affordable. The bodies and shells go into making this stock—the secret base to many favorite seafood recipes.

How you intend to use our lobster stock will determine whether you add the Asian or Mediterranean Spice Bundle. In either case, the delicate yet rich essence of lobster is so pleasing that adding just dumplings or cut vegetables yields a delicious meal. Stockpile quart-sized containers of this stock in the freezer for satisfying future meals, such as Capellini with Manila Clams, Lobster, and Asparagus in Lobster Broth (page 127). This recipe can be halved, if desired.

5 tablespoons olive oil

7 ribs celery, chopped

4 carrots, coarsely chopped

4 scallions, white and green parts, coarsely chopped

2 turnips, coarsely chopped

2 medium onions, coarsely chopped

1 head garlic, unpeeled but halved and crushed

5 pounds uncooked lobster bodies, crushed

4 quarts cold water

4 cups dry white wine

½ cup chopped fresh cilantro leaves

1 Asian Spice Bundle (page 6) or Mediterranean Spice Bundle (page 21)

1. Heat the olive oil in a large stockpot over medium heat. Add the celery, carrots, scallions, turnips, onions, and garlic and cook, stirring, until soft, about 15 minutes.

2. Add the crushed lobster bodies and cook over medium-high heat until they turn bright red, about 30 minutes.

3. Add the water, wine, cilantro, and spice bundle of choice and bring to a boil over high heat. Reduce the heat to low and simmer, uncovered, for 1 hour, skimming off any foam that forms on the surface.

4. Remove the pot from the heat and strain the stock through a fine sieve set over a large heatproof bowl. Press the solids with the back of a spoon to extract as much liquid as possible. Use immediately, or cool, transfer to airtight containers, and refrigerate for up to 1 week or freeze for 1 month.

Makes about 4 quarts

LOBSTER COCO LOCO BROTH

This fragrant broth walks that fine line between being a broth and a soup. Puréeing the solid ingredients helps to infuse the base with great flavor, and double straining the finished broth ensures a remarkable clarity. Serve as a soup, with wilted greens and Crabmeat Dumplings (page 156) added, or as a light, brothy sauce with grilled fish.

½ **cup chopped peeled fresh ginger**

¼ **cup tomato paste**

1 **medium red bell pepper, stemmed, seeded, and diced**

5 **stalks lemongrass (tops and bottoms), chopped**

4 **small-to-medium fresh jalapeño peppers, stemmed and halved with seeds**

4 **scallions, white and green parts, chopped**

6 **cups Lobster Stock (facing page)**

2 **cups unsweetened canned coconut milk**

1 **cup pineapple juice**

1 **tablespoon chili paste**

2 **pieces Kaffir lime leaves, fresh or dried**

Coarse (kosher) salt, to taste

1. Combine the ginger, tomato paste, bell pepper, lemongrass, jalapeños, and scallions in a blender or food processor and pulse until coarsely chopped.

2. Place the mixture in a stockpot and add the Lobster Stock, coconut milk, pineapple juice, chili paste, and lime leaves. Bring to a boil over medium heat, then reduce the heat to low and simmer for 1 hour.

3. Remove the pot from the heat and strain the broth through a fine sieve into a large heatproof bowl. Discard the solids. Return the broth to the pot, bring it back to a simmer, and continue to simmer it for about 30 minutes, until reduced by one fourth.

4. Strain again into a large bowl and season with salt. Use immediately, or cool, transfer to airtight containers, and refrigerate for up to 1 week or freeze for up to 1 month.

Makes about 5 cups

Serving family-style, from an all-purpose tureen with matching—or even nonmatching—bowls, always helps to relax a group and stimulate conversation.

ABOUT COCONUT MILK

The liquid you hear swishing around when you shake a coconut is coconut *water*, not coconut *milk*. So, since punching a hole in that coconut won't get you milk, where can you find it? There are four possibilities:

1. Purchase a can of unsweetened coconut milk from almost any market or grocery store. It comes ready to use. We prefer Chaokoh brand from Thailand.

2. Purchase coconut milk powder (available at Asian markets) and follow the instructions on the package.

3. Purchase unsweetened dried coconut meat (at ethnic markets and natural foods stores). Use 2 cups of hot half-and-half for every 8 ounces of dried coconut and make coconut milk as directed in number 4.

4. Purchase a fresh whole coconut.

Prepare the meat: Preheat the oven to 350°F. Pierce the "eyes" that are at one end of the coconut, using a screwdriver or icepick and a hammer, and drain off the liquid. (Drink this delicious, pure liquid—it's rich in minerals and vitamins.) Bake the coconut until the shell begins to crack, about 15 minutes, then remove from the oven and allow it to cool. Split the coconut by hitting it with a mallet or hammer, then remove the white flesh with a sharp paring knife. Shred the meat in a food processor fitted with the shredding disk. Remove the shredded coconut from the processor and replace the disk with the steel blade. Return the coconut to the processor.

Make the coconut milk: Bring 2 cups of whole milk just to a boil in a medium saucepan over high heat. Remove the pan from the heat and pour the boiling milk over the coconut in the processor. Pulse until the coconut is finely ground. Allow the blend to steep for 30 minutes, then strain the liquid through a fine sieve set over a bowl, pressing down on the pulp to squeeze out all the liquid. Return the pulp to the processor with the rest of the boiled milk and repeat the process. The milk is now ready to use. To store, transfer to an airtight container and refrigerate for up to 1 week.

SHELLFISH STOCK

Shellfish Stock in a Hurry

Knowing that even a small stash of uncooked shellfish shells may not be everybody's idea of a freezer staple, here's a quick-to-make shellfish stock that needs no shells at all.

6 bottles (8 ounces each) clam juice

1 Asian Spice Bundle (page 6) or Mediterranean Spice Bundle (page 21)

1. Combine the clam juice and spice bundle in a large saucepan and bring to a boil over medium heat. Reduce the heat to medium-low and simmer the mixture for 8 to 10 minutes.

2. Remove and discard the spice bundle. Use the stock immediately.

Makes 6 cups

Shrimp shells make an especially full-flavored stock, so ask your fishmonger to save them for you. Uncooked shells can be kept safely in the freezer for up to one month. Be sure to keep them in an airtight plastic bag and date it. Use this stock as a substitute for Lobster Stock and as a poaching liquid for fish.

> 3 tablespoons olive oil
> 1 pound uncooked shrimp or crayfish shells, rinsed
> 2 medium onions, chopped
> 2 ribs celery, chopped
> 8 cups cold water
> 3 cups dry white wine
> 4 sprigs fresh thyme
> 2 star anise
> 2 bay leaves

1. Heat the olive oil in a large stockpot over medium-high heat. Add the shrimp shells, onions, and celery, stir well, and cook until the vegetables brown slightly, stirring constantly.

2. Add the remaining ingredients and bring to a boil. Reduce the heat to low and simmer, uncovered, for about 1 hour, skimming off any foam that forms on the surface.

3. Remove the pot from the heat and strain the stock through a fine sieve set over a large heatproof bowl. Press the solids with the back of a spoon to extract as much liquid as possible. Cool, transfer to airtight containers, and refrigerate for up to 1 week or freeze for 1 month.

Makes about 6 cups

Chapter 2

SOUP BOWLS

ALL MANNER OF SOUPS

For us, there are no rules when it comes to serving soup. That's the fun of it. Soup, like so many of our other bowls, can lead off a meal, serve as an accompaniment, or follow as a main bowl. You may want to make it the center of attention, in which case you'd be opting for big bowls. Or you may choose to have smaller servings, in which case you may want to serve soup family style. Whichever you choose, consider making one or two of the side bowl suggestions. In several instances—Corn Soup with Ricotta and Spinach Dumplings, White Bean and Mushroom Soup with Chickpea Fritters, Roasted Garlic and Boniato Soup with Crispy Thai Mushroom Roll—we've already chosen the accompaniment. Most of the recipes here and many of the recipes in the Dumplings and Doodads chapter were made for each other. It's simply a matter of making the match.

We've included plenty of other soups that are especially light and brothy and very simply garnished—ideal, say, after a long hot day in the sun. Try our Cool Hand Cuke Soup or Chilled Pepper and Beet Soup with Lemongrass for a refreshing lift. With add-ons of grilled fish or shellfish, sliced roasted meats, or handfuls of freshly chopped greens just purchased from the market or local farmstand, the flexibility is endless.

No matter how or when or with what you eat them, we'd like to think that our soups will become a mainstay around your house.

TOMATO, MANGO, AND GINGER GAZPACHO

BASIL OIL
(page 230)

CHICKPEA FRITTERS
(page 185)

SHRIMP QUESADILLAS
(page 164)

AVOCADO WASABI
(page 260)

What's so wonderful about gazpacho during the hot summer months? For one, you don't have to turn on the stove—well, only very briefly (to blanch green beans)—yet you can create a satisfying main course for lunch in a surprisingly quick amount of time.

The mango in this version adds an unexpected but delightful flavor to this colorful celebration of summer's freshest.

2 ounces green beans, blanched and shocked (see box, page 214)
1 cup pineapple juice
½ cup roasted and peeled red bell peppers (see box, page 18)
¼ cup chopped peeled fresh ginger
3 fresh jalapeño peppers, stemmed, seeded, and chopped
2 tablespoons Sweet Soy Sauce (page 251)
4 cups tomato juice
1 medium zucchini, cut into ¼-inch dice
1 medium red onion, cut into ¼-inch dice
1 medium green bell pepper, stemmed, seeded, and cut into ¼-inch dice
1 small ripe tomato, seeded and cut into ¼-inch dice
¼ cup chopped fresh Italian (flat-leaf) parsley
3 tablespoons chopped fresh cilantro leaves
2 mangoes, peeled, pitted, and cut into ¼-inch dice
½ cup fresh lime juice
Salt and freshly ground black pepper, to taste

1. Cut the beans into ¼-inch rounds and set aside.

2. Combine the pineapple juice, roasted red peppers, ginger, jalapeños, and soy sauce in a blender or food processor and process until smooth.

3. Press the mixture through a fine sieve into a large bowl. Stir in the beans and the remaining ingredients and refrigerate, covered, until well chilled, about 2 hours.

4. To serve, stir the gazpacho, then ladle it into chilled bowls, dividing the vegetables and mango evenly.

Serves 4 to 6 as a main bowl

GREEN THUMB GAZPACHO

Gazpacho is virtually impossible to ruin if you remember one rule: Always use the freshest vegetables possible. This will automatically set the flavor and assure you of a naturally delicious soup. This recipe produces a lovely pale green soup that benefits visually from a red or dark green garnish, like minced red pepper or chopped parsley.

2 pounds (about 20) fresh tomatillos,
    husks removed

7 medium ribs celery, coarsely chopped

2 medium cucumbers, cut into 1-inch pieces

1 medium zucchini, coarsely chopped

1 large red onion, coarsely chopped

½ cup fresh lime juice

½ cup rice vinegar

½ cup water

¼ cup chopped fresh Italian (flat-leaf) parsley

2 fresh poblano chilies, stemmed,
    seeded, and chopped

1 fresh Scotch bonnet pepper or serrano chili,
    stemmed, seeded, and chopped

A Pinch for All Seasons (page 246), to taste

Integrate odd-shaped bowls among your more ordinary ones for fun and a touch of eccentricity.

YELLOW CURRY OIL
(*page 233*)

CRAB EMPANADAS
(*page 158*)

PICADILLO BUNS
(*page 169*)

**CHILI-MARINATED
GRILLED SHRIMP**
(*page 183*)

1. Preheat the oven to 350°F.

2. Place the tomatillos in a roasting pan and roast until soft, about 20 minutes. Remove from the oven and cool.

3. Transfer the tomatillos and all the remaining ingredients, except A Pinch for All Seasons, in batches to a blender or food processor and process until smooth. Pour the soup into airtight containers, and refrigerate until thoroughly chilled or for up to 3 days.

4. To serve, stir well, transfer to a big bowl, and season with A Pinch for All Seasons.

Serves 6 to 8 as a main bowl

ROAST THE GREEN LANTERN

The shape of the veined, paper-thin covering on a tomatillo resembles a festive Chinese lantern, another name by which tomatillos are known. Also called a Mexican green tomato, the tomatillo belongs to the same nightshade family as the tomato. But it is not a tomato. In fact, the tomatillo is more closely akin to a berry, especially the papery-husked gooseberry.

Tomatillos can be used raw, either chopped or thinly sliced, in salads, for example, for their slightly acidic taste and crunchy texture, but more often they are cooked. Poaching or roasting tomatillos whole softens their thick skins and brings out their citrus and herblike flavors. They blend well with spices and chilies, making them a great base for soups, sauces, and dressings.

Tomatillos can be found fresh in Latin markets and many supermarkets. Look for firm, pale small green fruits with tight papery skins and no sign of blemish. They hold remarkably well refrigerated for up to a month. They are also available in cans.

COOL HAND CUKE SOUP

The kitchen is the last place you want to be on a hot, hazy summer afternoon. But if you are making this soup, you won't mind a bit. Considered a mainstay of the summer recipe repertoire at Lola Bowla, this creamy concoction is a breeze to make, plus the spice and herb possibilities are limitless. Make a bowl of this a complete meal by serving it with dumplings, cornbread, or a crisp side salad. Chilled clay pots make for an attractive presentation, as does a rustic vegetable salsa garnish.

12 cups chopped unpeeled English
    (long, thin, unwaxed) cucumbers
    (about 10 cucumbers)
6 scallions, white and green parts, chopped
1 cup minced fresh cilantro leaves
3 cups regular or lowfat sour cream, if desired
½ cup fresh lemon juice
2 tablespoons chopped fresh mint leaves
1 tablespoon ground cumin
3 cups Chicken Stock for Mediterranean Bowls
    (page 20) or water, or as needed
Salt and freshly ground black pepper, to taste

1. Combine the cucumbers, scallions, cilantro, sour cream, lemon juice, mint, and cumin in large bowl. Transfer the mixture, in batches, to a blender or food processor and process until smooth.

2. Add chicken stock to the desired consistency. (For a thin soup, use all of it; if you prefer a thicker soup, add the stock gradually and stop when the soup is thin enough.) Season with salt and pepper. Refrigerate, covered, for 2 hours before serving.

Serves 8 as a main bowl

THE SIDE BOWLS

CRABMEAT DUMPLINGS
(page 156)

CRAB EMPANADAS
(page 158)

CHICKPEA FRITTERS
(page 185)

MANGO AND RUM-CURED SALMON ROLLS
(page 172)

HALIBUT CEVICHE SALAD
(page 211)

PUMPKIN SEED CRUMBS
(page 249)

Q-CUMBER CONUNDRUM

Q: What tube-shaped fruit has a shiny, slippery green skin and is *always* abundantly available in grocery stores?

A: Waxed cucumbers. However, these are not the preferred ones to purchase. Although waxed cucumbers always look fresh, they may not be the best choice.

MORAL: Appearances can be deceptive.

When it comes to cucumbers, always be on a quest for quality. The mild, moist, crisp flesh of fresh cucumber should never dominate the flavor of other ingredients; it can be refreshing and thirst quenching when eaten raw and a flavor-absorbing vehicle when cooked.

You'll find three kinds to choose from: short, stocky, sometimes knobby, always unwaxed ones a few inches in length, which are known as kirbies and are excellent for eating raw, skin on, alone or in salads, and for pickling; smooth, thin-skinned ones, several inches longer, which must be peeled if they are covered in wax; and long, skinny, unwaxed, nearly seedless ones, which are known as English cucumbers, and are best used in cooking because they are less watery and yield about twice as much pulp as the other varieties.

CHILLED BELL PEPPER AND BEET SOUP WITH LEMONGRASS

Either you love beets or you hate them. We suspect that many people who hate beets have only experienced them from a jar or can. Those of us who love fresh beets tolerate the canned ones, at best. In other words, for this Vietnamese-style "borscht" to be a win-them-over bowl, please don't even think about using anything other than fresh beets. Cool and light, this soup is a treat in summer—earthy, bright, and refreshing.

¼ cup olive oil

2 medium carrots, peeled and chopped

2 large fresh red beets, peeled and chopped

1 medium red onion, chopped

1 medium red bell pepper, stemmed, seeded, and chopped

1 cup chopped ripe tomatoes

¼ cup chopped peeled fresh ginger

3 stalks lemongrass bottoms, finely chopped

8 cups Vegetable Stock for Asian Bowls (page 27)

½ cup fresh lime juice

3 tablespoons grated lime zest

Salt and freshly ground black pepper, to taste

2 tablespoons Yellow Curry Oil (page 233)

Grilled flatbread, for serving

THE SIDE BOWLS

GARLIC OIL
(page 234)

MUSTARD-POTATO CREAM VINAIGRETTE
(page 223)

GARLIC AND HERB PASTE
(page 239)

HORSERADISH ROUILLE
(page 251)

SOUR CREMA
(page 263)

1. Heat the olive oil in a large stockpot over medium heat. Add the vegetables, ginger, and lemongrass. Cover and cook, stirring occasionally, until the vegetables are moderately softened, about 15 minutes. Add the vegetable stock and bring to a boil. Reduce the heat and simmer, uncovered, until the vegetables are completely tender, 30 minutes, skimming off any residue as it rises to the surface. Remove from the heat and cool to room temperature. Refrigerate until chilled, 1 hour.

2. Process the cooled soup, in batches, in a blender or food processor until smooth. Transfer to a large bowl, stir in the lime juice and lime zest, and season with salt and pepper. Serve in chilled bowls and drizzle with the curry oil before serving.

Serves 6 as a main bowl

Beauty and function: Don't let a stunning bowl just sit on your shelf as a decoration. This illustration of a hand-blown one-of-a-kind Swedish example is perfect for serving chilled soup.

CARROT CARDAMOM SOUP

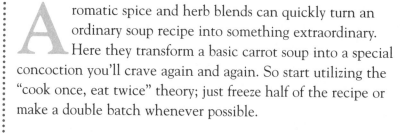

MINT OIL
(page 231)

PORCINI GARLIC PASTE
(page 242)

Aromatic spice and herb blends can quickly turn an ordinary soup recipe into something extraordinary. Here they transform a basic carrot soup into a special concoction you'll crave again and again. So start utilizing the "cook once, eat twice" theory; just freeze half of the recipe or make a double batch whenever possible.

2 tablespoons olive oil

I medium white onion, chopped

3 tablespoons chopped peeled fresh ginger

I tablespoon Cardamom Spice Blend (page 247)

5 large carrots, peeled and cut into ¼-inch dice

I red bell pepper, stemmed, seeded,
    and cut into ¼-inch dice

I medium Idaho potato, peeled and cut into ½-inch pieces

I medium sweet potato, peeled and cut into ½-inch pieces

8 cups Chicken Stock for Asian Bowls (page 5)

2 cups dry white wine

I tablespoon (packed) light brown sugar

½ cup fresh lime juice

½ cup chopped fresh Italian (flat-leaf) parsley

4 tablespoons (½ stick) unsalted butter, in pieces

Salt and freshly ground black pepper, to taste

Lime slices, for garnish

I. Heat the olive oil in a large nonreactive stockpot over medium heat. Add the onion, ginger, spice blend, carrots, red pepper, and potatoes. Stir to coat the vegetables with the spices, then sauté until the onion is translucent and the vegetables are tender, about 15 minutes.

2. Add the chicken stock, white wine, and brown sugar. Bring to a boil, reduce the heat to low, cover, and simmer until the vegetables are tender, 30 to 40 minutes. Remove from the heat.

3. Transfer the mixture, in batches, to a blender or food processor and process until smooth. Return the soup to the pot and reheat over low heat. Stir in the lime juice and parsley; add the butter and salt and pepper, and heat until the butter is melted. Serve in individual bowls, each garnished with a lime slice.

Serves 4 to 6 as a main bowl

DAL SOUP

Split peas, referred to as a type of *dal* in India, are often cooked with onions and spices, then puréed. They are high in carbohydrates and low in fat, as well as flavorful, and we often enjoy them in this Indian-inspired soup. In addition, this soup is so versatile that it also can be served as a sauce over rice or as a dip for grilled chicken cubes or shrimp. The Indian crisp flatbreads, poppadums, are a wonderful accompaniment.

3 tablespoons olive oil

1 onion, chopped

¼ cup roasted garlic (see box, page 48), chopped

1 teaspoon ground turmeric

1 teaspoon curry powder, preferably homemade (page 10)

1 teaspoon ground cumin

1 bay leaf

3 cups yellow split peas

4 fresh Kaffir lime leaves

2 cinnamon sticks (3 inches each)

8 cups Chicken Stock for Asian Bowls (page 5)

Salt and freshly ground black pepper, to taste

Crispy Shallots (see box, page 77), for garnish (optional)

PICADILLO BUNS
(page 169)

CHILI-MARINATED GRILLED SHRIMP
(page 183)

CHEESE-STUFFED POBLANOS
(page 174)

CHILI-ROASTED VEGETABLES
(page 96)

1. Heat the olive oil in a large stockpot over medium heat. Add the onion, roasted garlic, turmeric, curry powder, cumin, and bay leaf and stir to coat the onion with the spices. Sauté, stirring occasionally, until the onion is translucent, 5 to 10 minutes.

2. Add the split peas, lime leaves, cinnamon sticks, and chicken stock. Bring to a boil, reduce the heat to low, and simmer, uncovered, until the split peas are soft, about 45 minutes. Set aside to cool. Remove the lime leaves, bay leaf, and cinnamon sticks.

3. Transfer the mixture, in batches, to a blender or food processor and process until smooth. Season with salt and pepper. Reheat before serving. If you want to thin the soup, add a little water while reheating. Top with Crispy Shallots before serving, if desired.

Serves 4 to 6 as a main bowl

GARLIC, BEFORE AND AFTER THE ROAST

Before: Bitter in taste; dry

After: Nutty and sweet in flavor; soft and silky-smooth in texture

How to roast:

1. When buying garlic, look for uniformly shaped heads with tightly closed cloves. Avoid heads with dark bruises or soft spots, which can affect the taste of the entire head.

2. Preheat the oven to 350°F.

3. Loosen the papery outer skin by rolling the head of garlic back and forth across your cutting board. Remove the loose skin. When it no longer falls away easily, you've removed enough. Be sure not to pull off too much, or you'll loosen the cloves themselves.

4. Place the garlic head in a small roasting pan and drizzle ½ teaspoon olive oil over it to coat.

5. Roast the garlic until tender, for about 1 hour. Cool.

6. Cut the garlic head in half horizontally. With the back of the knife (if you don't want to use your hands), press the softened cloves out of their skins, rotating the head as you work to squeeze out all the garlic.

7. Store the roasted garlic, covered with a little olive oil, in a tightly closed jar in the refrigerator for up to 1 week.

CORN SOUP WITH RICOTTA AND SPINACH DUMPLINGS

We took the satisfying Southern combination of corn and bacon, created a chowder, then puréed it in order to highlight a feature of this soup we especially love—ricotta and spinach dumplings. Boniato, a sweet potato from South America, gives added body and makes an already thick soup even thicker and richer. It is available at Latin American or specialty markets.

2 tablespoons olive oil

2 ounces smoked slab bacon, rind removed,
   cut into ½-inch dice

1½ teaspoons curry powder, preferably homemade
   (page 10)

¼ teaspoon cayenne pepper

3 ribs celery, chopped

2 carrots, peeled and chopped

1 medium onion, chopped

1 medium boniato or sweet potato, peeled and
   cut into ½-inch dice

1 fresh jalapeño pepper, stemmed, seeded, and finely minced

3 cups fresh corn kernels

4 cups Chicken Stock for Asian Bowls (page 5)

1 cup dry white wine

2 tablespoons Hot Chili Oil (page 232),
   plus additional for serving (optional)

½ cup half-and-half

½ cup fresh lime juice, plus additional for serving

Salt and freshly ground black pepper, to taste

8 Ricotta and Spinach Dumplings (page 163)

4 ounces flat-leaf fresh spinach, rinsed and shredded

THE SIDE BOWLS

YELLOW CURRY OIL
(page 233)

CRISPY LEEKS
(see box, page 77)

49

1. Combine the olive oil, bacon, curry powder, cayenne, and all of the vegetables, except 1 cup of the corn, in a stockpot over medium heat. Cover and cook for 30 minutes. Add the chicken stock and wine, bring to a boil, and reduce the heat to low. Simmer, uncovered, for 15 minutes.

2. Meanwhile, heat the chili oil in a small skillet over medium-high heat. Add the remaining 1 cup corn, and sauté it until lightly browned, 1 to 2 minutes. Remove from the heat and set aside.

3. Remove the soup from the heat and transfer it, in batches, to a blender or food processor. Process until smooth. Pour the purée back into the pot and reheat the soup over medium heat. Stir in the half-and-half, reserved sautéed corn, the ½ cup lime juice, and salt and pepper to taste.

4. Divide the dumplings among 4 serving bowls and ladle the corn soup over them. Garnish with the shredded spinach. Serve with additional fresh lime juice and chili oil, if desired.

Serves 4 as a main bowl

GOLDEN DELICIOUS EGG DROP SOUP WITH CRABMEAT DUMPLINGS

At last, an egg drop soup that will leave you tipping your bowl to siphon out the last drops. Bands of egg swirl seductively through this broth made without cornstarch. Delicate Crabmeat Dumplings further enhance the silky broth. The naturally sweet flavor of crabmeat and the earthy taste of asparagus create the proverbial perfect blend of sea and earth.

6 cups Chicken Stock for Asian Bowls
   (page 5)

2 tablespoons mushroom soy sauce or
   regular soy sauce

2 carrots, peeled and chopped

5 sprigs fresh cilantro

4 cloves garlic, crushed

3 tablespoons chopped peeled fresh ginger

4 saffron threads

2 star anise

3 large eggs, beaten

2 tablespoons dry white wine

12 Crabmeat Dumplings (page 156)

4 ounces flat-leaf fresh spinach, rinsed

4 scallions, white and green parts, minced,
   for garnish

2 tablespoons Hot Chili Oil (page 232),
   plus additional for serving

1. Combine the chicken stock, soy sauce, carrots, cilantro sprigs, garlic, ginger, saffron, and star anise in a stockpot and bring to a boil over medium-high heat. Reduce the heat to low and simmer, uncovered, for 10 minutes.

2. Meanwhile, beat the eggs and white wine in a small bowl until blended.

3. Strain the broth through a fine sieve set over a large bowl. Press the solids with the back of a spoon to extract as much liquid as possible. Return the broth to the pot and heat over medium-low heat until it just comes to a simmer.

4. Reheat the crabmeat dumplings by steaming them in a small pan with a little salted water for 4 minutes until heated through. Remove with a slotted spoon to individual soup bowls.

5. Divide the spinach among the bowls.

THE SIDE BOWLS

GARLIC OIL
(page 234)

PARSLEY AND GARLIC OIL
(page 234)

SWEET SOY SAUCE
(page 251)

CHINESE SAUSAGE
(page 142)

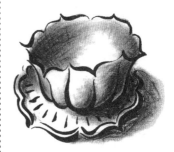

A delicate soup calls for a delicate presentation. A pretty bowl with a petal-like exterior and a fanciful underplate make our egg drop even lovelier.

6. While stirring the simmering broth, pour in the egg mixture in one slow, steady stream. Stir the broth again to break the cooked egg apart into strands.

7. Ladle the soup over the dumplings and spinach. Garnish with the chopped scallions and season with a drizzle of the hot oil.

Serves 4

THE SAFFRON STIGMA

Despite the fact that saffron is the most expensive spice on earth, it is a key ingredient in some of the world's most popular dishes—French bouillabaisse, Spanish paella, Italian risotto, Indian rice pilaf—for both its bright yellow color and complex, distinctive flavor.

Fortunately, a little goes a long way. Because flowering crocuses must be handpicked and the stigmas—which are the saffron threads—must be removed by hand, only about 1,100 flowers can be stripped by an experienced picker in one hour. And, because it takes approximately 250,000 flowers to equal one pound of saffron threads, a day's work is equivalent to no more than a couple of ounces of the spice. This is what makes it so precious: one pound of saffron is worth about $450 wholesale and $4,500 retail. Such a high price on such a small amount breeds greed. Some exporters do all sorts of unsavory things to add to the weight of saffron, such as coating it with molasses, honey, or wax.

When purchasing saffron, look for whole threads with a deep red color. If you are able to smell it, do; it should have a strong perfumey aroma. Good saffron should never taste sweet; rather, it will taste slightly bitter and floral. Having experimented with different types of saffron, we have found the Spanish varieties superior.

HOT-AND-SOUR CHOWDER

On a trip to Thailand, in pursuit of the hottest, most versatile hot sauce, we found ourselves at a soup stall on the outskirts of Bangkok. Interestingly, it was next to a roadside display of the latest in stoves, refrigerators, and other not-so-portable pieces of kitchen equipment. The soup we ordered was not memorable, but the hot sauce it was served with should have come with an antidote. The closest we've found here, in terms of flavor and intensity, is Sriracha Hot Chile Sauce. This all-occasion hot sauce can enliven any soup, but it is especially well-suited to this piquant, hearty chowder. Look for it here in Asian markets.

2 tablespoons Hot Chili Oil (page 232)

1 tablespoon peanut oil

2 large carrots, peeled and cut into ¼-inch dice

1 medium Spanish onion, thinly sliced

1 cup thinly sliced stemmed shiitake mushrooms

¾ cup chopped, rinsed white and green parts of leek

2 pounds skinless, boneless chicken breasts,
      cut into 1-inch strips

1 pound medium shrimp, peeled (leaving tails intact)
      and deveined

2 cups diced peeled Idaho potato

2 cups finely shredded Savoy cabbage

8 cups Hot-and-Sour Broth (page 14)

¼ cup fresh lime juice

Salt and freshly ground Sichuan peppercorns,
      to taste

12 ounces large spinach leaves, preferably flat-leaf,
      rinsed and julienned

¼ cup chopped fresh cilantro leaves, for garnish

Sriracha Hot Chile Sauce, for serving

THE SIDE BOWLS

CHOPPED SCALLIONS, WHITE AND GREEN PARTS

CRAB EMPANADAS
(page 158)

SHRIMP POT STICKERS
(page 162)

1. Heat the hot oil and peanut oil in a large nonreactive stock-pot over medium heat. Add the carrots, onion, mushrooms, and leek and sauté to soften slightly, 5 minutes.

2. Add the chicken strips, shrimp, potatoes, and cabbage. Cook, stirring, for 5 minutes more. Add the broth and bring to a boil. Reduce the heat to low and simmer, uncovered, until the chicken and vegetables are cooked through.

3. Remove the soup from the heat and stir in the lime juice. Season with salt and Sichuan pepper.

4. Divide the spinach among soup bowls, ladle the chowder over it, and garnish with the chopped cilantro. Pass the Sriracha Hot Chile Sauce separately.

Serves 4 to 6 as a main bowl

LATIN CHICKEN SOUP WITH NOODLES

This is not the chicken soup of days past—it's better because the chicken is marinated and sautéed rather than bland and boiled. The main theme of all chicken soups, though, is that they boast a "cure-all" reputation. Whether you're in San Juan or New York City, chicken soup is not only good for whatever ails you, but a delectable meal.

I chicken (3 pounds), trimmed of excess fat, cut into 16 pieces
Ancho Marinade (recipe follows)
4 tablespoons Garlic Oil (page 234)
2 onions, cut into ½-inch dice
I green bell pepper, stemmed, seeded, and cut into ½-inch dice
I red bell pepper, stemmed, seeded, and cut into ½-inch dice

I fresh poblano chili, stemmed, seeded,
   and cut into ½-inch dice

I cup cubed calabaza or winter squash

8 cups Chicken Stock for Asian Bowls (page 5)

I cup (loosely packed) fresh cilantro leaves

8 ounces angel hair pasta, broken into thirds

½ cup fresh lime juice

2 teaspoons finely chopped fresh thyme

Salt and freshly ground black pepper, to taste

2 cups coarsely chopped, rinsed fresh spinach

1. Toss the chicken pieces in a large bowl with the marinade. Refrigerate, covered, for at least 5 hours, preferably overnight.

2. Heat 2 tablespoons of the Garlic Oil in a large deep skillet over medium heat. Add half the chicken and sauté until browned on all sides. Using a slotted spoon, transfer the pieces to paper towels to drain. Sauté the remaining chicken in the remaining Garlic Oil and drain.

3. To the drippings in the skillet add the onions, bell peppers, poblano, and squash. Cook, stirring, over medium-low heat until the onions are softened and caramelized, about 10 minutes.

4. Return the chicken to the skillet along with the chicken stock and ¾ cup of the cilantro leaves, reserving the remaining ¼ cup leaves for garnish. Bring to a boil over medium-high heat, reduce the heat to low, and simmer, uncovered, skimming the surface occasionally, until the chicken is cooked through, 30 minutes.

5. Meanwhile, in a large pot of boiling water, cook the pasta according to the package directions until just al dente.

6. Remove the soup from the heat. Stir in the lime juice, thyme, and salt and pepper. Drain the pasta and divide it, with the spinach, among individual serving bowls. Ladle the soup and

THE SIDE BOWLS

ASIAN BABY BACK RIBS
(page 177)

PORCINI GARLIC PASTE
(page 242)

CHIPOTLE BUTTER
(page 250)

*Casual, brightly colored bowls
with amusing designs add a
festive note to any dinner.*

chicken pieces into the bowls and garnish with the remaining cilantro leaves. Be sure to have extra bowls on the table for the discarded chicken bones.

Serves 6 to 8

ANCHO MARINADE

While this full-bodied blend makes a great marinade for poultry, as in Latin Chicken Soup with Noodles (preceding recipe), and meats, as in Simmer My Juices and Give Me a Little Couscous (page 151), it also acts as a potent glaze on simple grilled fish or shrimp. If you can't find fresh mango, use mango purée, available in most specialty food markets. And, if you can't find ancho chili powder, you can still make a lively marinade using another pure ground chili.

> ½ **cup chopped mango**
> ¼ **cup rice vinegar**
> **10 cloves garlic, roasted (see box, page 48)**
> **3 tablespoons ancho chili powder**
> **2 tablespoons mirin, sweet sherry, or sweet vermouth**
> **2 teaspoons soy sauce**
> **Water, if necessary**

Combine all the ingredients, except the water, in a blender or food processor and process until smooth. The mixture should have the consistency of a milkshake. If it is too thick, add water a teaspoon at a time. Use immediately, or transfer to an airtight container and store in the refrigerator for up to 1 week.

Makes about 1 cup

Traditional Spanish clay bowls make perfect vessels for Mexican-style marinades and sauces.

LAMB WITH ORZO AND CURRY BROTH

Here's one for curry lovers: Three different curried components star here—oil deeply colored by turmeric, curry powder heated by cayenne, and broth sweetened with vegetables and more curry powder—each infusing its distinctive character into the dish. These rich Indian spices complement the strong flavor of lamb and produce an aromatic golden broth. We like to serve this in deep bowls with soft pita bread or *roti* for soaking up the liquid.

8 ounces orzo

¼ cup Yellow Curry Oil (page 233)

3 cloves garlic, chopped

2 tablespoons minced fresh ginger

2 fresh jalapeño peppers, stemmed, seeded, and chopped

2 teaspoons curry powder, preferably homemade (page 10)

1 teaspoon five-spice powder, toasted

3 bay leaves

1 pound ground lamb shoulder

2 tablespoons Sweet Soy Sauce (page 251)

2 cups Curry Broth (recipe follows)

1 cup cooked, diced potato (see Note)

2 cups (loosely packed) flat-leaf fresh spinach, rinsed

3 tablespoons fresh lemon juice

Salt and freshly ground black pepper, to taste

¼ cup Pumpkin Seed Crumbs (optional; page 249)

1. Prepare the orzo according to package directions. Drain and set aside, covered, to keep warm.

2. Heat the curry oil in a large skillet over medium heat. Add the garlic, ginger, jalapeños, spices, and bay leaves, stir to combine, and cook until fragrant, 2 minutes.

THE SIDE BOWLS

BASIL OIL
(page 230)

MINT OIL
(page 231)

VEGETABLE RICE
(page 149)

CRISPY PARSLEY
(see box, page 77)

3. Add the ground lamb, stirring to coat with the spices, then stir in the soy sauce. Reduce the heat to low and cook 5 minutes, stirring constantly to break up the lamb chunks.

4. Add the broth. Increase the heat to medium and simmer, uncovered, until the lamb is cooked through, 5 minutes. Remove the bay leaves.

5. Stir in the cooked orzo, potato, spinach, and lemon juice and remove the pan from the heat. Season with salt and pepper. Sprinkle with Pumpkin Seed Crumbs.

6. Serve in individual bowls.

Serves 4 to 6 as a main bowl, 8 to 10 as a small bowl

Note: Since no further cooking is required once the potato is added to the soup, it is best if the potato is freshly cooked and warm.

ONION SOUP WITH STILTON CHEESE

Five pounds of onions may seem like a lot, but onions have this amazing way of cooking down to one third their original volume. Large, pale yellow-skinned Vidalia onions, from Vidalia, Georgia, are exceptionally sweet and juicy and our first choice for this. Spanish onions, which are not as naturally sweet as Vidalias, can be substituted, but will need to be caramelized with a touch of brown sugar.

The French crown their bowls of onion soup with Gruyère to enrich and sweeten it. We prefer to enhance our onion soup with a sharp and pungent English Stilton. This creamy, crumbly blue-green-veined cheese counters the sweetness of the onions.

6 tablespoons (¾ stick) unsalted butter

5 pounds sweet onions, preferably Vidalia onions
(or substitute Spanish onions), thinly sliced

2 tablespoons (packed) brown sugar
(needed only if using Spanish onions)

3 tablespoons fennel seeds, toasted (see box, page 137)
and ground

3 tablespoons tomato paste

2 bay leaves

1 teaspoon chopped fresh thyme

6 threads saffron

1 cup dry white wine

1 cup dry red wine

½ cup brandy

¼ cup balsamic vinegar

8 cups Chicken Stock for Mediterranean Bowls
(page 20)

½ cup crumbled English Stilton cheese or
other good-quality blue cheese

Salt and freshly ground black pepper, to taste

Crusty bread, for serving

1. Melt the butter in a large nonreactive stockpot over medium heat. Add the onions and sugar (if using Spanish onions) and stir to combine. Reduce the heat to low and cover. Cook the onions until golden brown and caramelized, 10 to 20 minutes, stirring regularly.

2. Stir in the ground fennel seeds, tomato paste, bay leaves, thyme, and saffron. Add the wines, brandy, and vinegar and bring to a boil. Simmer, uncovered, for 10 minutes.

3. Add the chicken stock and bring to a boil. Reduce the heat to low and remove the bay leaves. Stir in the Stilton and season with salt and pepper. Remove from the heat and serve with crusty bread.

Serves 6 to 8 as a main bowl

THE SIDE BOWLS

SHRIMP AND YUCA FRITTERS
(page 184)

CREAMY POLENTA
(page 73)

APRICOT AND APPLE CHUTNEY
(page 266)

A deep round bowl holds plenty of caramelized onions and leaves room for dropping in thick chunks of crusty bread.

LENTIL SOUP WITH ROASTED GARLIC AND HERBS

Feel the Pulse

There is incredible variety when it comes to lentils, or pulses, and all are fine to use in our lentil soup. That includes the ordinary brown ones found in plastic bags in grocery stores, the green seed-coated Le Puy lentils from France (our first choice), available in specialty food stores, and the less common red and yellow lentils, found in Middle Eastern markets. Lentils cook quickly and, although you don't have to soak them, you do have to rinse and pick through them to remove any bits of grit before cooking them.

Did you ever wonder why you sometimes yearn for a bowl of soup filled with beans when you are in need of comfort and nurturing? The answer is in the beans. Beans, which include lentils, are high in minerals, calcium, and phosphorous (essential to maintaining strong bones and teeth) and vitamins A and B (great for body functioning). These little protein-packed legumes provide filling, nourishing sustenance.

8 ounces smoked slab bacon, rind removed,
    cut into ½-inch dice
5 ribs celery, finely diced
2 carrots, peeled and finely diced
1 large onion, finely diced
1 large celery root or white turnip, peeled and finely diced
2 tablespoons curry powder, preferably homemade
    (page 10)
2 cups lentils, preferably green Le Puy
3 tomatoes, seeded and chopped
½ cup sherry wine vinegar
1 sprig fresh rosemary
1 sprig fresh thyme
6 cups Chicken Stock for Mediterranean Bowls (page 20)
3 tablespoons Garlic Paste (recipe follows)
1 cup (loosely packed) chopped, rinsed fresh flat-leaf spinach
2 tablespoons unsalted butter
Salt and freshly ground black pepper, to taste

1. Cook the bacon in a medium nonreactive stockpot over low heat until crispy, about 5 minutes. Using a slotted spoon, transfer the bacon to paper towels to drain.

2. Add the celery, carrots, onion, celery root, and curry powder to the bacon fat in the pot. Sauté over medium heat until the celery root is tender, about 10 minutes.

3. Return the bacon to the pot, add the lentils, tomatoes, vinegar, rosemary, thyme, and chicken stock, and bring to a boil. Reduce the heat to low and simmer, uncovered, until the lentils are soft, about 30 minutes. Remove the herb sprigs.

4. Using the slotted spoon, transfer one third of the lentils to a blender or food processor and process until smooth. Return the purée to the pot and stir well to blend.

5. Stir in the Garlic Paste, spinach, and butter. Season with salt and pepper and heat until the butter is melted. Serve immediately.

Serves 4 to 6 as a main bowl

GARLIC PASTE

If you are a garlic lover, this simple recipe will become a staple in your kitchen. Having this paste on hand makes using garlic so easy—no peeling, no chopping. Drop a spoonful into a sauté pan when you're making pasta sauce or swirl it into a bowl of limpid broth. You can halve the recipe, if desired.

> **I cup garlic cloves, peeled**
> **½ cup olive oil, or more as needed**

I. Combine the garlic and oil in a small saucepan and simmer over medium-low heat until the garlic is lightly browned and soft, about 5 minutes. Remove from the heat and cool.

2. Process in a food processor or blender until smooth. If necessary, add more oil to achieve the desired consistency. Use immediately, or transfer to an airtight container and store in the refrigerator for up to 2 weeks.

Makes about I½ cups

CRAB EMPANADAS
(page 158)

THREE-ONION POTATO CAKES
(page 187)

ZUCCHINI PANCAKES
(page 188)

WHITE BEAN AND MUSHROOM SOUP WITH CHICKPEA FRITTERS

This filling winter soup is loaded with wild mushrooms. The greater the variety you use, the richer the flavor. When shopping for mushrooms, look for unblemished, relatively dry ones; they should not be spongy. Clean them just before you plan to use them and never immerse them in water. They will become soggy and lose not only texture but also flavor. Instead, wipe the caps and stems with a damp cloth or gently brush the mushrooms with a vegetable brush.

The choice of mushrooms is up to you. Shiitake, chanterelle, porcini, cremini, morel, hen-of-the-woods, and oyster are all excellent choices. And be sure you have the Porcini Garlic Paste on hand, even if you are using fresh porcini. The concentrated flavor of the paste intensifies even the most subtle mushroom flavor.

This soup is smooth and satisfying on its own. But with nutty, crispy Chickpea Fritters, you have a meal in a bowl. Make the fritters first, and keep them warm in a 200°F oven.

Use a casserole-style pot to serve a thick, hearty stew-like soup. Hold it in the oven at a low temperature and take it right to the table. And don't forget the wooden trivet!

4 tablespoons olive oil

8 ounces mixed wild mushrooms, wiped clean and trimmed

Salt and freshly ground black pepper, to taste

4 ounces smoked slab bacon, rind removed, diced

5 tablespoons Garlic Paste (page 61)

1 tablespoon Porcini Garlic Paste (page 242)

1 large carrot, peeled and cut into ½-inch dice

I large onion, cut into ½-inch dice

5 ribs celery, cut into ½-inch dice

2 bay leaves

6 cups Chicken Stock for Mediterranean Bowls (page 20)

3 cups cooked white beans (see box at right)

½ cup fresh lemon juice

12 Chickpea Fritters (page 185)

2 tablespoons Parsley and Garlic Oil (page 234),
   plus additional for serving (optional)

Chopped parsley, for garnish (optional)

1. Heat 2 tablespoons of the olive oil in a medium skillet over medium heat. Add the wild mushrooms and sauté them just until semisoft, about 3 minutes. They should still retain their shape and some crunch. Remove from the heat, season with salt and pepper, and set aside.

2. Heat the remaining 2 tablespoons oil in a large saucepan over medium heat and add the bacon. Sauté until slightly crispy, about 3 minutes. Add both garlic pastes and stir to combine.

3. Add the carrot, onion, celery, and bay leaves. Cover and cook until the vegetables are tender, about 20 minutes.

4. Add the chicken stock and 2 cups of the white beans. Cover and simmer for 15 minutes. Remove and discard the bay leaves.

5. Transfer the mixture, in batches, to a blender or food processor and process until smooth. Return the purée to the pan and add the remaining 1 cup beans, reserved mushrooms, and lemon juice. Season with salt and pepper, and simmer gently over medium heat until heated through.

6. Ladle the soup into serving bowls. Divide the fritters among the bowls and drizzle each serving with the Parsley and Garlic Oil. Garnish with chopped parsley, if desired.

Serves 4 to 6 as a main bowl, 8 to 10 as a small bowl

To Cook Dried White Beans

Prepare the beans a day ahead.

1. Rinse and sort through the beans thoroughly, discarding any pebbles or dirt.

2. Place the beans in a medium pot and add enough water to cover by 2 inches.

3. Bring to a boil, then reduce the heat to low and simmer, uncovered, for about 1½ hours, until the beans are tender.

4. Drain and set aside until ready to use, or store in an airtight container in the refrigerator overnight.

SAVORY ROASTED VEGETABLES WITH FAVA BEANS IN BLOND MISO BROTH

Roasting vegetables is a surefire way to enhance their flavor and retain their texture. The technique is so simple and the results so aromatic and tasty that you will be inspired to try vegetables you may have previously ignored. Here the low-key charm of salsify adds a subtle flavor similar to artichokes. Since salsify and fresh fava beans are specialty vegetables, they may be difficult to find. Peas make a fine substitute for the favas, while almost any root vegetable, like parsnip, can replace the salsify. Experiment by combining different vegetables for color, texture, and flavor.

Crusty bread or bowls of hot cooked jasmine rice make fine, simple accompaniments, as does any one of the very comforting side bowls.

I cup shelled fresh fava beans

I cup milk

4 salsify roots, peeled and cut into 2-inch lengths

6 scallions, white and green parts, cut into
    2-inch lengths

I cup thinly sliced red onion

I cup peeled baby carrots

I cup peeled baby white turnips

8 ounces unpeeled baby or new potatoes,
    scrubbed, quartered if large

¼ cup vegetable oil, preferably peanut

Salt and freshly ground black pepper,
    to taste

I cup Blond Miso Broth (page 28)

1. Preheat the oven to 375°F. Have ready a bowl of ice water.

2. Bring a large saucepan of water to a boil over medium heat. Add the fava beans and cook until bright green, 4 minutes. With a slotted spoon, remove the beans and plunge them into the ice water. Drain and set aside in a bowl.

3. Pour the milk into a small saucepan and bring to a boil over medium heat. Add the salsify and reduce the heat to low. Cover and cook until tender, about 10 minutes. Drain and put in a medium roasting pan.

4. Add the scallions, red onion, baby carrots, turnips, and potatoes to the roasting pan with the salsify. Add the oil and salt and pepper and toss well. Roast until the vegetables can be easily pierced with a knife but still show some resistance, about 30 minutes.

5. Meanwhile, in a saucepan, bring the broth to a simmer.

6. Divide the roasted vegetables among 4 shallow serving bowls. Sprinkle the reserved fava beans over the vegetables and ladle about ¼ cup hot broth into each bowl.

Serves 4 as a main bowl, 6 as a small bowl

THE SIDE BOWLS

CREAMY POLENTA
(page 73)

MASHED POTATOES
(page 189)

SESAME NOODLEHEAD
(page 133)

Unique bowls made by artisan potters help show off a colorful array of ingredients such as the delicate baby vegetables in this miso broth.

ROASTED GARLIC AND BONIATO SOUP WITH CRISPY THAI MUSHROOM ROLL

To add dimension to this silken smooth purée of sweet potatoes and roasted garlic, we like to serve a flaky, pastry-like roll in the bowl or alongside it. Either way, the roll creates a marvelous contrast in texture. The large amount of garlic, because it has been roasted, along with the boniato, contributes to the mildly sweet, nutty taste of the soup. Serve this full-flavored, hearty, but healthful vegetarian bowl drizzled with Garlic and Parsley Oil for added flavor and color. Boniatos are Latin American sweet potatoes and are available in specialty food markets. If you have difficulty finding them, simply substitute regular sweet potatoes.

3 pounds boniatos or sweet potatoes,
    peeled and chopped

1 large onion, chopped

½ cup chopped, roasted and peeled red peppers
    (see box, page 18)

5 tablespoons Garlic Paste (page 61)

8 cups Vegetable Stock for Asian Bowls
    (page 27)

1 cup unsweetened coconut milk (see box, page 35)

¼ cup Sweet Soy Sauce (page 251)

½ cup fresh lime juice

1 tablespoon Asian sesame oil

Salt and freshly ground black pepper, to taste

Crispy Thai Mushroom Roll (page 176),
    cut into 8 pieces

Parsley and Garlic Oil (page 234), for serving

Not only pitchers have lips. Large, lipped bowls like this one are practical. Just pour off the leftovers into an airtight container and refrigerate for another meal.

1. Combine the boniato, onion, roasted red peppers, Garlic Paste, vegetable stock, coconut milk, and soy sauce in a large stockpot and bring to a boil over medium heat. Reduce the heat to low, cover, and simmer until the vegetables are tender, 30 minutes.

2. Remove the pot from the heat. Transfer the soup, in batches, to a blender or food processor and process until smooth. Return the purée to the pot and simmer, uncovered, for 30 minutes. Stir in the lime juice and sesame oil. Season with salt and pepper.

3. Ladle the soup into bowls and serve with a piece of the mushroom roll. Pass the Parsley and Garlic Oil separately.

Serves 8 as a main bowl

CHOPPED PARSLEY

CRISPY LEEKS

(see box, page 77)

Coconut-Shrimp Soup with Cellophane Noodles

In many Asian countries, soup holds the central spot on the table at a family meal. Served in a large tureen, it is ladled into individual bowls and eaten over the course of the meal. At the end of the meal, any soup that remains is customarily poured over rice to flavor it. Diners then savor the flavored glutinous starch filler.

Served in large individual white porcelain bowls that are first warmed in the oven, this soup creates a stunning final effect: Green cilantro leaves float like lily pads on a pastel pink pond that glistens with a drizzle of curry oil. A confetti of chopped scallion dazzles the surface. And leftovers, if any, make a delicious topping for rice.

6 cups Lobster Coco Loco Broth (page 33)

¼ cup nam pla (Asian fish sauce)

3 Kaffir lime leaves

2 stalks lemongrass bottoms, finely chopped

2 tablespoons tomato paste

8 ounces cellophane noodles

1 pound small shrimp, peeled and deveined

Salt and freshly ground black pepper, to taste

5 scallions, white and green parts, finely chopped

¼ cup (loosely packed) fresh cilantro leaves

2 tablespoons Yellow Curry Oil (page 233)

THE SIDE BOWLS

CHOPPED TOASTED PEANUTS
(see box, page 137)

SAFFRON AND WASABI MASHED POTATOES
(page 190)

ZUCCHINI PANCAKES
(page 188)

SPICY CILANTRO SOY PASTE
(page 239)

1. Combine the broth, *nam pla*, lime leaves, lemongrass, and tomato paste in a nonreactive stockpot over medium heat. Bring to a boil over medium-high heat, reduce the heat to low, and simmer, uncovered, for 30 minutes.

2. Meanwhile put the noodles in a medium bowl and pour in very hot water to cover them. Let stand until softened, about 10 minutes.

3. Remove the broth from the heat and strain through a fine sieve set over a large heatproof bowl. Return the broth to the pot and bring back to a simmer. Simmer, uncovered, for 2 minutes. Add the shrimp and cook until just opaque, from 2 to 4 minutes. Season with salt and pepper.

4. Drain the noodles and divide them among 4 serving bowls. Ladle the broth and shrimp over the noodles and garnish with cilantro leaves. Sprinkle the chopped scallions over them, drizzle on the curry oil, and serve.

Serves 4 as a main bowl, 8 as a small bowl

Chapter 3

SOME OF OUR
FAVORITE HEARTY
BOWLS

STEWS

A stew should be memorable. Worth calling your own. Worth looking forward to serving again—and soon. Here we've gathered some of our favorites, reflecting our nontraditional and eclectic food passions.

Come to either of our homes for a meal during the fall and celebrate the harvest with a deep bowl of hearty winter squash stewed with fish, shrimp, and squid, as in our Seafood Stew in Tamarind Broth. Or come after the trees clarify their branches and share comforting bowls of Mustard-Rubbed Chicken Thighs and Yellow Split Pea Stew or Chili-Roasted Vegetables. These are the bowls that satisfy the soul as well as the stomach.

Because cooking a stew can sometimes be a slow process, use the waiting time to prepare a side bowl or two. Whether it's Cilantro Oil or Spicy Tomato Glaze for Ropa Vieja, or Ginger's Hot Broth or Vegetable Rice for Roasted Pork Loin with Honey-Hoisin Marinade, the side bowls are generally easy to prepare and always add something unexpected and exciting to an already delectable meal.

The stews and other hearty recipes in this chapter represent our biggest bowls. Their rich and satisfying aromas will fill your home and arouse hunger—and possibly some impatience—as they cook. Always choose serving bowls unique in character to make an exciting presentation with these dishes.

ROPA VIEJA

A Pepper Primer

Pepper, the world's most popular spice—and one of the oldest—derives from the peppercorn, the fruit of the pepper plant, a climbing perennial vine native to India and widely cultivated in hot, moist areas of tropical Asia.

The fruit takes the form of a berry and is processed to produce three basic kinds of peppercorns: black, green, and white. Green peppercorns have been harvested while still immature and are preserved in brine to remain soft and edible. Black peppercorns, picked when almost ripe, are dried, at which point the skins turn brown to black. The white peppercorn is a berry that has been soaked in water, then rubbed, which removes its outer covering. It is then dried until pale in color—hence, the name.

▶

This recipe is steeped in Latin American flavors and tradition. Said to have been brought to Cuba by the Spanish, *ropa vieja* describes the texture of meat after a long cooking time—it shreds easily, like old clothes or rags. The more vegetables and spices you add, the richer the aroma and flavor. Serve with our creamy polenta (facing page) if desired.

1 pound flank steak, trimmed

2 medium carrots, peeled and chopped

2 ribs celery, chopped

1 medium white or yellow onion, chopped

2 bay leaves

3 tablespoons olive oil

1 medium red onion, thinly sliced

1 medium green bell pepper, stemmed, seeded,
    and cut into ½-inch dice

1 medium red bell pepper, stemmed, seeded,
    and cut into ½-inch dice

4 cloves garlic, chopped

1 whole fresh Scotch bonnet pepper or serrano chili

6 green peppercorns

1 teaspoon chopped fresh thyme

1 teaspoon chopped fresh oregano

½ teaspoon ground allspice

1 cup diced fresh tomatoes, or canned, drained

½ cup dry red wine

½ cup red wine vinegar

3 tablespoons (packed) dark brown sugar

Salt and freshly ground black pepper, to taste

1. Combine the flank steak, the chopped carrots, celery, onion, and 1 of the bay leaves in a flameproof nonreactive casserole or Dutch oven. Add water to cover and bring to a boil over medium heat. Reduce the heat to low and simmer, uncovered, until the meat is very tender, about 1 hour, adding more water if necessary.

2. Transfer the meat to a cutting board. Strain the cooking liquid, reserving 1 cup. Discard the vegetables. Shred the meat with two forks and set aside on a plate.

3. Heat the olive oil in a medium skillet over medium heat. Add the sliced red onion, the bell peppers, garlic, Scotch bonnet pepper, peppercorns, remaining bay leaf, thyme, oregano, and allspice. Stir, cover, and reduce the heat to low. Cook the vegetables until they are tender, about 10 minutes.

4. Uncover and add the reserved shredded meat, the reserved cooking liquid, tomatoes, wine, vinegar, and salt and pepper. Cover and simmer for 30 minutes. Adjust the seasoning and discard the Scotch bonnet pepper before serving.

Serves 4 to 6 as a main bowl, 8 to 10 as a small bowl

CREAMY POLENTA

Polenta is customarily a simple combination of cornmeal and water. Here we've dressed it up a bit with cream, lots of butter, and cheese. For the creamiest results, the polenta and the liquid should be blended with care; otherwise you may end up with a lumpy lot. The moral here is to take your time, ponder the pot, and stir, stir, stir. Serve this as a filling accompaniment to anything with a flavorful broth or sauce, such as Stewed Short Ribs (page 76), Seared Steak Salad with Roasted Tomatoes (page 196), Grilled Ratatouille Salad (page 216), and the foregoing recipe for Ropa Vieja.

6 cups water

½ cup heavy (whipping) cream

1½ cups instant polenta

6 tablespoons (¾ stick) unsalted butter, in pieces

½ cup freshly grated Parmesan cheese

¼ cup finely chopped fresh Italian (flat-leaf) parsley

Salt, to taste

Green peppercorns have the freshest flavor, the least pungency, and the lowest heat, and can be eaten whole in food preparations because they are soft and mild. Black and white peppercorns can only be used whole in stocks, broths, or poaching liquids that will be strained. When ground, white pepper is considered the hottest.

Pink peppercorns are an altogether different story; they are the dried berries of a rose plant cultivated in Madagascar. They are used more for their color and less for their spice since they are not as pungent as true peppercorns.

FOR ROPA VIEJA:

LENTIL SOUP WITH ROASTED GARLIC AND HERBS
(page 60)

CREAMY POLENTA

CHEESE-STUFFED POBLANOS
(page 174)

Combine the water and cream in a medium saucepan and bring to a boil over high heat. Reduce the heat to medium and slowly pour in the polenta, stirring constantly. Reduce the heat to low and continue stirring until the mixture is thickened and smooth, about 15 minutes. Remove from the heat and stir in the butter, cheese, parsley, and salt until thoroughly blended. Serve immediately.

Serves 4 to 6 as a small bowl

POLENTA

Polenta is an Italian preparation made from dried ground corn cooked in liquid until the starches have had time to hydrate or swell. We frequently see it in a solid state—in pieces that have been sautéed, fried, or grilled, then served with salads and soups. In northern Italy, polenta is more often served in a soft, steaming mound, similar to the way we serve mashed potatoes. It is great for soaking up gravy, too.

To make polenta in the authentic manner is a laborious, time-consuming task. But it does not have to be. Although Italian grandmothers would insist upon the old-world method, we take the couch-polenta route, and avail ourselves of an instant brand that requires 15 minutes of stirring. Instant polenta, which has been cooked once and then dried, does not share the same corn flavor as the original kind that is made in a double boiler with an hour of constant stirring. But when we prepare it as we do in the recipe for Creamy Polenta, strict authenticity isn't our primary concern.

DUCK ROPA VIEJA

Ropa vieja means "old clothes." Traditionally flank steak is used (see page 72 for recipe) because it shreds easily, like rags. Duck meat shreds well, too, and makes a perfect alternative to red meat. Here it is combined with Caribbean accents—coconut milk and a Scotch bonnet pepper. So very versatile, this duck ropa vieja can be served on pasta or with rice, used as a stuffing for tamales or as a variation for the beef filling in Picadillo Buns (page 169). Or you can serve it simply over a bed of crisp greens.

10 duck legs (available at butcher)

1 cup unsweetened canned coconut milk

3 cups water, or as needed

2 medium carrots, peeled and chopped

2 ribs celery, chopped

1 medium yellow onion, chopped

1 large red onion, thinly sliced

1 medium green bell pepper, stemmed, seeded, and cut into ½-inch dice

1 medium red bell pepper, stemmed, seeded, and cut into ½-inch dice

1 cup diced fresh tomatoes or drained canned tomatoes

6 cloves garlic, chopped

¼ cup olive oil

1 teaspoon chili paste

2 tablespoons (packed) dark brown sugar

1 teaspoon chopped fresh thyme

2 bay leaves

1 fresh whole Scotch bonnet pepper or serrano chili

5 green peppercorns

THE SIDE BOWLS

HOT CHILI OIL
(page 232)

MASHED POTATOES
(page 189)

VEGETABLE RICE
(page 149)

Fiestaware, new or old, in various vibrant colors, makes a playful presentation for this Caribbean-style Ropa Vieja. A great party dish!

1. Preheat the oven to 375°F.

2. Combine the duck legs, coconut milk, and enough water to cover in a large roasting pan with a lid. Cover and braise in the oven until the meat easily peels away from the bone, about 1½ hours.

3. Transfer the duck legs to a cutting board and let stand until cool enough to handle. Meanwhile, strain the liquid, skimming off the fat, and reserve 1 cup of the liquid. Remove the meat from the bones and shred. Discard the fat, skin, cartilage, and bones.

4. Combine the shredded duck meat, reserved defatted cooking liquid, and remaining ingredients in a flameproof nonreactive casserole or Dutch oven. Bring to a simmer, cover, and simmer for 45 minutes.

5. Remove from the heat, skim off the fat, and discard the Scotch bonnet pepper. Using a slotted spoon, remove the duck and vegetables from the cooking liquid to a serving bowl.

6. Ladle some of the cooking liquid over the duck and vegetables and serve.

Serves 4 to 6 as a main bowl, 8 to 10 as a small bowl

Stewed Short Ribs

BONIATO, CARROT, AND JALAPEÑO PURÉE
(page 167)

CRISPY SHALLOTS
(see box on facing page)

CREAMY POLENTA
(page 73)

Short ribs are often passed over for choicer cuts of beef, which baffles us. Cooked properly, short ribs are as tender as a filet, as succulent as a slow-cooked roast, and as delicious as the most perfectly tended-to grilled steak. Reasonably priced, they also make ideal party fare. Serve these on a raw night with a steaming bowl of Creamy Polenta, our absolutely favorite accompaniment. Sautéed or steamed kale makes a good side bowl, too.

8 beef short ribs (about 8 ounces each)

1 tablespoon A Pinch for All Seasons (page 246)

½ cup all-purpose flour

¼ cup olive oil

3 medium Vidalia or Spanish onions, chopped

3 medium carrots, peeled and cut into medium dice

4 whole fresh jalapeño peppers, plus 1 sliced into rounds

2 cups chopped fresh tomatoes or canned whole tomatoes in purée

**4 cups Chicken Stock for Mediterranean Bowls
(page 20)**

1 cup fresh orange juice

3/4 cup fresh lime juice

1/4 cup rice vinegar

4 tablespoons grated lime zest

Salt and freshly ground black pepper, to taste

Creamy Polenta (page 73), for serving

Lime slices, for garnish

1. Preheat the oven to 375°F.

2. Season the ribs generously on both sides with A Pinch for All Seasons, then dredge them in the flour, shaking off the excess.

3. Heat the olive oil in a large cast-iron skillet until hot. Add the ribs and sear on all sides until brown and crispy, 10 to 15 minutes. Transfer to a roasting pan.

4. Add the onions, carrots, and whole jalapeños to the hot skillet and brown on all sides. Transfer to the roasting pan with the seared ribs.

5. Add the tomatoes, chicken stock, orange juice, lime juice, vinegar, and lime zest to the roasting pan. Cover the pan with aluminum foil and roast for 1 hour, skimming periodically. Check after 30 minutes and, if the liquid is evaporating too quickly, add up to 1 cup water. When done, the meat should be almost falling off the bones. Season with salt and pepper.

6. Place 2 ribs in each of 4 bowls. Strain the sauce and serve it separately to ladle over the ribs and around the polenta. Garnish with jalapeño rounds and lime slices.

Serves 4 as a main bowl, 8 as a small bowl

Crispy Variations

Frying thin slices of shallots and leeks or sprigs of delicate herbs, such as parsley, heightens their flavor and brightens their color. Sprinkling a little of any of them on top of one of our savory bowls makes the bowl even better.

Pat the shallots, leeks or parsley sprigs dry. Pour vegetable oil to a depth of 2 inches in a deep, heavy pot and heat it to 360°F on a deep-frying thermometer. Fry garnish until crisp—2 minutes for shallots and leeks, 10 to 20 seconds for parsley. Remove with a slotted spoon and drain on paper towels. Season lightly with salt. Use immediately or transfer to an airtight container and store in a cool, dry spot for up to 4 days.

For each recipe use:
3 medium shallots *or*
2 leeks (white and light green parts only) *or*
1 bunch parsley (curly or flat-leaf), large stems removed

PICADILLO

Translated from Spanish, *picadillo* means hash. This full-flavored, pungent, sweet, and salty mix of meat, spices, fruit, and olives is traditionally used to fill Mexican empanadas. It performs equally well served over rice or as a savory filling for Chinese-style buns (page 169).

1 tablespoon Annatto Oil (page 232)

2 tablespoons olive oil

1 large onion, finely chopped

1 large green bell pepper, stemmed, seeded, and finely chopped

1 fresh Scotch bonnet pepper or serrano chili, stemmed, seeded, and finely chopped

4 cloves garlic, minced

1 teaspoon ground cumin

2 pounds lean ground chuck

2 cups undrained canned plum tomatoes, chopped

½ cup dark rum

½ cup green olives, pitted and chopped

¼ cup dark raisins

¼ cup capers, chopped

¼ cup fresh lime juice

Salt and freshly ground black pepper, to taste

1. Heat the oils in a large nonreactive skillet over medium heat. Add the onion, green and Scotch bonnet peppers, garlic, and cumin and sauté until the vegetables are tender, about 10 minutes. Add the meat, tomatoes, and rum and cook for 10 minutes, stirring frequently to break up the meat. Reduce the heat to low, cover, and simmer for 1 hour until most of the liquid has evaporated.

2. Stir in the olives, raisins, capers, and lime juice and cook until heated through. Remove from the heat, season with salt and pepper, and serve.

Serves 4 to 6 as a main bowl, 8 to 10 as a small bowl

THE SIDE BOWLS

CILANTRO OIL
(*page 230*)

CREAMY POLENTA
(*page 73*)

MASHED POTATOES
(*page 189*)

TOMATO-GARLIC VINAIGRETTE
(*page 226*)

SPICY TOMATO GLAZE
(*page 263*)

DREAMY CREAMY CORN
(*page 264*)

ROASTED PORK LOIN WITH HONEY-HOISIN MARINADE

Our Honey-Hoisin Marinade delivers the salty sweet taste that is characteristic of many Chinese recipes, including spareribs. Here we've replaced the ribs with a tender meaty pork loin. But the marinade is so good you'll want to use it on other roasted or braised pork preparations. So feel free to double the recipe, transfer the surplus to an airtight container, and store it in the refrigerator for up to 2 weeks. For this bowl, be sure to set aside at least 10 hours or overnight for marination to get truly successful results.

HONEY-HOISIN MARINADE

I cup soy sauce

½ cup dry sherry

½ cup hoisin sauce

¼ cup sugar

¼ cup honey

¼ cup chopped peeled fresh ginger

I tablespoon ground cinnamon

6 star anise

4 cloves garlic, chopped

PORK

I boneless pork loin (about 2 pounds)

Chopped scallions, for garnish

I. Make the Honey-Hoisin Marinade: Combine all the marinade ingredients in a medium skillet and bring to a boil over medium heat. Reduce the heat to low and simmer, uncovered, until the liquid is reduced to about 2 cups, about 30 minutes. Remove from the heat and cool.

THE SIDE BOWLS

GINGER'S HOT BROTH
(page 11)

DAL SOUP
(page 47)

HALF MOON OVER MANCHEGO
(page 165)

TOMATO SOY SAUCE
(page 252)

VEGETABLE RICE
(page 149)

ROASTED RED PEPPER AND CILANTRO SAUCE
(page 261)

2. Place the pork in a large bowl, add the marinade, and turn the meat to coat. Cover and refrigerate for at least 10 hours.

3. Preheat the oven to 350°F.

4. Remove the pork from the marinade and place on a rack in a roasting pan. Reserve the marinade. Roast the pork until an instant-read thermometer registers 140°F when thrust into the center, 40 to 50 minutes. Baste the pork three or four times with the marinade while it roasts. Remove from the oven and let rest for about 10 minutes.

5. Meanwhile, strain the marinade into a small saucepan and bring to a boil over medium heat. Boil for 3 to 4 minutes. Drizzle the hot marinade over the pork before slicing. Serve garnished with the chopped scallions.

Serves 4

Mojo-Marinated Chicken

Whether you call it a Cuban *mojo* or a Brazilian *molho*, this salsa-like marinade of Spanish descent leaves room for plenty of imagination. The main ingredients are almost always garlic, citrus juice, olive oil, and some kind of herb, and they remain so here. However, we give the marinade an Asian twist by spicing it with green curry paste—available at Asian markets—and turmeric. Although traditionally used as a sauce, it can also be put into service as a vinaigrette. For this dish, we really get our mojo working—first as a marinade for chicken, then as a drizzle to top the chicken after it has grilled—it's so good, we use it twice.

1 cup fresh orange juice

½ cup olive oil

½ cup chopped fresh tomato, or canned, drained

¼ cup fresh lime juice

¼ cup distilled white vinegar

2 tablespoons chopped garlic

2 tablespoons chopped peeled fresh ginger

1 teaspoon crushed red pepper flakes

¼ teaspoon green curry paste

1 teaspoon ground turmeric

4 whole boneless, skinless chicken breasts, cut in half

Salt and freshly ground black pepper, to taste

1. Combine the orange juice, oil, tomato, lime juice, vinegar, garlic, ginger, red pepper flakes, curry paste, and turmeric in a blender or food processor and process until blended.

2. Place the chicken in a large glass baking dish. Pour the marinade over the chicken and turn the chicken to coat it. Cover and refrigerate for at least 5 hours, and as long as 8.

3. Preheat a grill until hot.

4. Drain the chicken, reserving the marinade. Arrange the chicken on the grill grate and cook until cooked through, about 20 minutes total time, turning once. Slice into 1-inch-thick pieces. Season with salt and pepper, then transfer to individual serving bowls.

5. Just before the chicken is done, bring the marinade to a boil in a medium saucepan over medium-high heat. Boil for 3 to 4 minutes. Drizzle over the chicken and serve.

Serves 6

THE SIDE BOWLS

ZUCCHINI PANCAKES
(page 188)

GRILLED RATATOUILLE SALAD
(page 216)

APRICOT AND APPLE CHUTNEY
(page 266)

Serve individual bowls of Mango and Coconut Rice (page 147) along with this punchy chicken dish.

African Chicken and Peanut Stew

This one-pot recipe finds its roots in North Africa, where poultry and peanuts, or peanut sauces, are often teamed to make stews. This moist-heat cooking method of stewing extracts juices from the ingredients as they simmer gently in seasoned stock. The result is well-blended, robust flavor.

3 cups Chicken Stock for Asian Bowls
   (page 5)
1 cup Spicy Peanut Sauce
   (page 254)
2 tablespoons tomato paste
1 tablespoon African Spice Blend
   (recipe follows)
1 cup coarsely grated zucchini
1 cup julienned cabbage
½ cup coarsely grated peeled carrot
2½ pounds skinless, boneless chicken breasts,
   cut into 1-inch strips
3 cups julienned rinsed fresh spinach
¼ cup fresh lime juice
Salt and freshly ground black pepper, to taste

THE SIDE BOWLS

STEAMED HOT RICE

CHOPPED CILANTRO

CHOPPED PEANUTS

HOT CHILI OIL
(page 232)

CRISPY SHALLOTS
(see box, page 77)

1. Combine the chicken stock, peanut sauce, tomato paste, and spice blend in a medium nonreactive Dutch oven or saucepan, stirring well to mix. Bring to a boil over medium heat. Reduce the heat to medium-low and simmer, uncovered, for 10 minutes.

2. Add the zucchini, cabbage, and carrot, and simmer just until tender, 2 to 3 minutes. Add the chicken, spinach, and lime juice, cover, and simmer until the chicken is cooked through, about 10 minutes.

3. Remove from the heat, season with salt and pepper, and serve in bowls.

Serves 6 as a main bowl, 10 as a small bowl

AFRICAN SPICE BLEND

The aromatic blending of spices, such as cinnamon and cardamom, can transform even the simplest stew into a rich and sensual feast. Use a small amount of this blend to awaken the flavors of an otherwise uninspired dish. And remember, the secret to any spice blend is to use only the freshest spices available and to toast them to release their fragrance. Adjust the heat in this mix by adjusting the amount of cayenne pepper.

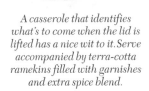

- **4 teaspoons cayenne pepper**
- **4 teaspoons ground ginger**
- **2 teaspoons dry mustard**
- **2 teaspoons ground cumin**
- **2 teaspoons ground turmeric**
- **1 teaspoon ground cinnamon**
- **1 teaspoon ground allspice**
- **½ teaspoon ground cardamom, preferably freshly ground**

A casserole that identifies what's to come when the lid is lifted has a nice wit to it. Serve accompanied by terra-cotta ramekins filled with garnishes and extra spice blend.

Combine all the spices in a dry medium skillet over medium heat and heat, shaking the pan continuously to prevent burning, until the spices are fragrant and just beginning to smoke, 1 to 2 minutes. Transfer the blend to a bowl to cool. Use immediately, or transfer to an airtight container and store in a cool, dry place for up to 2 months.

Makes about ⅓ cup

Mustard-Rubbed Chicken Thighs and Yellow Split Pea Stew

Mild in flavor, split peas are a healthful and pleasant-tasting addition to any number of soups or stews. Here they are combined with spicy mustard-coated chicken that is further accented with chunks of red tomato. The small amount of coconut milk in the sauce contributes substantially to its smooth texture and imparts a subtle, yet exotic note. For more mustard flavor overall, you can marinate the chicken overnight. For a lighter, lower-in-fat dish, remove the skin from the chicken thighs before sautéing.

Serve the chicken with the greens of your choice. We like it over a bed of uncooked fresh spinach that gently wilts under the steamy stew. And garlic breadsticks or flatbreads are excellent for soaking up the liquid.

Always be on the lookout for unusual bowls of every shape and size. Tag or yard sales are great sources for big bowls like this one and the cost is often practically nothing.

¾ cup yellow split peas

12 chicken thighs

1 tablespoon salt

1 teaspoon freshly ground black pepper

½ cup **Mustard Rub (recipe follows)**

¼ cup olive oil

2 medium carrots, finely diced

1 large onion, cut into 1-inch pieces

1 medium Idaho potato, peeled and finely diced

1 medium turnip, peeled and finely diced

1 tablespoon Garlic Paste (page 61)

1 whole fresh Scotch bonnet pepper or
    serrano chili

4 cups Chicken Stock for Mediterranean Bowls
    (page 20)

1 can (13½ ounces) unsweetened coconut milk

2 fresh ripe tomatoes, seeded and finely diced,
   or 1 cup canned tomatoes, drained, seeded,
   and chopped
3 tablespoons Porcini Garlic Paste (page 242)
¾ cup fresh lemon juice
2 whole scallions, finely chopped
Salt and freshly ground black pepper, to taste

1. Place the split peas in a small saucepan and add water to cover by 2 inches. Bring to a boil over medium-high heat. Reduce the heat to low, cover, and simmer until tender, about 1 hour. Drain.

2. Meanwhile, rub the chicken thighs all over with the Mustard Rub. Cover and refrigerate for 30 minutes.

3. Preheat the oven to 350°F.

4. Heat half the olive oil in a large ovenproof nonreactive skillet over medium heat. Add half the chicken thighs and sauté until well browned on all sides, about 10 minutes. Using tongs, remove the thighs to a plate. Repeat with remaining thighs and oil.

5. Add the carrots, onion, potato, turnip, Garlic Paste, and Scotch bonnet pepper to the drippings in the skillet and sauté until brown, about 10 minutes. Stir in the chicken stock, coconut milk, split peas, tomatoes, and porcini paste. Return the chicken thighs to the skillet and bring to a boil over medium heat.

6. Remove the skillet from the heat, cover, and place in the oven. Bake until the chicken falls easily away from the bone, about 30 minutes.

7. Remove the skillet from the oven, uncover, and skim off any fat that has accumulated on the surface. Remove the Scotch bonnet. Stir in the lemon juice and chopped scallions. Season with salt and pepper.

THE SIDE BOWLS

YELLOW CURRY OIL
(page 233)

**APRICOT AND APPLE
CHUTNEY**
(page 266)

8. Place 2 thighs in each of 6 serving bowls. Ladle the stew on top and serve.

Serves 6 as a main bowl, 12 as a small bowl

MUSTARD RUB

This rub was specially created for the Mustard-Rubbed Chicken Thighs and Yellow Split Pea Stew (preceding recipe), but it creates a stalwart impression on any meat. When used as a marinade and left on overnight, its lime-juice base aids in tenderizing.

Serve stews with hearty chunky ingredients in sturdy, wide-open bowls. It's much easier to get at all the good food. If the dish has bones or shells, place pretty smaller bowls alongside to hold them, once they no longer have food attached.

½ **cup fresh lime juice**

½ **cup water**

10 **cloves garlic, roasted (see box, page 48)**

4 **tablespoons freshly ground black pepper**

1 **tablespoon ground turmeric**

1 **tablespoon dry mustard**

1 **tablespoon ground cumin**

1 **tablespoon imported sweet paprika**

1 **tablespoon honey**

1 **tablespoon salt**

1 **cup olive oil**

Combine the lime juice, water, garlic, pepper, turmeric, mustard, cumin, paprika, honey, and salt in a blender or food processor and process until smooth. With the motor running, add the olive oil in a slow, steady stream and blend until thoroughly incorporated. Use immediately, or transfer to an airtight container and store in the refrigerator for up to 2 weeks.

Makes about 2 cups

SEAFOOD STEW IN TAMARIND BROTH

This simple stew requires no browning, which means no added fat calories from oil or butter. Simmering the seafood in the Tamarind Broth gives it a fullness of flavor as it adds delicate sweetness. Feel free to substitute any fresh fish or shellfish that suits your palate, pocketbook, or both.

Ladle the stew over steamed greens, such as bok choy, Chinese broccoli, or Swiss chard. Then mop up the broth with a crusty roll. This is also wonderful served with bowls of fragrant hot jasmine rice.

> 4 carrots, peeled and cut into 3-inch lengths
> 2 pounds calabaza or winter squash, peeled, seeded, and cut into 6 large wedges
> 4 cups Tamarind Broth (page 18)
> ¼ cup hoisin sauce
> 2 pounds thick white fish fillets (bass, halibut, or snapper), cut into 2-ounce pieces
> 1 pound medium shrimp, peeled and deveined
> 1 pound squid, cleaned (see box, page 90) and cut into 1-inch strips
> Salt and freshly ground black pepper, to taste
> 5 scallions, white and green parts, chopped, for garnish
> 1 fresh jalapeño pepper, stemmed and minced, with seeds, for garnish

1. Preheat the oven to 250°F.

2. Bring a medium saucepan of salted water to a boil over medium heat. Add the carrots and simmer until softened, about 5 minutes. Using a slotted spoon, transfer the carrots to a large ovenproof bowl and keep warm in the preheated oven.

Hoisin Sauce

Widely used in South China, this thick, dark, jamlike sauce has a concentrated, fruity flavor. Hoisin is made from soybeans, vinegar, sugar, and spices and is reddish-brown in color. Because of its mighty twang, hoisin should be blended with other ingredients to balance its flavor. Add it to sautés, along with stock, sesame oil, ginger, and scallions, to make a quick, full-flavored sauce. It's also great in marinades for pork or beef, or brushed on top of fish after grilling. Sold in jars or cans in Asian markets and most grocery stores, hoisin can last for months if refrigerated tightly covered.

MUSTARD OIL

ROASTED GARLIC
(page 48)

BONIATO, CARROT, AND JALAPENO PUREE
(page 167)

SPICY CILANTRO SOY PASTE
(page 239)

3. In the same pan of boiling water, simmer the calabaza until softened, about 5 minutes. Transfer to the bowl with the carrots and keep warm. Discard the cooking water.

4. Combine the broth and hoisin in the saucepan and bring to a boil over medium heat. Reduce the heat to low and simmer for 3 minutes. Add the fish pieces and cook until just cooked through, 3 minutes.Using a slotted spoon, transfer the fish to the bowl with the vegetables. Repeat the cooking procedure with the shrimp, then the squid, cooking the shrimp and squid for 3 minutes.

5. Strain the hot cooking liquid over the vegetables and seafood. Sprinkle with the scallions and jalapeño and serve.

Serves 4 to 6 as a main bowl

SQUID WITH SOFRITO

A *sofrito* is a basic sauce made with onions, garlic, green peppers, and herbs that can be added to soups and sauces for flavor. The Spanish-style sofrito that we serve with squid is made with Annatto Oil, which is the major difference between it and its Italian cousin, *soffrito*. The addition of the squid turns it into a stew that is sumptuous when ladled over rice or tossed with pasta. Because the squid is not integral to this sofrito and is added at the end, you can always substitute shrimp or another shellfish at that time, if you prefer. However, squid is high in protein and relatively inexpensive when compared with other seafood. It can be disappointing, though, if not cooked properly. Here it is slowly simmered, which maintains tenderness. Don't be tempted to cook it longer than we suggest because it will break down and lose its texture.

SOFRITO

⅓ cup Annatto Oil (page 232)

I large onion, cut into ½-inch dice

¼ cup Garlic Paste (page 61)

1½ tablespoons chili paste

8 ounces ground pork butt or bacon, finely diced

I teaspoon chopped fresh thyme

I teaspoon crushed red pepper flakes

½ teaspoon dried oregano leaves

6 cups chopped canned tomatoes, drained and seeded

2 cups tomato juice

2 cups dry white wine

½ cup red wine vinegar

SQUID

2 pounds squid, cleaned (see box, page 90) and cut into
    1-inch rings; leave tentacles whole or cut in half, if large

½ cup (loosely packed) chopped fresh basil leaves

Salt and freshly ground black pepper, to taste

Bowls make great vacation souvenirs. A trip to Mexico can yield particularly inviting serving pieces.

1. Make the sofrito: Heat the Annatto Oil in a large nonreactive saucepan over medium heat. Add the onion and sauté, stirring, until softened, 5 minutes. Add the Garlic Paste and chili paste and stir to combine. Add the ground pork and sauté for 10 minutes, stirring to break up the meat. Stir in the thyme, pepper flakes, and oregano. Add the chopped tomatoes, tomato juice, wine, and vinegar. Raise the heat and bring to a boil. Reduce the heat to medium-low and simmer, uncovered, skimming off the fat, until the liquid is reduced by half, about 20 minutes.

2. Add the squid and cook, uncovered, until tender when tested, about 40 minutes.

3. Remove from the heat and season with salt and pepper. Transfer to a large serving bowl, sprinkle with the basil, and serve in shallow bowls.

Serves 6 as a main bowl, 10 as a small bowl

THE SIDE BOWLS

WILTED SPINACH

JASMINE RICE

ZUCCHINI PANCAKES

(page 188)

TRUE GRITS WITH GRILLED MARINATED SQUID

How to Clean Squid

In selecting fresh squid to cook with, choose small, whole ones with clear eyes and a mild ocean scent. Fresh or frozen, these ten-armed mollusks need to be cleaned before they are ready to cook. You can purchase them already cleaned; failing that, here is how to do it:

1. Pull the head, with the tentacles, out of the squid body; with a chef's knife, cut the tentacles off the head just above the eyes.

2. Pull out the hard "beak" in the middle of the tentacles. Discard. Set the tentacles aside for later use, if desired.

3. Pull out the hard cartilage from inside the sac of the squid body. Discard.

4. Lay the squid body on the cutting surface. Pressing firmly, slide the dull side of your knife

▶

Growing up in the Northeast, our winter breakfasts consisted of farina, Cream of Wheat, and Maypo. The first time either of us heard the word "grits," it was in association with a John Wayne movie. We now know better. *True* grits are served at any meal, any time of the year, hot or just warm. If you haven't already, plan to expand your repertoire with the addition of these mild-tasting, coarsely ground, hulled kernels of dried corn, oats, or rice. Grits will quickly become a strong culinary shoulder you can lean on, freeing you to experiment. Here we serve bowls of warm corn grits topped with grilled squid on a bed of peppery greens—a variation on a traditional Mediterranean combination— polenta (cornmeal) and squid.

> 2 pounds squid, cleaned (see box, this page), tentacles reserved for another use
>
> ⅓ cup balsamic vinegar
>
> ¼ cup extra virgin olive oil
>
> 3 large cloves garlic, finely minced
>
> 2 teaspoons crushed red pepper flakes
>
> I cup regular or quick-cooking (not instant) yellow grits
>
> I large red bell pepper, roasted and peeled (see box, page 18), finely chopped
>
> ¼ cup finely chopped pitted black olives, preferably Kalamata
>
> 3 tablespoons capers, drained and chopped
>
> ½ cup chopped fresh Italian (flat-leaf) parsley
>
> Salt, to taste
>
> 12 ounces arugula leaves, rinsed and patted dry
>
> I cup Tomato-Garlic Vinaigrette (page 226)

1. Cut the squid bodies open so they lie flat, then score them on each side as directed in the box on these pages (step 6).

2. Combine the vinegar, olive oil, garlic, and pepper flakes in a large nonreactive bowl and beat with a fork to blend. Add the squid and toss well to coat. Cover and refrigerate for 1 to 1½ hours.

3. Preheat the grill and oil the grill rack. (Or preheat the broiler.)

4. Meanwhile, cook the grits according to package directions. Remove from the heat and stir in the roasted bell pepper, olives, capers, ¼ cup of the parsley, and water, if needed, for a smooth consistency. Taste and season with salt. Cover and set aside in a warm spot.

5. Drain the squid, reserving the marinade. Grill the squid 5 to 6 inches from the heat until lightly charred, about 1 minute on each side. (Or broil the squid on the rack of a broiler pan about 3 inches from the heat for about the same amount of time.) Remove, and season with salt, then transfer to a cutting board and cut into 1-inch strips.

6. Divide the arugula among individual serving bowls. Spoon the grits mixture over the arugula, then drizzle the Tomato-Garlic Vinaigrette over the grits and around the inside edge of each bowl. Arrange the squid strips on top of the grits and sprinkle some of the remaining ¼ cup parsley over each serving.

7. Bring the reserved marinade to a boil in a small nonreactive saucepan and simmer a minute or so. Remove from the heat and drizzle over the squid. Serve.

Serves 4 to 6 as a main bowl, 8 as a small bowl

from tip to opening along the length of the body to force out the viscera and to remove some of the outer purple skin; the remaining skin can be peeled off easily.

5. Rinse the squid body, inside and out, under cold running water. It is now ready for scoring, cutting into strips, slicing into rings, or stuffing whole.

6. To score squid, place the squid bodies on a flat surface and cut open lengthwise along one side. Make shallow cuts in a gridlike pattern on the inside of the squid body, then again along the outside surface.

Latin-style ceramics are festive enough to perk up any table. Don't save them for South American dishes.

African White Fish Stew

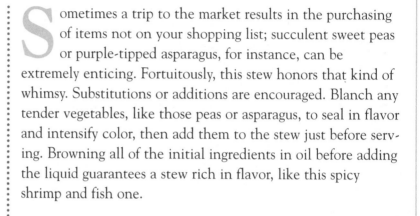

Sometimes a trip to the market results in the purchasing of items not on your shopping list; succulent sweet peas or purple-tipped asparagus, for instance, can be extremely enticing. Fortuitously, this stew honors that kind of whimsy. Substitutions or additions are encouraged. Blanch any tender vegetables, like those peas or asparagus, to seal in flavor and intensify color, then add them to the stew just before serving. Browning all of the initial ingredients in oil before adding the liquid guarantees a stew rich in flavor, like this spicy shrimp and fish one.

THE SIDE BOWLS

PARSLEY AND GARLIC OIL
(page 234)

BONIATO, CARROT, AND JALAPEÑO PUREE
(page 167)

I cup jasmine rice

¼ cup olive oil

I tablespoon Garlic Paste (page 61)

2 medium shallots, minced

2 tablespoons imported sweet paprika

I tablespoon African Spice Blend
    (page 83)

3 pounds sea bass or other white fish fillets,
    cut into 4-ounce pieces

4 ribs celery, cut ¼ inch thick on the diagonal

2 medium onions, cut into small dice

I medium red bell pepper, stemmed, seeded,
    and cut into ½-inch dice

I medium green bell pepper, stemmed, seeded,
    and cut into ½-inch dice

I fresh poblano chili, stemmed and
    cut into ½-inch dice with seeds

I cup fresh corn kernels (from 2 ears)

2 cups Chicken Stock for Asian Bowls (page 5)

2 cups chopped and seeded fresh tomatoes,
    or canned, drained

I pound medium shrimp, peeled
(leaving tails intact) and deveined
½ cup fresh lime juice
I tablespoon chopped fresh thyme
Salt and freshly ground black pepper, to taste
¼ cup Pumpkin Seed Crumbs (page 249)

I. Cook the rice according to package directions. Set aside.

2. Meanwhile, heat the olive oil until it ripples in a large skillet over medium heat. Add the Garlic Paste, shallots, paprika, and spice blend. Cook, stirring, until fragrant, 1 minute.

3. Add the fish in batches and sauté until lightly brown on both sides, about 3 minutes. Using a slotted spoon, remove the fish to a platter.

4. Add the celery, onions, bell peppers, poblano, and corn to the drippings in the pan. Sauté, stirring occasionally, to soften, about 5 minutes. Stir in the chicken stock, reserved cooked rice, and tomatoes and simmer for 5 minutes.

5. Return the fish to the skillet and simmer until it is almost cooked through, about 8 minutes. Add the shrimp, lime juice, thyme, and salt and pepper. Simmer until the shrimp are just opaque, about 3 minutes.

6. Serve in bowls and sprinkle with the Pumpkin Seed Crumbs before serving.

Serves 6 to 8 as a main bowl

A fish bowl for a fish stew. Serve condiments like the Pumpkin Seed Crumbs called for here in small, shallow fish-shaped bowls.

No Choke Artichoke Stew

Cut to the Heart

The artichoke is the bud of a thistle family plant. The bigger artichokes shield their tender hearts with thick, tightly formed, triangular-shaped leaves that some-times project nasty thorns at their apex. How do you get past this armor if you're inter-ested only in the heart? The technique is simple, provided you purchase fresh, crisp artichokes, which are the easiest to handle.

1. Hold the artichoke in one hand while you tear off the outer leaves with the other hand. Pull each leaf down toward the base so that it snaps off.

2. Lay the artichoke on your cutting surface, and with a large sharp knife, cut off the top third of the inner leaves and the stem at the base of the

▶

In this hearty shrimp, white bean, and artichoke stew, the beans plump up and use their flavor-trapping and thick-ening power to make this a hearty, delicious meal-in-one. The artichoke-infused stock gives this stew its dominant fla-vor, and the tartness of the lemon and the texture of the shrimp round out its character.

2 cups dried white beans
1 Mediterranean Spice Bundle (page 21)
2 lemons, cut in half
16 fresh baby artichokes or 8 fresh large artichokes
5 cups Chicken Stock for Mediterranean Bowls (page 20)
6 tablespoons extra virgin olive oil
2 carrots, peeled and cut into ¼-inch dice
1 cup diced, peeled, and seeded fresh tomatoes,
    or canned, drained
2 tablespoons chopped shallots
2 tablespoons chopped garlic
1 cup dry white wine
¼ cup chopped fresh basil leaves
1 pound small shrimp, peeled and deveined
3 tablespoons minced fresh chives or
    green part of scallion
2 tablespoons unsalted butter, softened
Salt and freshly ground black pepper, to taste

1. Put the beans in a large bowl and add enough cold water to cover them by 2 inches. Let soak at room temperature overnight, then drain and rinse.

2. Transfer the beans to a medium saucepan and cover with cold water. Add the spice bundle and bring to a boil. Reduce the heat to low, cover, and simmer until the beans are tender but not mushy, about 1 hour. Drain, remove and discard the spice bundle, and set the beans aside.

3. Meanwhile, fill a large bowl with water and squeeze the juice of 1 lemon into the water. If using baby artichokes, cut off the outer leaves, trim the tops of the remaining leaves, and halve. Drop the prepared artichokes into the acidulated water. If using large artichokes, follow the preparation instructions in the box next to this recipe. Quarter the larger artichokes before dropping them into the bowl of water.

4. Drain the artichokes and combine with the chicken stock in a medium saucepan. Bring to a boil over high heat, reduce the heat to low, cover, and simmer until you can easily pierce the artichokes with a knife, about 20 minutes. Using a slotted spoon, remove them to a bowl. Continue to simmer the liquid, uncovered, in the saucepan until it is reduced by half, 20 to 30 minutes more. Remove from the heat and set aside.

5. Heat 3 tablespoons of the olive oil in a large nonreactive saucepan or Dutch oven over medium-high heat. Add the carrots, tomatoes, shallots, and garlic and sauté until the carrots are tender, about 8 minutes. Add the artichokes, artichoke-infused stock, wine, beans, and basil and simmer, uncovered, until the beans soften and the stock thickens, about 15 minutes. Add the shrimp, the remaining 3 tablespoons oil, and the chives and cook until the shrimp are cooked through, about 7 minutes more. Thin with water, if necessary, to the desired consistency. Juice the remaining lemon and stir it and the butter into the stew. Season with salt and pepper and serve in wide bowls.

Serves 4 to 6 as a main bowl, 8 as a small bowl

artichoke and pare around the bottom until the heart is exposed.

3. Using a spoon, scrape or scoop out the prickly choke from the heart.

4. Place the heart in a bowl of water acidulated with lemon juice to prevent browning from oxidation. When ready to cook, drain. The heart is now ready to use in a recipe.

WILTED SPINACH

CRISP SALAD

CRUSTY BREAD

HORSERADISH ROUILLE
(page 251)

POURABLE PESTO
(page 260)

CHILI-ROASTED VEGETABLES

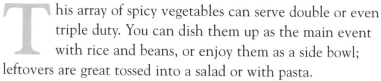

This array of spicy vegetables can serve double or even triple duty. You can dish them up as the main event with rice and beans, or enjoy them as a side bowl; leftovers are great tossed into a salad or with pasta.

The small, extra step of toasting the spice seeds in the marinade delivers brilliant fragrance. Don't skip it. Look for annatto seeds and red curry paste in large, well-stocked supermarkets.

JASMINE RICE

CRAB EMPANADAS
(page 158)

PICADILLO BUNS
(page 169)

CREAMY POLENTA
(page 73)

**FIERY RED CURRY
SAUCE**
(page 124)

MARINADE

½ cup cider vinegar

½ cup fresh orange juice

¼ cup olive oil

10 cloves garlic, roasted (see box, page 48) and chopped

1 tablespoon fennel seeds, toasted (see box, page 137) and ground

1 teaspoon annatto seeds, toasted (see box, page 137) and ground

½ teaspoon red curry paste

VEGETABLES

3 cups diced peeled chayote (1-inch pieces)

3 cups diced zucchini (1-inch pieces)

2 cups diced Japanese eggplant (1-inch pieces)

2 cups diced peeled calabaza or winter squash (1-inch pieces)

2 cups diced red onion (1-inch pieces)

1. Preheat the oven to 375°F.

2. Make the marinade: Whisk together all of the marinade ingredients in a large stainless-steel or glass bowl.

3. Add the vegetables to the marinade and toss to coat. Cover and marinate at room temperature for 30 minutes.

4. Drain the vegetables and place in a roasting pan. Roast until soft and caramelized, about 20 minutes, stirring halfway through the cooking time. Serve.

Serves 4 to 6 as a main bowl, 8 to 10 as a small bowl

Chapter 4

NOODLE, PASTA, AND RICE BOWLS

SILKY NOODLES AND FRAGRANT RICE

A quick look at the cuisines of the world and, right off, you glean the importance of noodles and rice, both as foodstuff and as a way of life. In parts of China, at open-air shops, the noodles are made fresh and cooked streetside, with lunchtime crowds cramming around makeshift tables to eat steaming hot bowls of soup; in Italy, a meal is unthinkable without a pasta course. And where would the national diet of China (and the rest of Asia, for that matter) or Italy (think risotto) or Latin America be without magnificent rice?

Popular doesn't really begin to describe noodles. It goes beyond taste; it has much to do with culture, of course, and pleasure, lots of it. Noodles can be slurped up, twirled around, shoveled in. They can be made of wheat flour, rice flour, mung bean flour, to name a few. They can be chewy in texture, slithery, or silky. They can be thickly sauced or loosely brothed, hot or cold, fat or thin, fresh or dried. Cooking them is almost as much fun as eating them, because sometimes you go to Asia; at other times you could swear from that first mouthful you're on the Amalfi Coast. We've cooked up bowls of noodles to do just that, to take you worldwide: Shanghai Noodles, Soba Noodles with Clams and Fiery Red Curry Sauce, or in a nod to just how easily certain flavors interplay, Capellini with Manila Clams, Lobster, and Asparagus in Lobster Broth. For us, there can never be enough bowls of really good noodles, including something as simple and comforting as one of our flavorful broths with a mound of egg noodles swirled in before serving.

Like noodles and pasta, there are a lot of rices available in the markets now from which to choose. Get to know the differences. The ubiquitous extra-long grain is different from basmati; basmati does not taste like jasmine or Arborio, and sticky rice is different still. Appreciating the subtleties makes for better bowls of rice. A selection of completely different-tasting rice bowls follows, ranging from fried rice to a Thai Paella to an almost sweet Mango and Coconut Rice. Delicious, each and every one.

USE YOUR NOODLE

Noodles can be a confusing lot—so many types, so many uses. You may have wondered: Is a particular noodle best for a particular preparation or can you substitute one kind of noodle for another? The answer to both of these is yes, with a little understanding. Fettuccine, for example, offers a smooth, flat surface for a creamy rich Alfredo sauce to coat evenly and luxuriously. Because both linguine and Chinese egg noodles are flat wheat noodles, you can substitute one for another without any worry.

When presented with the choice between fresh Chinese wheat noodles or dried, you can always use dried in place of fresh. But fresh are superior in taste and texture. You can find them in the refrigerated section of any Chinese market or other Asian food stores. When you get them home, keep them refrigerated until you're ready to use them; they hold well for three to four days.

Rice noodles are a little different. There are dried varieties that cannot be replaced with fresh, and fresh rice sheets—that you make into wide rice noodles—which cannot be replaced by the dried.

There's very little difference among cellophane noodles, glass noodles, and bean threads, aside from length, thickness, and type of bean starch used in making them. Where they come from, say, China, Thailand, or Vietnam, usually dictates what they are called in English.

To help answer any questions that may be lingering in your mind, we've attempted to simplify the wonderful world of noodles, by grouping them into four types based on the flour, or starch, used to create them.

Once you familiarize yourself with the choice of noodles available and their particular characteristics—plump and chewy, crisp and crunchy, or soft and delicate—you will know which noodles are best suited to a particular preparation.

TYPE	VARIETIES	USE
RICE (rice flour and water)	• rice vermicelli—dried • rice sticks—dried • rice sheets—fresh for cutting your own noodles	• stir-fry, soup, salad
BEAN (bean starch and water)	• mung bean—dried • fava bean—dried • bean threads (vermicelli)—dried • broad cellophane—dried • broad glass noodles—dried	• stir-fry, soup salad
EGG (wheat flour, egg, and water)	• thin dried egg noodles • thin egg noodles—fresh • fat egg noodles—dried or fresh • thin egg noodle clusters—dried • some Italian pastas—dried or fresh	• soup • pan or deep-fry
FLOUR (wheat flour and water)	• udon—fat, dried • soba—buckwheat, dried • somen—thin, dried • flat noodles—dried • thin noodles—dried • some Italian pastas—dried	• soup • soup or salad

NUTTY RICE NOODLES WITH TANGY BEEF AND WATERCRESS

Some things never change. It's amazing, but there are still people who request that their food not touch. This is easier to achieve when you're not serving it layered in a bowl as we suggest here. However, a series of five small bowls can work very nicely. In fact, it's a fun way to eat. Try this one both ways—as in more than one or an all-in-one bowl.

TOASTED SESAME SEEDS
(page 137)

CHOPPED PEANUTS

1 pound flank steak, trimmed and sliced
    on an angle against the grain into thin strips
Tangy Marinade (recipe follows)
10 ounces dried rice stick noodles
½ cup chopped scallions, white and green parts
2 tablespoons peanut oil
½ cup canola oil
¼ cup fresh lime juice
Salt and freshly ground black pepper, to taste
3 bunches watercress or arugula, stemmed
1 cup Spicy Peanut Sauce (page 254)
Orange segments, for garnish (optional)
Chopped green part of scallion, for garnish
    (optional)

1. Place the steak in a medium bowl, add the marinade, and toss to coat. Cover and marinate in the refrigerator for 1 hour.

2. Meanwhile, put the rice sticks in a large bowl and add very hot water to cover. Soak until softened, about 20 minutes. Drain well, then cut the noodles in half with scissors or a knife. Return to the bowl and toss with the scallions. Set aside.

3. Remove the beef from the marinade with a slotted spoon and transfer the marinade to a small saucepan. Bring to a boil over high heat. Reduce the heat to medium-low and simmer, uncovered, until slightly thickened, about 4 minutes. Remove from the heat and set aside.

4. Heat the peanut oil in a large skillet over medium heat until it begins to smoke. Add the beef and quickly sear, 1 to 2 minutes on each side. Remove from the skillet to paper towels to drain.

5. Combine the canola oil, lime juice, and salt and pepper in a medium nonreactive bowl and beat with a wire whisk to blend. Add the watercress and toss well. Divide among 6 serving bowls.

6. Heat the peanut sauce in a medium saucepan over low heat until warm and thinned, about 5 minutes, stirring occasionally.

7. Top the salad in each bowl with noodles, dividing them evenly, and top the noodles with the beef strips. Ladle peanut sauce over the beef in each bowl, then drizzle with the reserved marinade. Garnish with orange segments and scallion green, if desired.

Serves 6 as a main bowl, 10 as a small bowl

TANGY MARINADE

This is a simple-to-assemble marinade that can be reduced to a sauce and drizzled over grilled swordfish, mako shark, or other rich fish steaks. A mix of tomato juice and lemon juice is a satisfactory substitute for the tamarind concentrate in color, texture, and tang, but like any stand-in it's just not quite the same. Hold out for the pucker and order tamarind concentrate by mail if necessary. It is easy to use—just open the jar and scoop it out.

Handcrafted bowls with plenty of imperfections are perfect for lots of noodles.

½ cup unsweetened canned coconut milk

½ cup tamarind concentrate

½ cup dry sherry

2 tablespoons soy sauce

¼ teaspoon crushed red pepper flakes

¼ cup (packed) dark brown sugar

Combine all the ingredients in a medium bowl, whisking to dissolve the sugar and to blend thoroughly. Use immediately, or transfer to an airtight container and refrigerate for up to 2 weeks.

Makes about 1½ cups

RICE NOODLES WITH SPICY PORK AND MANGO

Once upon a time, pork was considered a fatty meat and took bad press because of it. But pork producers got the message and produced leaner hogs. Calling pork the "other white meat," the pork producers boast that pork tenderloin is no fattier than chicken meat. We use pork in this noodle concoction because we like its natural mild, sweet flavor in combination with a sweet and spicy glaze. However, if you're still not convinced, you can substitute chicken.

8 ounces pork loin, cut into ½-inch thick slices,
   then julienned

½ recipe Honey-Hoisin Marinade (page 79)

8 ounces flat dried rice noodles

4 tablespoons Hot Chili Oil (page 232)

4 cloves garlic, minced

2 tablespoons chopped peeled fresh ginger

2 tablespoons minced lemongrass bottoms

½ cup Thai Dipping Sauce (page 253)

¼ cup Spicy Peanut Sauce (page 254)

2 cups thinly sliced napa or Savoy cabbage

2 ripe mangoes, peeled, pitted, and cut into thin strips

Salt and freshly ground black pepper, to taste

¼ cup peanuts, toasted (see box, page 137)
   and chopped

6 scallions, white and green parts, chopped

¼ cup fresh lime juice

1. Place the pork in a medium bowl, add the marinade, and toss to coat the pork. Cover and marinate in the refrigerator for 30 minutes.

2. Meanwhile, bring a large pot of salted water to a boil. Add the rice noodles and cook just until soft, about 4 minutes. Drain in a colander, rinse under cool running water, drain again, and set aside.

3. Heat the hot oil in a wok or large skillet over high heat until hot but not smoking. Add the garlic, ginger, and lemongrass. Stir to prevent burning.

4. Remove the pork from the marinade and add it to the wok. Stir-fry until cooked through, about 3 minutes. Remove with a slotted spoon to a plate and set aside.

5. Add the noodles and the two sauces to the wok and toss well to combine, coating the noodles thoroughly. Toss until heated through, about 2 minutes.

6. Return the pork to the wok and add the cabbage and mangoes. Toss to heat through, about 1 minute. Season with salt and pepper and toss well. Remove from the heat and toss with the peanuts, scallions, and lime juice. Serve in individual bowls.

Serves 6 as a main bowl, 10 as a small bowl

Noodles tossed with thinly sliced savory cabbage find an expressive home in a cabbage bowl like this one.

PAPPARDELLE WITH LAMB AND SHIITAKE MUSHROOMS IN PORCINI BROTH

The woodsy flavors of shiitake mushrooms and porcini mushroom broth combine with the assertiveness of lamb in this hearty, complex dish. We like serving this over pappardelle, or substitute regular wide egg noodles. Serve warm, crusty bread and freshly grated Parmesan alongside.

2½ pounds boneless lamb shoulder or leg,
    cut into 1½-inch cubes
Salt and freshly ground black pepper, to taste
3 tablespoons extra virgin olive oil
3 carrots, peeled and chopped
3 ribs celery, cut into medium dice
1 large onion, cut into medium dice
3 tablespoons Porcini Garlic Paste
    (page 242)
6 cups Chicken Stock for Mediterranean Bowls
    (page 20)
2 cups dry sherry
1 can (16 ounces) diced tomatoes, undrained
1 tablespoon Garlic Paste (page 61)
1 sprig fresh rosemary
1 pound fresh shiitake mushrooms, stemmed
    and thinly sliced
½ cup red wine vinegar
1½ pounds dried pappardelle or wide egg noodles
2 cups (packed) coarsely chopped fresh spinach
3 tablespoons Parsley and Garlic Oil
    (page 234)
1 bunch Italian (flat-leaf) parsley, finely chopped

1. Season the lamb pieces all over with salt and pepper. Heat the olive oil in a large saucepan over medium-high heat. Add the lamb, in batches (do not overcrowd the pan), and sear until browned on all sides, 3 to 5 minutes per batch. Using a slotted spoon, remove each batch as it is browned to paper towels to drain.

2. Add the carrots, celery, onion, and porcini paste to the pan, stirring to combine well. Cook until the vegetables are soft and lightly browned, about 10 minutes. Return the lamb to the pan and add the chicken stock, sherry, tomatoes, garlic paste, and rosemary sprig. Bring to a boil, reduce the heat to medium-low, and cover. Simmer until the meat is almost tender, 1 hour.

3. Add the shiitake mushrooms and ¼ cup of the vinegar to the lamb mixture and simmer, covered, for 45 minutes.

4. Meanwhile, bring a large pot of salted water to a boil over medium-high heat. Add the pappardelle and cook until just tender, about 8 to 12 minutes. Drain the pasta and transfer it to a large bowl. Add the spinach, the remaining vinegar, and the garlic oil and toss well. Season with salt and pepper and toss well again.

5. Stir the chopped parsley into the lamb mixture and season with salt and pepper. Remove from the heat and transfer to a large bowl. Serve over the pappardelle in large bowls.

Serves 6 to 8 as a main bowl

Use an elegant Provence-style casserole for an elegant yet hearty bowl of lamb, noodles, and wild mushrooms. Ladle out bowlfuls at the table.

GLASS NOODLES WITH SPICY GRILLED CHICKEN AND SPINACH

Prepare this bowl in stages, first the noodles, then the chicken, and finally the vegetables. Assemble just before serving. Garnish with more cilantro and chopped scallions, if desired, and serve with plenty of cold beer on a hot summer night.

3 ounces thin cellophane noodles

1½ pounds skinless, boneless chicken breasts

5 tablespoons Sweet Soy Sauce
   (page 251)

Shichimi togarashi (see box, page 115), to taste

4 cups (loosely packed) fresh spinach leaves,
   preferably flat-leaf, thinly sliced

1 cup thinly sliced napa cabbage

½ cup unpeeled cucumber matchsticks

½ cup (loosely packed) fresh cilantro leaves

1 small red onion, very thinly sliced

½ fresh poblano chili, stemmed, seeded,
   and finely minced

1 cup Ginger Dressing (page 228)

¼ cup white sesame seeds, toasted
   (see box, page 137)

THE SIDE BOWLS

HOT CHILI OIL
(*page 232*)

CRISPY SHALLOTS
(*see box, page 77*)

1. Preheat the grill to high and place the rack 5 to 6 inches from the heat. Or preheat the broiler.

2. Put the noodles in a bowl and add very hot water to cover. Soak until softened and pliable, about 15 minutes. Drain well in a colander. With scissors or a chef's knife, cut the noodles in thirds. Set aside.

3. Brush the chicken breasts on both sides with 3 tablespoons of the Sweet Soy Sauce, and season with the *shichimi togarashi*. When ready to grill, oil the grill rack. Grill the chicken until cooked through, about 7 minutes on each side. (Or broil the breasts on the rack of a broiler pan about 3 inches from the heat for about the same amount of time.) Remove, cool, slice into thin strips, and put in a large shallow bowl.

4. Add the noodles, spinach, napa cabbage, cucumber, cilantro, onion, and poblano to the bowl. Pour on enough of the dressing to coat and toss well.

5. Divide the noodle mixture among 4 serving bowls. Sprinkle with the sesame seeds, drizzle with the remaining 2 tablespoons Sweet Soy Sauce and the Ginger Dressing, and serve.

Serves 4 as a main bowl

When you use a wide, low-sided bowl for noodles, they appear relaxed and visually striking.

RICE NOODLES WITH CHICKEN, SHRIMP, AND SPICY PEANUT SAUCE

Rice stick noodles, everyday fare in Vietnam and Thailand, couldn't be easier to prepare. A soak in warm water makes them tender; these silky noodles require no cooking. In combination with creamy Spicy Peanut Sauce, they make a slithery complement to the pieces of chicken and shrimp in this tasty bowl.

Keep things simple by preparing the elements of this ahead of time; it takes only minutes to assemble.

8 ounces dried rice stick noodles

½ cup coconut milk

½ cup **Spicy Peanut Sauce (page 254)**

½ cup **Chicken Stock for Asian Bowls (page 5)**

3 tablespoons **Hot Chili Oil (page 232)**

2 tablespoons nam pla (Asian fish sauce)

2 tablespoons **Sweet Soy Sauce (page 251)**

I tablespoon minced lemongrass bottoms

I teaspoon red curry paste

   (available at Indian or Asian markets)

½ teaspoon ground turmeric

3 tablespoons peanut oil

I pound skinless, boneless chicken breasts,

   cut into I-inch strips

I pound medium shrimp, peeled, deveined, and

   coarsely chopped

I cup thinly shredded napa cabbage

½ cup chopped scallions, white and green parts

¼ cup peanuts, toasted (see box, page 137)

   and ground

2 tablespoons dark sesame seeds, toasted

   (see box, page 137), for garnish

These natural-color clay bowls were hand-crafted. Their organic shape is ideal for the earthy tones of this recipe.

1. Put the rice sticks in a medium bowl and add very hot water to cover. Soak until softened, about 20 minutes.

2. Meanwhile, combine the coconut milk, peanut sauce, chicken stock, chili oil, *nam pla*, soy sauce, lemongrass, red curry paste, and turmeric in a large skillet and bring to a boil over medium-high heat. Reduce the heat to medium and simmer, stirring constantly to combine the flavors, about 10 minutes.

3. Heat the peanut oil in another large skillet over high heat until hot but not smoking. Add the chicken and stir-fry for 3 minutes; add the shrimp and stir-fry for 2 minutes. Add the peanut sauce mixture, lower the heat to medium-low, and simmer to cook and heat through, about 2 minutes more.

4. Drain the noodles thoroughly in a colander, then cut the noodles in half with scissors or a knife. Transfer them to a large bowl and add the cabbage, scallions, and chopped peanuts. Toss thoroughly to mix.

5. Divide the noodle mixture among individual serving bowls and ladle the chicken, shrimp, and peanut sauce over them. Sprinkle with sesame seeds and serve.

Serves 6 to 8 as a main bowl

GLAZED SALMON WITH CELLOPHANE NOODLES AND ONIONS

You have probably never tasted anything like this, so unusual is the combination of ingredients. Sweet, mildly pungent onions, cooked until buttery soft, play a perfect complement to the rich succulent salmon, and together they stand successfully against the tartness of the mustard and tamarind.

3 tablespoons olive oil

1 tablespoon Asian sesame oil

18 cipollini onions or shallots, peeled

½ cup sherry vinegar

¼ cup (packed) dark brown sugar

6 cups Tamarind Broth (page 18)

1 tablespoon soy sauce

10 ounces thin cellophane noodles

2¼ pounds salmon fillets, cut into six 6-ounce portions

½ cup Mustard Rub (page 86)

6 scallions, white and green parts, finely chopped

1. Heat 1 tablespoon of the olive oil and the sesame oil in a large heavy saucepan over medium heat. Add the onions and cook until golden brown on all sides, about 15 minutes, stirring frequently.

2. Add the vinegar and brown sugar to the onions and stir until blended and the onions are coated. Cook until the liquid is reduced by half, for about 5 minutes.

3. Add the Tamarind Broth and soy sauce to the onions and bring to a boil. Reduce the heat to medium-low and simmer, uncovered, until the liquid is reduced by half, about 20 minutes. Keep warm, covered.

4. Meanwhile, put the noodles in a bowl and add very hot water to cover. Soak until softened and pliable, about 15 minutes. Drain well in a colander. Set aside in a large bowl.

5. Preheat the broiler.

6. Heat the remaining 2 tablespoons of olive oil in a large ovenproof skillet. Add the salmon, skin side up, and cook until browned, about 3 minutes. Remove from the heat.

7. Turn the salmon pieces over and brush with the Mustard Rub. Place the skillet under the broiler 4 inches from the heat and broil the salmon until it is just cooked through and the rub begins to bubble, 3 to 5 minutes. Remove and set aside.

8. Add the chopped scallions to the noodles in the bowl and toss to combine. Place some noodles in each of 6 serving bowls and top with a piece of the salmon. Ladle some of the broth and onion mixture over each serving.

Serves 6 as a main bowl

Note: Cipollini are distinctive disk-shaped onions, available in specialty markets, especially ones in Italian neighborhoods.

A bowl with a classic shape can give a certain familiarity to a classy, out-of-the-ordinary dish.

CELLOPHANE NOODLES WITH CRACKER-CRUSTED MUSTARD-FRIED BASS

Working in stages—softening the noodles, preparing the vegetables, then frying the fish—keeps all the components of this vibrant bowl at their optimum until the last-minute assembly. The refreshing noodle salad provides a colorful bed for the bass, with its slightly aggressive, pungent mustard flavor. If you wait to toss the vegetables with the noodles until just before serving, they won't become soggy.

NOODLES

8 ounces thin cellophane
noodles

⅓ cup peanut oil

2 cups zucchini matchsticks

2 cups (loosely packed) fresh
spinach leaves, preferably
flat-leaf, cut into ½-inch strips

I cup thinly sliced napa
cabbage

I cup thinly sliced stemmed
fresh shiitake mushrooms

5 shallots, thinly sliced

2 large cloves garlic, minced

Salt, to taste

I tablespoon dark mustard
seeds, toasted
(see box, page 137)

½ cup thinly sliced, roasted
and peeled red bell pepper
(see box, page 18)

½ cup (loosely packed)
fresh cilantro leaves

MUSTARD-FRIED BASS

½ cup Dijon mustard

4 tablespoons mustard oil or
2 tablespoons dry
mustard

2 tablespoons light soy sauce

I cup all-purpose flour

I cup graham cracker
crumbs

2 teaspoons cayenne pepper

½ cup vegetable oil

6 sea bass fillets (about 5
ounces each) or red
snapper fillets

Salt, to taste

Sweet-and-Sour Red Pepper
Drizzle (page 119)

THE SIDE BOWLS

CILANTRO OIL
(page 230)

HOT CHILI OIL
(page 232)

YELLOW CURRY OIL
(page 233)

1. Put the noodles in a large bowl and add very hot water to cover. Soak until softened and pliable, about 15 minutes. Drain well in a colander, cut the noodles in half with scissors or a knife, and set aside.

2. Meanwhile, heat a large skillet over medium heat. Add the peanut oil and heat until it begins to shimmer, then add the zucchini, spinach, napa cabbage, mushrooms, shallots, and garlic and sauté until tender, 2 to 3 minutes. Season with salt, remove from the heat, transfer to a large bowl, add the mustard seeds, and cool.

3. When the vegetables are cool, add the drained noodles, roasted red pepper strips, and cilantro and set aside.

4. Prepare the fish: Combine the mustard, 2 tablespoons of the mustard oil, and the soy sauce in a shallow dish. In another shallow dish, toss together the flour, graham cracker crumbs, and cayenne pepper until combined.

5. Heat the vegetable oil in a large sauté pan over medium-high heat.

6. Meanwhile, dredge the fish fillets first in the mustard mixture, then in the flour mixture, making sure they are completely coated. Carefully place the fish in the hot oil. Fry until golden brown on both sides and the fish flakes easily when tested with a fork, 2 to 3 minutes per side. Remove to paper towels to drain, then season with salt.

7. Place a mound of the noodle mixture in the middle of each of 6 shallow serving bowls and arrange a piece of fish on top. Drizzle some of the pepper drizzle over each fillet. Just before serving, drizzle with the remaining mustard oil. Serve at room temperature.

Serves 6 as a main bowl

When serving a selection of side-bowl oils, avoid confusion by placing them in three different small-bowl styles.

SHICHIMI TOGARASHI

A sprinkle of this Japanese seven-spice mix on noodles, rice, soups, vegetables, grilled meat and fish, or you name it, adds a unique, peppy accent. It is composed of dried ground *togarashi* (red pepper flakes), *sansho* (brown pepper pods), mandarin orange peel, black hemp seeds, white poppy seeds, *nori* (dark green seaweed), and white sesame seeds, and is available in mild, medium, and hot strengths at Japanese markets. Which one you choose to use is a matter of individual taste. We like it hot.

The berries, flowers, and leaves of the *sansho,* or Japan pepper—a handsome, graceful-looking small tree with spiny branches and fine leaves—are a prime ingredient of this traditional spice mix. The young red fruits are dried, and the bitter black seeds extracted. In China, the dried seedless berries, which have a wood-spicy flavor, are known as Sichuan pepper, and the plant is thought to have medicinal value for digestive disorders.

Although there is no substitute, if you want to attempt your own blend we suggest toasting (see box, page 137):

    1 tablespoon white sesame seeds

    1 tablespoon Sichuan peppercorns

    1 small dried hot red chili

Then grind together with:

    ½ teaspoon dried orange peel

    ½ teaspoon crushed dried dark green seaweed

Or you can simply substitute cayenne pepper, but it is no match for either the real thing or your own blend.

Fish-shaped bowls come in all sizes from minnow on up.
They are easy to find in tableware shops and
it's worthwhile having a selection on hand.

FARFALLE AND LOBSTER WITH RAMPS AND SPICY BREAD CRUMBS

The scallion-thin wild leeks called ramps that we use here can be found in the produce section of specialty food markets. Available only in spring, ramps offer an unabashed garlicky-onion flavor that we can only long for the rest of the year. If you cannot find ramps, then leeks, scallions, or onions are all good, albeit tamer, substitutes.

If you plan ahead by precooking the lobster and making the Parsley and Garlic Oil and bread crumbs in advance, you will be free to enjoy this sensational bowl at the dinner table with your guests instead of after dinner in the kitchen!

> 1 pound farfalle (bowtie) pasta
> 2 tablespoons olive oil
> 1 bunch ramps (see Note)
> 2 cups cooked lobster meat, cut into 1-inch pieces
> 1 bunch fresh chives, chopped
> ½ cup Parsley and Garlic Oil (page 234)
> ¼ cup fresh lemon juice
> 1 tablespoon grated lemon zest
> ¾ cup Spicy Bread Crumbs (recipe follows)
> Salt and freshly ground black pepper,
>   to taste

1. Bring a large pot of salted water to a boil over medium-high heat. Add the farfalle and cook until just tender, about 8 to 12 minutes.

2. Meanwhile, heat the olive oil in a medium skillet over medium heat. Add the ramps and cook until softened, about 5 minutes, stirring occasionally.

3. Remove the ramps from the heat and transfer to a large bowl. Add the lobster, chives, garlic oil, and lemon juice and zest and stir to combine.

4. Drain the pasta and add it to the lobster mixture; toss thoroughly. Slowly sprinkle the bread crumbs over the pasta, tossing as you add and trying to sprinkle evenly to prevent lumps. Season with salt and pepper. Divide among individual serving bowls.

Serves 4 to 6 as a main bowl, 8 to 10 as a small bowl

Note: To use ramps, peel off the outer layer of skin on each bulb, trim off the root, and rinse well under cold running water. Drain and pat dry. For this recipe, cut into 2-inch lengths. If ramps are not available, substitute 3 medium leeks; cut lengthwise in half, rinse thoroughly, drain, and pat dry. Cut crosswise into ¼-inch slices. Cook as directed in Step 2.

SPICY BREAD CRUMBS

Fresh bread crumbs provide a much lighter coating than the dried store-bought variety. If you want seasoned but not spicy fresh crumbs, omit the cayenne pepper.

Here's a shape that appeals to all cultures, from Mexico to Japan. This bowl is statuesque and makes a notable display of a delectable meal.

> **2 cups freshly dried bread crumbs**
> **1 tablespoon imported sweet paprika**
> **1 tablespoon freshly ground black pepper**
> **1 tablespoon finely chopped fresh thyme**
> **½ teaspoon cayenne pepper**

Combine all the ingredients in a bowl and toss thoroughly to combine. Use immediately, or transfer to an airtight container and refrigerate for up to 1 month.

Makes about 2 cups

PAN-SEARED SCALLOPS WITH EGG NOODLES

S ea scallops are best when quickly seared on the outside and slightly undercooked within. Overdone, their natural juices cook off, changing their texture from moist and succulent to dry and tough. Properly cooked, they match up beautifully to the robust syrup-like sauce featured here.

CILANTRO OIL
(page 230)

CRISPY LEEKS
(see box, page 77)

CRISPY SHALLOTS
(see box, page 77)

Contrasting colors and shapes—fluted, stark white porcelain filled with pearly white scallops and bright red broth.

3 tablespoons (packed) light or dark brown sugar

3 tablespoons nam pla (Asian fish sauce)

½ teaspoon chili paste

1½ pounds sea scallops, rinsed and cut horizontally into
¼-inch-thick disks

8 ounces thin fresh egg noodles

3 tablespoons peanut oil

2 cloves garlic, minced

1 shallot, minced

1 tablespoon minced peeled fresh ginger

1 red bell pepper, roasted and peeled (see box, page 18),
thinly sliced

1 large ripe tomato, seeded and cut into medium dice

1 cup diagonally cut asparagus pieces (1-inch pieces),
blanched and shocked (page 214)

1 cup Chicken Stock for Asian Bowls (page 5)

½ cup Sweet-and-Sour Red Pepper Drizzle (recipe follows)

2 scallions, white and green parts, chopped

Salt and freshly ground black pepper, to taste

1. Combine brown sugar, *nam pla*, and chili paste in a medium bowl and beat with a fork to blend. Add the scallops and toss well to coat. Let stand for 15 minutes.

2. Meanwhile, bring 2 quarts of water to a boil in a large saucepan. Add the noodles, return to a boil, and boil until tender, about 3 minutes. Drain in a colander, rinse under cool running water, drain again, and set aside.

3. Drain the scallops. Heat the peanut oil in a wok or large skillet over medium-high heat until hot but not smoking. Add the scallops and sear them quickly for about 1 minute on each side. You may want to do this in 2 batches to avoid steaming. Remove to a plate and set aside.

4. Increase the heat under the wok to high and add the garlic, shallot, and ginger. Stir for 10 seconds. Stir in the roasted red pepper, tomato, asparagus, chicken stock, and pepper drizzle and heat through.

5. Add the noodles, scallops, and chopped scallions. Toss the mixture until thoroughly combined and heated through, about 1 minute. Season with salt and pepper and serve immediately.

Serves 4 as a main bowl, 6 to 8 as a small bowl

SWEET-AND-SOUR RED PEPPER DRIZZLE

    I cup roasted, peeled, and seeded red bell peppers
        (4 large peppers; see box, page 18)
    5 tablespoons rice vinegar
    ¼ cup Thai Dipping Sauce (page 253)
    ¼ cup honey
    ¼ cup fresh lime juice
    ½ teaspoon cayenne pepper

Combine all the ingredients in a blender or food processor and process until smooth. Use immediately, or transfer to an airtight container and store in the refrigerator for up to 2 weeks.

Makes about 2 cups

It's Just Drizzling

The tangy red pepper drizzle accompanying the scallops adds contrasting flavors to other preparations as well. Try it with Cellophane Noodles with Cracker-Crusted Mustard-Fried Bass (page 113) and Hot-and-Sour Chowder (page 53). In fact, it adds dazzle to just about anything. Just try it as a dipping sauce with Crabmeat Dumplings (page 156) and see. Once you have, you'll come to depend on it as a pantry staple.

ON-THE-FLY NOODLES WITH SHRIMP

It's eight P.M., cold and windy and as dark as midnight. You've just arrived home. The dog must be walked, the kids are starving, and you have a work deadline. Take heart. Comfort—a warming bowl—is not far off. Admittedly, you have to have a few possibly atypical pantry ingredients on hand. But, if you've been cooking regularly from this book, you already know the value of having sake, mirin, and *shichimi togarashi* in the cupboard. While the nutritional value of this dish is remarkably high, it is its flavor and ease of preparation that secure its popularity. Water never tasted so good!

Yes, it's a dog bowl! But no dog has used it for his dinner. Instead, it's a quirky way to serve noodles. Entice the kids with a new approach!

6 cups water

1 cup soy sauce

1 cup sake

½ cup mirin, sweet sherry, or sweet vermouth

Pinch of shichimi togarashi (see box, page 115)

1 cup cooked chopped spinach

6 jumbo shrimp, in shells but deveined

1 pound skinless, boneless chicken breasts, thinly sliced on the diagonal

1 medium onion, thinly sliced

2 scallions, white and green parts, cut into 2-inch pieces

12 ounces dried soba (buckwheat) noodles

3 tablespoons fresh lemon juice

2 tablespoons Asian sesame oil

Hot Chili Oil (page 232), to taste

¼ cup white sesame seeds, toasted (page 137), for garnish

1. Combine the water, soy sauce, sake, mirin, and *shichimi togarashi* in a large nonreactive saucepan and bring to a boil over high heat. Reduce the heat to low, and simmer to cook off the alcohol and let the flavors blend, about 30 minutes.

2. Meanwhile, bring 2 quarts of salted water to a boil in another large saucepan over medium-high heat. Add the noodles, return to a boil, and cook until just tender, 2 to 3 minutes. Drain thoroughly in a colander. Divide the noodles and the spinach among 6 serving bowls.

3. Add the shrimp, chicken, onion, and scallions to the simmering broth and cook until the shrimp and chicken are tender, about 10 minutes.

4. Remove the broth mixture from the heat. Add 1 shrimp to each serving of noodles and spinach, then add chicken and vegetables, dividing them evenly. Ladle the broth into the bowls, then drizzle each serving with lemon juice, sesame oil, and hot oil. Garnish the bowls with the sesame seeds and serve.

Serves 6 as a main bowl

TAGLIATELLE WITH FRESH CORN AND LUMP CRAB

Make this pasta and seafood bowl at the height of corn season, May through September. If the corn isn't fresh and sweet, the delicacy and simplicity of the flavors in this light summer pasta will be lost. And if you have the opportunity, buy corn at a local farmstand as soon after it has been picked as possible. Once corn has been picked, its sugar begins to change to starch, reducing the corn's natural sweetness and tenderness. Look for ears with tight, bright green husks and golden-brown silk.

You can choose here to steam live blue crabs for their meat. We kept it simple and recommend purchasing high-quality lump crabmeat from a reliable fish market near you. Be sure to pick the crab over carefully to remove any bits of shell and cartilage.

8 ounces fresh tagliatelle

I small bunch fresh chives, chopped

7 tablespoons olive oil

I small red bell pepper, stemmed, seeded,
    and cut into small dice

2 medium ribs celery, cut into ¼-inch diagonal slices

2 shallots, minced

1½ cups fresh corn kernels (about 3 large ears)

I cup Chicken Stock for Mediterranean Bowls (page 20)

I tablespoon Garlic and Herb Paste (page 239)

I small tomato, seeded and diced

¼ cup chopped scallions, white and green parts

¼ cup fresh lemon juice

I pound lump crabmeat, picked over for cartilage

Salt and freshly ground black pepper, to taste

*A large, wide serving bowl
that sits on a metal stand, gives
everyone a full view of the
crabmeat and corn in this recipe.
Serve accompanied by
a stack of smaller bowls and
serving utensils.*

I. Bring a large pot of salted water to a boil over medium-high heat. Add the tagliatelle and cook until just tender, 8 to 12 minutes. Drain well, then transfer to a large ceramic serving bowl and toss with 3 tablespoons of the olive oil and the chives. Cover, set aside, and keep warm.

2. Heat the remaining 4 tablespoons of the olive oil in a large deep skillet over medium heat. Add the red pepper, celery, and shallots and cook until slightly translucent, about 5 minutes, stirring occasionally.

3. Stir in the corn, chicken stock, and herb paste. Bring to a simmer and cook for 1 to 2 minutes, then add the tomato, scallions, and lemon juice and simmer for another minute.

4. Stir in the crabmeat and cook until just heated through, 1 to 2 minutes. Season with salt and pepper.

5. Remove the corn and crab mixture from the heat and pour over the pasta. Serve at once.

Serves 4 as a main bowl, 8 as a small bowl

SOBA NOODLES WITH CLAMS

A restaurateur visiting from Japan stopped by Lola Bowla one day and tried a bowl of these out of curiosity. He had never eaten soba noodles this way. Just one look at the expression on his face secured the longevity of the recipe! The coolness of the cilantro garnish, along with the coconut milk and lime juice in the curry sauce, offers the perfect contrast to the distinctive flavor of the curry paste.

>
> **Double recipe (4 cups) Fiery Red Curry Sauce**
> **(recipe follows)**
> **4 dozen small clams (Manila or littleneck), rinsed and scrubbed**
> **12 ounces dried soba (buckwheat) noodles**
> **2 tablespoons Asian sesame oil**
> **1 tablespoon Sweet Soy Sauce (page 251), for garnish**
> **½ cup (loosely packed) fresh cilantro leaves, for garnish**

CHOPPED SCALLIONS

STEAMED RICE

SAUTÉED GREENS

HOT CHILI OIL

(page 232)

1. Bring the curry sauce to a simmer in a stockpot over low heat. Add the clams and increase the heat to medium. Cover and cook until the clams open, about 4 minutes. Using a slotted spoon, remove the clams to a bowl; discard any that did not open. Cover the clams to keep them warm.

2. Continue to simmer the sauce, uncovered, over low heat until slightly thickened, another 15 to 20 minutes.

3. Meanwhile, bring 2 quarts of salted water to a boil in a large saucepan over medium-high heat. Add the noodles, return to a boil, and cook until just tender, 4 to 5 minutes. Drain thoroughly in a colander, transfer to a large bowl, and toss with the sesame oil.

4. Divide the noodles and clams evenly among 6 serving bowls. Then top with a ladleful of sauce. Drizzle with the Sweet Soy Sauce, garnish with the cilantro leaves, and serve.

Serves 6 as a main bowl

FIERY RED CURRY SAUCE

We like it hot, hot, hot! And because heat is a subjective matter, we urge you to adjust the heat here according to your own taste. If you like it less hot, substitute a not-so-fiery curry blend such as our Curry Powder (page 10) for the intensely flavored red curry paste. Concocted specially for Soba Noodles with Clams, this sauce is wonderful with Chili-Roasted Vegetables (page 96) or Squid Stuffed with Shrimp and Ginger (page 171).

> 2 cups Chicken Stock for Asian Bowls (page 5)
> 1 cup unsweetened canned coconut milk
> ¼ cup tomato juice
> ¼ cup chopped fresh ginger
> 2 stalks lemongrass, finely chopped
> 1 tablespoon red curry paste
>   (available at Indian or Asian markets)
> ¼ cup fresh lime juice
> 1 tablespoon Sweet Soy Sauce (page 251)
> Salt and freshly ground black pepper, to taste

1. Combine the chicken stock, coconut milk, tomato juice, ginger, and lemongrass in a medium nonreactive saucepan and bring to a boil over medium heat. Add the red curry paste, stirring to dissolve, then reduce the heat to low, and simmer, uncovered, about 25 minutes.

2. Remove from the heat and strain the sauce through a fine sieve into a medium heatproof bowl, pressing the solids with the back of a spoon to extract the liquid.

3. Stir in the lime juice and Sweet Soy Sauce and season with salt and pepper. Use immediately, or store in an airtight container in the refrigerator for up to 1 week.

Makes about 2 cups

SPICY STIR-FRIED SQUID WITH ORANGE SEGMENTS AND EGG NOODLES

Mild-tasting squid absorbs the sweet, salty, and slightly spicy flavors of the marinade, which also helps to tenderize the squid, making it adaptable to quick cooking methods. Here it is stir-fried in a flash, leaving it tender and succulent.

4 tablespoons Hot Chili Oil (page 232) ,
    plus additional for serving

3 tablespoons nam pla (Asian fish sauce)

2 tablespoons (packed) light or dark brown sugar

2 pounds squid, cleaned (see box, page 90) and
    cut into 1-inch strips

8 ounces thin fresh egg noodles

½ cup Chicken Stock for Asian Bowls (page 5)

½ cup fresh orange juice

1 tablespoon minced peeled fresh ginger

2 shallots, minced

½ teaspoon crushed red pepper flakes

¾ cup fresh orange segments

½ cup fresh green peas, blanched and shocked
    (see box, page 214), or frozen, thawed

1 medium cucumber, peeled, seeded, and
    cut into matchsticks

3 scallions, white and green parts, chopped

¼ cup fresh lime juice

2 tablespoons white sesame seeds, toasted
    (see box, page 137), plus additional for serving

Grated zest of 1 lime

Salt and freshly ground black pepper, to taste

Lime wedges, for serving

Here, an Asian-style pedestal bowl stands tall on the table, like an offering to the gods.

125

1. Combine 2 tablespoons of the chili oil, the *nam pla*, and brown sugar in a large bowl and beat with a fork to blend. Add the squid and toss well to coat. Cover and marinate in the refrigerator for 30 minutes.

2. Meanwhile, bring 2 quarts of water to a boil in a large saucepan. Add the noodles, return to a boil, and boil until tender, about 3 minutes. Drain in a colander, rinse under cool running water, drain again, and set aside.

3. Heat the remaining 2 tablespoons chili oil in a wok or large skillet over high heat until hot but not smoking. Add the squid with the marinade and stir-fry until opaque, no more than 2 minutes. Remove the squid to a bowl and set aside.

4. Add the chicken stock, orange juice, ginger, shallots, and pepper flakes to the wok. Bring to a boil, stirring, and cook for 1 minute.

5. Add the egg noodles to the wok and toss to coat thoroughly.

6. Add the following ingredients, one at a time, tossing to incorporate before adding the next: the orange segments, peas, cucumber, scallions, lime juice, sesame seeds, lime zest, and salt and pepper. Then remove from the heat.

We almost never serve anything savory without citrus wedges. This small Japanese rectangular-shaped platter, traditionally used for small portions of food like sushi or pickled vegetables, is an ideal way to present them.

7. Divide the noodle mixture among 4 serving bowls, place a portion of squid on top of each serving, and sprinkle with additional toasted sesame seeds and chili oil. Serve with lime wedges.

Serves 4 as a main bowl, 8 as a side bowl

CAPELLINI WITH MANILA CLAMS, LOBSTER, AND ASPARAGUS

This light seafood pasta is a delight to eat in summer. All of the cooking is done stovetop, which keeps you and the kitchen cool. And much of the preparation can be done ahead, including cooking the lobster and blanching the vegetables, provided they are held, covered, in the refrigerator. If you don't have lobster stock available, substitute Shellfish Stock. Failing that, chicken stock will still give you a great-tasting pasta. The clam liquid, however, is integral to the sauce, offering as it does the deep flavor of the sea.

Be sure to serve with a loaf of crusty fresh bread.

8 ounces dried capellini

4 dozen small clams (Manila or littleneck),
    rinsed and scrubbed

2 cups water

2 cups Lobster Stock (page 32), Shellfish Stock
    (page 36), or Chicken Stock for Mediterranean Bowls
    (page 20)

I tablespoon tomato paste

I cup cooked lobster meat, in chunks

4 fresh medium asparagus spears, trimmed,
    blanched and shocked (see box, page 214),
    and cut into I-inch diagonal pieces

I small ripe tomato, seeded and cut into medium dice

½ cup fresh corn kernels, blanched and shocked
    (page 214)

½ cup Parsley and Garlic Oil (page 234)

I bunch fresh chives, finely chopped, for garnish

Salt

Lime wedges, for serving (optional)

Coaxing Clams

Clams that don't open after they have been properly cooked either were dead or are just plain stubborn. To determine which it is, rap the clams in question sharply once or twice with the handle of a knife. This should convince the clams to open; if it doesn't, discard them.

BASIL OIL
(page 230)

GARLIC OIL
(page 234)

1. Bring a large pot of salted water to a boil over medium-high heat. Add the capellini and cook until just tender, about 8 to 12 minutes. Drain in a colander, rinse well, and set aside.

2. Meanwhile, combine the clams and water in a stockpot. Cover, bring to a boil over medium heat, and steam until the clams pop open, 5 to 10 minutes, removing them from the pan to a bowl as they open. Discard any that do not open.

3. Strain the clam broth through a sieve lined with a coffee filter into a large wide saucepan. Add the stock and tomato paste and bring to a boil. Reduce the heat to medium and simmer, uncovered, for 10 minutes, stirring occasionally.

4. Add the lobster, asparagus, tomato, corn, and garlic oil to the broth mixture and stir to combine. When the liquid returns to a simmer, add the pasta, toss thoroughly to mix, and cook until the pasta is heated through, 1 to 2 minutes, tossing occasionally. Season with salt and remove from the heat.

5. Divide the capellini mixture among 4 serving bowls. Divide the clams among the bowls and sprinkle with the chives. Serve at once.

Serve each guest their portion in bowls of the same basic design but different color glazes.

Serves 4 as a main bowl

SHANGHAI NOODLES

Considered street food in southern regions of China, this kind of noodle preparation is a quick, satisfying, savory yet sweet vegetable meal in a bowl. The soft, flat rice noodles capture the essence of the soy, sherry, and lime juice.

5 Japanese eggplants (6 to 8 ounces each)

8 ounces flat dried rice noodles

½ cup soy sauce

¼ cup dry sherry

¼ cup (packed) light brown sugar

1 teaspoon chili paste

1 tablespoon nam pla (Asian fish sauce)

2 cups thinly sliced Savoy cabbage

½ cup fresh green peas, blanched and shocked (see box, page 214), or frozen, thawed

5 scallions, white and green parts, chopped

¼ cup fresh lime juice

Salt and freshly ground black pepper, to taste

1. Preheat the oven to 375°F.

2. Place the whole eggplants on a baking sheet and bake until soft, about 20 minutes.

3. Meanwhile, bring a large pot of salted water to a boil. Add the noodles and boil just until soft, about 4 minutes. Drain in a colander, rinse under cool running water, drain again, and set aside.

4. Combine the soy sauce, sherry, sugar, chili paste, and *nam pla* in a small bowl and, with a wire whisk, beat until blended and the sugar is dissolved. Set aside.

5. Remove the eggplant from the oven. When cool enough to handle, roughly chop, leaving the skin on but discarding the ends.

A basic, smaller-than-usual wok makes a rustic presentation for noodles with an Asian flair.

6. Heat a wok or large skillet over high heat until hot and add the soy sauce mixture. Add the rice noodles and toss to coat thoroughly. Incorporate the chopped eggplant, cabbage, peas, and scallions and combine well, 1 minute. Remove from the heat and toss with the lime juice and salt and pepper.

7. Serve in individual bowls.

Serves 4 as a main bowl

PENNE WITH ZUCCHINI AND TOMATO-GARLIC VINAIGRETTE

Penne is so popular you can find it in any grocery store and in countless variations—smooth on the outside or ridged on the outside, narrow or wide, short or long. Goat cheese, which adds a creamy, slight thickness to the tomato sauce, makes this tube-shaped pasta the perfect choice. It seeps deep into the noodle's round hollow, making every bite pleasing.

1½ pounds penne

2 cups Tomato-Garlic Vinaigrette (page 226)

4 ounces crumbled goat cheese

½ cup dry white wine

¼ cup extra virgin olive oil

2 tablespoons Parsley and Garlic Oil (page 234)

1 teaspoon Basil Paste (recipe follows)

1 pound zucchini, cut in half lengthwise,
    then into very thin slices crosswise

¼ cup finely chopped Italian (flat-leaf) parsley

Salt, to taste

Pinch of crushed red pepper flakes

1. Bring a large pot of salted water to a boil over medium-high heat. Add the penne and cook until just tender, 8 to 12 minutes.

2. As the pasta cooks, hold a stainless-steel bowl over the pasta pot to warm it. Add the vinaigrette, goat cheese, wine, oils, and Basil Paste to the bowl. While holding the bowl over the cooking pasta, blend the mixture with a wooden spoon until smooth. Set aside.

3. Drain the pasta and transfer it to the bowl with the warm vinaigrette mixture. Add the zucchini and chopped parsley and toss thoroughly to mix. Season with salt and pepper flakes and toss again before serving.

Serves 6 as a main bowl

BASIL PASTE

This paste can turn an ordinary pasta dish into a magnificent summer memory—even in the dead of winter. Make a few batches when basil is in season, store in airtight containers, label and date them (so they don't get lost or forgotten), then put them in the freezer and you'll have summer at the tips of your fingers all winter long.

> 1 bunch Italian (flat-leaf) parsley, stemmed and rinsed
> 1 cup (tightly packed) fresh basil leaves, rinsed
> 1 tablespoon roasted garlic (see box, page 48)
> ½ cup extra virgin olive oil

1. Bring a large pot of salted water to a boil. Have a bowl of ice water ready on the counter.

2. Drop the parsley and basil leaves into the boiling water and blanch for about 10 seconds. Drain, then plunge into the ice water to refresh and set the color. Drain again, then squeeze with your hands to remove the remaining water.

What could be better suited to a heaping serving of Italian-style pasta than a classic Italian pasta bowl?

3. Roughly chop the parsley and basil and transfer to a blender or food processor. Add the roasted garlic and process until smooth. With the motor running, add the olive oil in a slow, steady stream and blend until incorporated. Use immediately, or transfer to an airtight container and store in the refrigerator for up to 1 week or freeze for up to 4 months.

Makes about I cup

PEARL PASTA WITH FRESH PEAS AND GORGONZOLA

The ultimate comfort food, pearl pasta (also called *acini di pepe*) is similar to the tiny alphabet pasta Mom used to add to soup. The miniature size causes the "pearls" to act like grains rather than pasta, making pearl pasta an excellent choice for a creamy risotto-like creation like this.

I pound pearl pasta

2 cups Chicken Stock for Mediterranean Bowls (page 20)

2 tablespoons roasted garlic (see box, page 48)

I cup fresh peas, blanched and shocked (see box, page 214)

½ cup finely chopped, roasted, seeded, and peeled red bell peppers (2 large peppers; see box, page 18)

4 ounces Gorgonzola cheese, crumbled

2 tablespoons red wine vinegar

½ cup crème fraîche

I teaspoon chopped fresh thyme leaves

Salt and freshly ground black pepper, to taste

1. Bring a large pot of salted water to a boil over medium-high heat. Add the pasta and cook until just tender, 8 to 12 minutes. Drain in a colander, run under cold water, and drain again. Set aside, covered.

2. Bring 1½ cups of the chicken stock to a boil in a large saucepan over medium heat. Add the roasted garlic and cook, uncovered, until reduced by half, about 10 minutes. Add the pasta, peas, roasted peppers, Gorgonzola, and vinegar and toss well. Stir in the crème fraîche, the remaining ½ cup stock, and the thyme. Season with salt and pepper. Divide the pasta among 6 serving bowls and serve at once.

Serves 6 as a main bowl, 10 as a small bowl

Attractive pot-style bowls often have lips—a good place to rest a spoon or fork. These bowls are also good for hearty servings of onion soup.

SESAME NOODLEHEAD

Eating noodles has, we're sure, always brought on waves of giggles among children; no matter how these long coils make their way—be it finger, fork, or chopsticks—to their mouths, a lone strand or two always seems to be left dangling for a sumptuous slurp. It was probably at noodle meals like that that names such as "noodlehead" came into our vernacular. You'd have to be a real non-noodlehead not to appreciate this dish, with its nutty flavors and smooth textures. The rich, creamy sesame sauce generously coats slithery egg noodles and tender, wilted green chard for a homey rewarding meal.

You can also use fresh thin egg noodles for this; if so, cook only 3 minutes.

1 pound fat fresh egg noodles

2 tablespoons olive oil

2 cups (tightly packed) thinly sliced Swiss chard leaves

10 scallions, white and green parts, blanched and shocked
  (see box, page 214), cut into 2-inch pieces

1 fresh poblano chili, stemmed, seeded, and chopped

4 tablespoons white sesame seeds, toasted (see box, page 137)

2 cups Sesame Sauce (recipe follows)

Salt, to taste

Juice of 1 lime

2 tablespoons Garlic Oil (page 234)

½ teaspoon Asian sesame oil

1. Bring 2 quarts of water to a boil in a large saucepan. Add the noodles, return to a boil, and boil until tender, 4 to 6 minutes. Drain in a colander, rinse under cool running water, drain again, and set aside.

2. Heat the olive oil in a medium saucepan over medium-low heat. Add the Swiss chard, blanched scallions, poblano, and 3 tablespoons of the sesame seeds. Stir for 1 minute, add the sesame sauce, and cook, stirring, until heated through, 30 seconds more. Remove from the heat and season with salt and the juice of half the lime.

3. Divide the noodles among individual serving bowls and top with the Swiss chard mixture. Drizzle 2 or 3 drops each of the garlic and sesame oils over each serving of noodles, then sprinkle each bowl with some of the remaining sesame seeds and lime juice.

Serves 6 to 8 as a main bowl, 12 to 14 as a small bowl

SESAME SAUCE

The right sesame seed paste is integral to the success of this sauce. Some pastes are bitter and lack a distinct toasted sesame flavor, which is why we specifically recommend Lan Chi brand here.

There seems to be an endless variety of shapes in little Asian-made bowls. Mix and match these shapes and colors when serving a variety of dipping sauces. Each person can have their own set. If bowls are to be shared, be sure each has its own little (demitasse) spoon so that there's no double-dipping.

It lends rich flavor and thick creamy texture. You can find sesame seed paste in any Asian market. Be sure to check the expiration date on the jar and choose one that has not been sitting on the shelf too long. The Middle Eastern sesame seed paste tahini is not a substitute for Asian sesame seed paste. Smooth peanut butter, however, is.

3 cups Chicken Stock for Asian Bowls
    (page 5)
¼ cup sesame seed paste, preferably Lan Chi
    (see headnote), or 2 heaping teaspoons smooth
    peanut butter
2 tablespoons soy sauce
1½ tablespoons sugar
1 tablespoon Chinese rice wine or dry sherry
½ teaspoon green curry paste
    (available at Indian or Asian markets)
1 star anise
½ tablespoon Asian sesame oil
Juice of 1 lime

1. Combine the chicken stock, sesame seed paste (or peanut butter), soy sauce, sugar, rice wine, green curry paste, and star anise in a medium nonreactive saucepan and bring to a boil over medium heat, stirring occasionally. Reduce the heat to low and simmer, uncovered, until smooth and slightly thickened, about 30 minutes.

2. Remove from the heat. Press the sauce using the back of a spoon through a fine sieve into a medium heatproof bowl. Add the sesame oil and lime juice, stir, then cool.

3. Use immediately, or transfer to an airtight container and store in the refrigerator for up to 1 week.

Makes about 2 cups

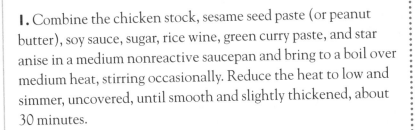

GOING HEAD TO HEAD

Sometimes identifying different types of cabbage can be confusing. We've even gone head to head about one or two of them ourselves. For example, Chinese cabbage is the same as napa cabbage, which is the same as Peking cabbage. White Chinese cabbage, which differs from Chinese cabbage, is most often known as bok choy.

No matter their specific name, cabbages are high in fiber and potassium and contain large amounts of vitamins C and E. And cabbage is great for adding to soups and broths at the last minute to enliven the recipe with color, flavor, and texture. Because cabbages vary in type, size, shape, and degree of compactness, it's worth noting those we favor.

NAPA CABBAGE: At any size, longish, compact heads of napa cabbage are excellent for slicing thin and tossing into stir-fries, rolling up in spring rolls and in vegetable pot stickers, and using as the wrappers themselves. Because the head is tightly formed, you need to rinse only the outer leaves to clean away any soil that may linger. Napa cabbage heads vary dramatically in size, but the cream-and-pale-green leaves are always tightly formed.

BOK CHOY: On the other hand, bok choy, with its long, crisp white stalks topped with deep green leaves, is loose leafed and must be rinsed of its grit. However, you can slice the head lengthwise into halves or quarters, then rinse and steam in a matter of minutes. Bok choy is especially nice when purchased small, or young. The deep green leaves are tender yet hearty, and the stalks are edible as well.

SAVOY CABBAGE: Another favorite, Savoy cabbage is round with loose, crinkled light green inner leaves and darker green outer leaves that are great for making cabbage rolls. Because of its delicate flavor, some cooks consider it the best of its kind.

MUSTARD-SCENTED RICE NOODLES WITH NAPA CABBAGE

Crisp, fresh napa cabbage combined with toasted peanuts, sesame seeds, and mustard seed makes an easy crunchy dressing for softened rice sticks. Mustard oil adds a unique, arousingly aromatic kick to whatever it is combined with. Although you can make this pungently flavored oil yourself by steeping toasted ground yellow mustard seeds in canola oil, we recommend purchasing it. The commercial variety has a much stronger flavor. You can find mustard oil in any Indian market or specialty food store.

> **8 ounces dried rice stick noodles**
> **½ cup rice vinegar**
> **¼ cup mustard oil (see headnote)**
> **3 tablespoons olive oil**
> **2 cups very thinly sliced napa cabbage**
> **3 ounces fresh shiitake mushrooms, stemmed**
>   **and thinly sliced**
> **I bunch fresh chives, finely chopped**
> **¼ cup peanuts, toasted (see box, this page) and ground**
> **3 tablespoons white sesame seeds, toasted**
>   **(see box, this page)**
> **I tablespoon dark mustard seeds, toasted**
>   **(see box, this page)**
> **I teaspoon shichimi togarashi (see box, page 115)**
> **Salt and freshly ground black pepper, to taste**

1. Put the rice sticks in a bowl and add very hot water to cover. Soak until softened, about 20 minutes.

2. Meanwhile, combine the vinegar, mustard oil, and olive oil in a large bowl. Beat well with a wire whisk to blend.

3. Drain the noodles thoroughly in a colander, then cut the noodles in half with scissors or a knife. Add to the dressing with the cabbage. Toss thoroughly to coat.

4. Add the mushrooms, chives, peanuts, sesame seeds, mustard seeds, and *shichimi togarashi* and toss again. Season with salt and pepper. Serve in individual bowls.

Serves 4 as a main bowl, 8 as a small bowl

To Toast and Pan-Roast Seeds and Nuts

1. Put the seeds or nuts in a small dry skillet and set over medium-high heat. For seeds, keep the lid at the side of the skillet. Use it to prevent the seeds from popping out of the pan as the heat rises. For nuts, stir them occasionally to color all sides.

2. As soon as the seeds begin to pop, 2 to 3 minutes, or the nuts smell fragrant and start to color, 3 to 4 minutes, remove the skillet from the heat, transfer the seeds or nuts to a bowl, and let cool.

RISOTTO WITH BRAISED DUCK AND SPICY GINGER BROTH

D uck is as easy to prepare as chicken and has a much richer flavor, but many cooks steer away from it because they think it's hard to work with or too high in fat. It is higher in fat than chicken, but here only the legs are braised and the skin is removed, which eliminates a lot of the concern. The leg meat and a stock made from the duck bones flavor this robustly seasoned, creamy risotto.

BRAISED DUCK LEGS

I tablespoon salt

I tablespoon freshly ground Sichuan peppercorns

I fresh Scotch bonnet pepper or serrano chili, stemmed, seeded, and chopped

2 teaspoons ground cumin

I teaspoon star anise, ground

8 duck legs

4 cups Chicken Stock for Asian Bowls (page 5)

I cup dry white wine

½ cup finely chopped peeled fresh ginger

½ cup fresh Thai basil leaves

¼ cup roasted garlic (see box, page 48)

RISOTTO

3 tablespoons olive oil

I small red onion, finely chopped

2 tablespoons minced garlic

I tablespoon finely chopped peeled fresh ginger

Pinch saffron threads

2 cups Arborio rice

2 cups duck stock (from braising duck legs)

I cup water

2 scallions, white and green parts, finely chopped

½ teaspoon chopped fresh mint leaves

Salt and freshly ground black pepper, to taste

1½ cups Ginger's Hot Broth (page 11)

Lime wedges, for serving

1. Preheat the oven to 400°F.

2. Prepare the duck legs: Combine the salt, Sichuan peppercorns, chili, cumin, and star anise in a small bowl. Rub the duck legs with the mixture and place in one layer in a roasting pan. Roast, uncovered, for 20 minutes, reduce the heat to 325°F, and roast until cooked through, 40 minutes more. Let cool.

3. When cool enough to handle, remove the duck meat from the bones, reserving the bones, and shred the meat into bite-size pieces, discarding the cartilage and skin. Set the duck meat aside.

4. Place the leg bones in a medium saucepan, add the stock, wine, ginger, basil, and garlic, and bring to a boil over medium heat. Reduce the heat to low and simmer, uncovered, until reduced to 2 cups, about 30 minutes. Remove from the heat, strain the stock into a heatproof bowl, and let cool. Remove as much fat as possible from the stock, then set aside.

5. Prepare the risotto: Heat the olive oil in a large heavy skillet over medium heat. Add the onion and garlic and sauté until the onion is softened, about 5 minutes. Add the ginger, saffron, and rice and sauté, stirring to coat the rice, about 3 minutes.

6. Add the duck stock, ½ cup at a time, stirring constantly, until each portion of stock is absorbed before adding the next. Add the reserved duck meat, then add ½ cup of the water, stirring until it is absorbed. Add the remaining water and stir until it is absorbed. The risotto will be creamy and the rice should be cooked al dente (just tender to the bite). This will take about 1 hour of cooking time.

7. Remove the pan from the heat and stir in the scallions and mint. Season with salt and pepper.

8. Spoon the risotto into individual serving bowls and drizzle some of the ginger broth over and around each serving. Serve at once accompanied by lime wedges.

Serves 6 as a main bowl

At first glance, you may see a fruit bowl here, but don't pass it by. It makes a good bowlfood serving dish—as long as it's heat resistant. This one, with its lavish grape art, is a wonderful, even a little eccentric, way to present duck risotto. Remember, there are no rules.

THAI PAELLA

Once again, we buck tradition by offering a variation on paella, the famous Spanish dish. Our version is neither cooked in a *paella*—the wide, shallow two-handled pan in which the seafood, meat, and rice combination is customarily served and after which it is named—nor flavored with saffron. This interpretation, however, boasts a delectable combination of shellfish and meat simmered in liquids and spices, many of them associated with Thai cooking.

Although it isn't necessary to prepare paella in a traditional paella pan, it can be used to serve a hot, steamy, very nontraditional version of the dish.

⅔ cup jasmine rice, rinsed and drained

1⅓ cups water

½ cup finely chopped lemongrass bottoms

¼ cup finely chopped peeled fresh ginger

¼ cup dried shrimp (see box, page 29)

2 tablespoons tomato paste

1 tablespoon chili paste

1 tablespoon Garlic Paste (page 61)

1 teaspoon freshly ground Sichuan peppercorns

4 Kaffir lime leaves

2 shallots, chopped

¼ cup Hot Chili Oil (page 232)

6 cups Lobster Stock (page 32)

4 cups unsweetened canned coconut milk

2 whole lobsters (about 1 pound each), cut into 16 pieces, lightly cracked with a cleaver

1 pound skinless, boneless chicken breasts, cut into 1-inch strips

½ cup cooked Chinese Sausage (recipe follows)

2 dozen littleneck clams, rinsed and scrubbed

8 ounces medium shrimp, peeled and deveined (leaving tails intact)

1 pound squid, cleaned (see box, page 90) and cut into rings, tentacles left whole or cut in half, if large

Salt and freshly ground black pepper, to taste (optional)

2 small bunches fresh chives, chopped

1. Put the rice and water in a medium saucepan and bring to a boil over medium heat. Stir once, reduce the heat, cover, and simmer until the water is absorbed and the rice is al dente (just tender to the bite), about 15 minutes. Set aside, covered, to keep warm.

2. Combine the lemongrass, ginger, dried shrimp, tomato paste, chili paste, ground Sichuan peppercorns, lime leaves, and shallots in a blender or food processor and process until a paste forms.

3. Heat the chili oil in a nonreactive stockpot over medium heat. Add the paste mixture and sauté for 5 minutes, being careful not to let it burn. Stir in the stock and coconut milk and bring to a boil. Reduce the heat to low and simmer, uncovered, for 15 minutes. Strain the liquid through a fine sieve set over a large bowl, then return the liquid to the pot. Add the lobster, chicken, and sausage and bring to a simmer over medium heat. Cover and simmer for 8 minutes.

4. Meanwhile, place the clams in a medium skillet and add water to come halfway up their sides. Set the skillet over medium heat, cover, and bring to a boil. Steam for 5 to 10 minutes, until the shells pop open. Remove to a paella pan or a wide shallow serving bowl for the paella. Discard any clams that do not open.

5. When all of the clams have been removed from the skillet, strain the liquid into the pot with the lobster, chicken, and sausage mixture. Add the shrimp, squid, and cooked rice and cook until the shrimp and squid are just opaque, about 2 minutes. Check the seasonings and add the chives. Ladle into a paella pan or serving bowl with the clams and serve at once.

Serves 6 as a main bowl

Rice Rules

In America, as we've come to savor ethnic cuisines, more flavorful varieties of rice have begun to play an interesting role in our diets. There was a time when its only place was to plainly sit beside a piece of fish or broiled chicken. Well, all that has changed. Say "hello" to basmati, jasmine, and pearl.

It would be impossible to list every kind of rice available, for there are thousands of varieties. The key types to know are long grain and short grain. The longer the grain—basmati and jasmine—the fluffier the rice; the shorter the grain—Chinese *bai fan* (pearl, or sticky or glutinous), Italian Arborio, and Japanese *mochi*—the creamier the rice.

CHINESE SAUSAGE

Chinese sausage, which is dry and hard in texture, can be purchased in Chinese markets. It is delicious but extremely fatty. That's why we believe it's always best to make your own, without a lot of fat. Made in bulk, without the casing, the mixture can be divided into portions, wrapped airtight, and frozen. Then it is just a matter of defrosting as needed. It is a major flavor component in Thai Paella and is wonderful with noodles and in stir-fries.

2 pounds ground pork butt
½ cup soy sauce
5 tablespoons Hot Chili Oil (page 232)
¼ cup minced peeled fresh ginger
¼ cup minced garlic
¼ cup rice vinegar
2 tablespoons crushed red pepper flakes
2 tablespoons Asian sesame oil

1. Combine the pork, soy sauce, 2 tablespoons of the chili oil, ginger, garlic, vinegar, red pepper flakes, and sesame oil in a large bowl. Stir well to mix, cover, and refrigerate overnight.

2. Heat the remaining 3 tablespoons of chili oil in a large nonreactive skillet over medium heat. When the oil begins to shimmer, add the pork mixture and sauté, breaking it up with a wooden spoon and stirring until the meat is cooked through, about 10 minutes.

3. Remove from the pan with a slotted spoon to a bowl. Use immediately, or transfer to an airtight container and store in the refrigerator for up to 4 days. The sausage can also be frozen for up to 1 month.

Serves about 6 as a small bowl

RICE TAMALES WITH SHRIMP, BLACK OLIVES, AND ALMONDS

These Mediterranean-flavored tamales are some of our favorites. The olives will perfume the rice with a distinctive savoriness, so prepare them a day in advance of serving. If you are planning on serving these at a party, wait until the party is in full swing, then just pop them on a preheated hot grill or into a steamer. If you do opt to steam them, follow these tips to ensure safe and thorough heating: Fill the bottom of the steamer with as much water as it will hold without touching the food when the water boils. Once you've placed the tamales on the steaming tray, be sure to cover the steamer tightly; only a minimum amount of steam should escape. When it's time to remove the tamales, lift the lid slowly and away from you to protect your face from the steam.

    33 dried corn husks
    8 ounces medium shrimp, peeled and deveined
    2 cups cooked jasmine rice (1 cup raw), cooled
    ½ cup Kalamata olives, pitted and finely chopped
    ½ cup almonds, toasted and chopped
    ¼ cup finely chopped scallions, white and
        green parts
    5 tablespoons fresh lime juice
    ¼ cup Tomato Soy Sauce (page 252)
    2 tablespoons Tabasco sauce
    ¼ cup fresh cilantro leaves, finely chopped

1. Place the corn husks in a large bowl and cover with hot water. Place a plate directly on the husks to keep them submerged. Soak for 30 minutes.

THE SIDE BOWLS

SOUR CREMA
(*page 263*)

PUMPKIN SEED SAUCE
(*page 256*)

Hot Tamales!

Steamed until hot, these popular food wraps are extremely versatile. Traditional Mexican and Cuban tamales are chopped meat and vegetables coated with masa or cornflour dough, and wrapped in a corn husk or banana leaf.

But don't limit yourself—there are few rules and countless variations. You can use the husks of fresh corn or buy dried corn husks or frozen banana leaves at Latin markets. If you use dried corn husks, be sure to soften them in hot water to cover for about 1 hour before using. If using banana leaves, cut them into pieces about 10 by 6 inches.

As to the fillings, combine your favorite seafood, poultry, or meat with a choice of vegetables—anything goes! Our favorites are fat- and cholesterol-free. You can omit the masa and shortening and what you will have is a splendid interpretation in a little package.

2. Bring a pot of salted water to a boil. Drop in the shrimp and poach until just opaque, 2 to 3 minutes. Drain well, then cut into medium dice. Combine the shrimp in a medium bowl with the remaining ingredients. Toss thoroughly to mix, cover, and let stand at room temperature for 30 minutes.

3. Remove the husks from the water, lay them flat in one layer on paper towels, and pat thoroughly dry. Tear one husk lengthwise into 16 strands. The strands will be used for tying tamales.

4. Place 2 corn husks side by side, overlapping the long sides. Spoon ¼ cup of the rice mixture into the center, then fold the top edge down over the filling and the bottom edge up to overlap the top. Fold in the ends and tie the bundle with a strand of husk. Fill and wrap the remaining husks in the same manner.

5. Arrange the tamales, in batches, in one layer in the top of a steamer set over simmering water and steam for 15 to 20 minutes. Or arrange the tamales on a hot grill and cook, turning several times, until heated through, about 10 minutes.

6. Remove the tamales from the steamer or grill to a work surface, cut open the ties, unfold the leaves, and place the opened husks in a broad shallow bowl. Serve with a sauce or bright, cooling salsa of choice.

Makes 16 tamales, serving 8 as a main bowl, 16 as a small bowl

Children shouldn't be the only ones allowed to use bowls with kid-friendly designs. Shallow ones are great for serving tamales to grown-ups, as well as to the younger set.

NOT-SO-FRIED RICE

Scoop up a big bowl of this hearty, colorful rice on a cold day or when the night holds you hostage. The sunny yellow mixture dotted with flavorful mustard seeds is a comforting meal in a bowl. The Pineapple-Sake Marinade, which can be made in advance, combines with fresh lime juice for a memorably tart but sweet punch. The finishing touch of a ladleful of flavored stock to each bowl guarantees moistness without added fat.

2 cups basmati or jasmine rice, rinsed
    and drained

4 cups water

3 large eggs

1 tablespoon light soy sauce

¼ cup peanut oil

5 ribs celery, finely chopped

2 carrots, peeled and finely chopped

1 large onion, diced

½ cup diced peeled daikon radish

4 cloves garlic, chopped

2 tablespoons dark mustard seeds

1 tablespoon finely chopped peeled fresh ginger

2 teaspoons curry powder, preferably homemade
    (page 10)

1 cup fresh green peas, blanched and shocked
    (see box, page 214), or frozen, thawed

½ cup chopped scallions, white and green parts

1¾ cups Pineapple-Sake Marinade
    (page 180)

2 tablespoons Hot Chili Oil (page 232)

Salt and freshly ground black pepper, to taste

1 cup Chicken Stock for Asian Bowls
    (page 5)

Lime wedges, for garnish

THE SIDE BOWLS

GRILLED CHICKEN SKEWERS
(page 179)

1. Put the rice and water in a medium saucepan and bring to a boil over medium heat. Stir once, reduce the heat, cover, and simmer until the water is absorbed and the rice is al dente (just tender to the bite), about 15 minutes. Set aside, covered, to keep warm.

2. Meanwhile, whisk the eggs with the soy sauce in a small bowl and cook flat, omelet style (see box, facing page), in a 6-inch nonstick omelet pan, 2 to 3 minutes. Remove the omelet to a plate to cool slightly. Cut into ½-inch dice and set aside.

3. Heat the peanut oil in a large heavy skillet over medium-high heat. Add the celery, carrots, onion, daikon radish, garlic, mustard seeds, ginger, and curry powder and sauté, stirring, until the vegetables are crisp-tender and coated with the spices, about 5 minutes.

4. Add the hot rice, peas, scallions, diced omelet, and ¾ cup of the Pineapple-Sake Marinade. Stir gently over low heat until thoroughly combined and heated through, about 2 minutes. Add the chili oil and salt and pepper to taste.

5. Bring the stock and the remaining 1 cup marinade to a boil in a small nonreactive saucepan over high heat. Meanwhile, spoon the warm fried rice into 6 large serving bowls. Ladle some of the hot broth mixture around each serving of rice, then garnish with lime wedges and serve.

There's no better way to eat rice, especially if it's moistened with broth, than from a deep, all-purpose bowl.

Serves 6 as a small bowl

OMELET WANNABE

No matter what type of omelet you plan to make, the objective is always the same: to transform a viscous egg mixture into a smooth-textured omelet. No need to be intimidated, because it's a cinch to turn out an omelet, provided you use a nonstick pan. A nonstick surface has already been "seasoned," which means you don't need to add fat (great—no unnecessary calories there!) and the eggs won't stick to the pan. And here is another reason to be confident: There is no such thing as the exactly "right" heat for cooking an omelet. Low heat lengthens the cooking time, whereas medium to high heat cooks the eggs quickly. For the purposes of Not-So-Fried Rice, a light golden color is fine.

Follow these basic steps:

1. Beat the eggs with a fork or whisk until well mixed.

2. Preheat the pan, then pour the egg mixture into it. When the eggs are cooked on the bottom, lift sides of the set eggs with a spatula while tilting the pan to allow uncooked egg to run underneath. Continue to do this until the eggs are no longer runny and an omelet has formed, 2 to 3 minutes.

3. Remove the pan from the heat and slip the omelet onto a plate. (The only difference between a "real" omelet and this one is that this one isn't folded over on itself.)

MANGO AND COCONUT RICE

What makes a bowl of this so special is the rice itself—sweet sticky rice—also known as pearl or glutinous rice. Sticky rice comes both long and short grain; here we use a short variety. When cooked properly, it becomes tender and moist, with enough bite to sink your teeth into, and it is just sticky enough to grasp in clumps between chopsticks. When blended with fresh mango, shallots, and coconut milk, it takes on paradoxical characteristics, being mildly sweet, yet savory; creamy, yet full of texture.

GINGER'S HOT BROTH
(page 11)

GRILLED SHRIMP ON SUGARCANE
(page 181)

CRISPY LEEKS
(see box, page 77)

TOASTED COCONUT

2 tablespoons olive oil

½ cup finely chopped shallots

2 cups sticky (pearl) rice, rinsed, drained and air-dried
   (see box, this page)

3 cups water

1 cup unsweetened canned coconut milk

Salt and freshly ground black pepper, to taste

1 cup diced ripe mango

¼ cup chopped scallions, white and green parts

1. Heat the olive oil in a medium saucepan over medium heat. Add the shallots and sauté until translucent, about 5 minutes.

2. Add the rice and stir for 5 minutes. Add the water and coconut milk, season with salt and pepper, and bring to a boil. Reduce the heat to low, cover, and simmer, until all liquid has been absorbed, 15 to 20 minutes.

3. Remove from the heat and fold in the mango. Spoon the rice into individual serving bowls and sprinkle with the scallions.

Serves 4 as a small bowl

STICKY RICE

To cook sticky rice properly requires some know-how. Here are a few tips:

1. Use ½ cup uncooked rice per serving. (It expands 75 percent when cooked.)

2. Rinse the rice thoroughly and repeatedly in a sieve under cold water until the water runs clear, about 5 minutes. (The milky run-off comes from powdered bran and polishing compound on the grains and disappears with rinsing.)

3. Drain the rice in a colander in the open air for about 30 minutes.

4. Place the rice in a heavy pot and add enough water to cover by 1 inch (or use 1 cup washed rice to 2 cups water). Set over medium heat until the water begins to boil, then turn the heat up to high to bring the water to a vigorous boil. A white starchy liquid will bubble up and shake the pot lid. When the bubbling stops, reduce the heat to low, and continue to cook the rice until all the water is absorbed. Turn off the heat and let stand on the burner for 15 to 20 minutes, without lifting the lid. Fluff and serve.

VEGETABLE RICE

This colorful preparation can be presented in any number of ways: Serve it hot or cold, as a stand-alone or paired with seafood or poultry. The more you improvise here, the better. If you have yellow bell peppers on hand, add in a quarter cup, finely diced. Or turn to your garden and select something fitting from there.

3 tablespoons plus ¼ cup olive oil

5 cloves garlic, roasted (see box, page 48) and
  mashed with a fork

2 tablespoons finely chopped peeled fresh ginger

1 teaspoon curry powder, preferably homemade (page 10)

½ teaspoon ground annatto seeds
  (available at Latin markets)

3 cups jasmine rice, rinsed and drained

6 cups water

1 cup finely diced calabaza or winter squash

¾ cup snow peas, thinly sliced crosswise

½ cup finely diced chayote

½ cup finely diced red onion

½ cup finely diced red bell pepper

½ cup finely diced and seeded fresh poblano chili

Salt and freshly ground black pepper, to taste

¼ cup finely diced scallion, white and green part, for garnish

3 tablespoons dark mustard seeds, toasted
  (see box, page 137), for garnish

A recipe that's full of color and texture—like Vegetable Rice— asks to be served in a more modestly designed bowl.

1. Heat the 3 tablespoons olive oil in a large heavy saucepan over medium heat. Add the garlic, ginger, curry powder, and annatto seed and sauté, stirring, until the mixture turns a golden red, about 2 minutes.

2. Add the rice and stir well to coat. Cook, stirring, until the rice turns toasty brown in color, about 5 minutes. Add the

THE SIDE BOWLS

ROASTED RED PEPPER BROTH
(page 24)

DUCK ROPA VIEJA
(page 74)

STEWED SHORT RIBS
(page 76)

water and bring to a boil. Reduce the heat, cover, and simmer until all the water is absorbed and the rice is al dente (just tender to the bite), about 15 minutes.

3. Meanwhile, heat the remaining ¼ cup oil in a large skillet over medium heat. When the oil is hot (a piece of vegetable dropped into the pan will sizzle on contact), add the calabaza, snow peas, chayote, onion, bell pepper, and poblano and sauté until tender, about 7 minutes.

4. Remove from the heat and stir in the rice. Season with salt and pepper.

5. If serving immediately, spoon the rice mixture into individual serving bowls and garnish with diced scallion and mustard seeds. Or cool to room temperature before garnishing and serving.

Serves 6 to 8 as a main bowl, 10 to 12 as a small bowl

ABOUT CHAYOTES

An irresistible member of the gourd family, the chayote, a.k.a. mirliton and vegetable pear, has been grown and eaten in Mexico since the time of the Aztecs. Curiously, this versatile and accommodating vegetable made its way around the world before gaining recognition in the United States. Chayote is now grown in California, Louisiana, and Florida.

Pale green in color, chayotes look like oversized pears, usually weighing in at anywhere from 8 ounces to 1 pound. With fairly smooth skin and crisp, smooth flesh, they taste similar to zucchini, only sweeter. They can be purchased virtually year-round in Latin markets.

Like most squashes, chayotes can be prepared in many ways: They can be sautéed, steamed, braised, baked, grilled, puréed. They can also be sliced paper thin and eaten raw. Our favorite way to enjoy chayote is sliced ¼ inch thick (seed in), brushed lightly with olive oil, seasoned, and grilled. Remove the seed pieces before serving.

SIMMER MY JUICES AND GIVE ME A LITTLE COUSCOUS

Passions run high over this bowl—we've seen it turn reluctant meat eaters into meat lovers. The couscous explodes with the unusual mouthwatering and savory flavors featured here. Garnish with chopped scallion or cilantro.

2 pounds New York strip steak, 1 inch thick, trimmed of
    two thirds of the fat (there should be enough for
    6 portions, each 2 inches wide)

1 cup Ancho Marinade (page 56)

4 cups Chicken Stock for Mediterranean Bowls (page 20)

5 carrots, peeled and cut into ½-inch dice

2 medium leeks, white part only, cut in half lengthwise and
    thoroughly rinsed

2 medium onions, each cut into 6 wedges

2 tablespoons chopped peeled fresh ginger

2 tablespoons chopped fresh cilantro leaves

1 tablespoon Garlic Paste (page 61)

½ fresh jalapeño pepper, stemmed, seeded,
    and finely chopped

1 teaspoon ancho chili powder

1 teaspoon sweet paprika, preferably Hungarian

1 medium zucchini, cut into ½-inch dice

¼ cup rice vinegar

2 tablespoons unsalted butter

3½ cups couscous

Coarse (kosher) salt, to taste

Freshly ground Sichuan peppercorns, to taste

Tomato-Garlic Vinaigrette (page 226)

Fresh lemon juice, to taste

Brightly patterned collectible bowls from the 1930s and 1940s can still be found at yard sales, often with lids. Many of these cheerful bowls started life as refrigerator storage bowls. Today they look particularly good mixed and matched on the table.

CHOPPED PEANUTS

CRUSTY BREAD

**STEAMED GREEN
VEGETABLE**

HORSERADISH ROUILLE
(page 251)

1. Put the strip steak in a rectangular glass baking dish and pour the marinade over it. Cover and refrigerate for at least 1 hour, or overnight, turning occasionally.

2. Preheat the grill to high and place the rack 5 to 6 inches from the heat. Or preheat the broiler.

3. Combine the chicken stock, carrots, leeks, onions, ginger, cilantro, Garlic Paste, jalapeño, chili powder, and paprika in a large heavy saucepan. Bring to a boil, stirring to combine. Reduce the heat to low, cover, and simmer until the vegetables are tender, about 10 minutes. Add the zucchini, vinegar, and butter, stirring to mix, then remove from the heat.

4. Place the couscous in a large heatproof bowl and pour the hot stock and vegetables over it. Cover tightly with plastic wrap and set aside for 20 minutes.

5. Meanwhile, remove the steak from the marinade and slice it against the grain into 6 thick portions. Season with a little salt on both sides.

6. When ready to grill, oil the rack. Grill the steak pieces for 1 to 2 minutes on each side for medium-rare. (Or broil the portions on the rack of a broiler pan about 3 inches from the heat for about the same amount of time.)

7. Remove the steak from the grill (or broiler) to a cutting board and allow to rest for several minutes. Sprinkle each portion with salt and Sichuan pepper. Slice each in half on the diagonal.

8. Fluff the couscous, then spoon it, the stock, and the vegetables into 6 deep serving bowls. Arrange 2 pieces of steak over each serving, then ladle the vinaigrette over the steak. Squeeze a few drops of lemon juice over each portion and serve.

Serves 6 as a main bowl

Chapter 5

DUMPLINGS AND DOODADS

BITS AND BITES

The dumplings and doodads in this chapter represent all those utterly irresistible "little" foods that go by a variety of different names, including finger foods, accompaniments, hors d'oeuvres, appetizers, and snacks. Mostly, they are exquisitely delicious, self-contained creations. Usually, when the two of us talk about eating little snacks, our inspiration strays first to China, where the Cantonese are famous for their *dim sum*, or little snacks. But we don't stop there. We mix and match ideas with inspirations from the Mediterranean, where dumplings and doodads are called *tapas* and *mezes*. And from Mexico, where they pass around wonderful pies called *empanadas* and flat, toasted sandwiches called *quesadillas*. In Southeast Asia, it's the little bamboo skewers, or *satays*, that are popular and eaten with an array of dipping sauces. And on it goes, country by country. You'll find variations of many of the world's little foods in this chapter. And although you might not automatically think of serving some of them in bowls, let's just say, think again.

Some of our recipes, like Pot Stickers, can be frozen, which means you can cook today for good eating in your future. Others, for example, Grilled Shrimp on Sugarcane, a dish with Vietnamese roots, require very little effort, but you may have to go looking for sugarcane. And still others, like soul-warming Mashed Potatoes, require little work *and* no ingredient search . . . and have a very tasty return.

In short, dumplings and doodads are quintessential bowlfood—pleasing, satisfying delicious little bites. Moreover, they go with all kinds of other bowlfoods, like broths and soups and salads and rice and noodles. So, savor the following medleys of savory and sweet tastes. We promise you'll have fun eating them.

Mostly Stuffed Stuff

CRABMEAT DUMPLINGS

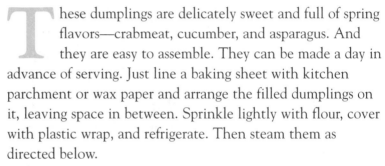

These dumplings are delicately sweet and full of spring flavors—crabmeat, cucumber, and asparagus. And they are easy to assemble. They can be made a day in advance of serving. Just line a baking sheet with kitchen parchment or wax paper and arrange the filled dumplings on it, leaving space in between. Sprinkle lightly with flour, cover with plastic wrap, and refrigerate. Then steam them as directed below.

In China, steamed dumplings are customarily served in bamboo baskets and are accompanied by a variety of dipping sauces. We suggest three different sauces and one oil as side bowls. Try them all!

SWEET SOY SAUCE
(*page 251*)

TOMATO SOY SAUCE
(*page 252*)

MANGO VINAIGRETTE
(*page 221*)

HOT CHILI OIL
(*page 232*)

I pound lump crabmeat, picked over
    for shell and cartilage
½ cup minced scallions, white and green part
½ cup minced raw asparagus
½ cup minced, peeled, and seeded cucumber
I tablespoon fresh lemon juice
I teaspoon Asian sesame oil
I teaspoon Hot Chili Oil (page 232)
I teaspoon nam pla (Asian fish sauce)
Salt and freshly ground black pepper,
    to taste
24 gyoza wrappers
Vegetable oil, for oiling the steamer
All-purpose flour, for dusting

I. Combine the crabmeat, scallions, asparagus, cucumber, lemon juice, sesame oil, 1 teaspoon chili oil, *nam pla*, and salt and pepper in a medium bowl. Stir gently but thoroughly to mix.

2. Lay the wonton wrappers a few at a time on a flat surface. Place approximately 1 tablespoon of the crabmeat filling in the center of each. Dampen the outer edge of each wrapper with water, fold the wrapper over the filling to make a half moon, and press the edges of the wrapper together to seal. Make dumplings with the remaining filling and wrappers in the same way.

3. Sprinkle the dumplings lightly with a little flour to prevent them from sticking.

4. Pour water into a wok or large pot. When a steamer is placed in the wok, there should be 1 inch space between it and the top of the water. Bring the water to a boil.

5. Lightly oil a steamer with vegetable oil. Place just enough dumplings to fit comfortably in a single layer in the steamer and place the steamer in the pot. Make sure the boiling water doesn't come up into the steamer. Cover the pot and steam the dumplings until they are heated through, about 10 minutes. Repeat until all the dumplings are cooked, re-oiling the steamer if the dumplings start to stick. Serve them immediately in rimless bowls.

Makes 24 dumplings, serving 4 to 6 as a small bowl

A sectioned or divided bowl—this one a Fiestaware multiserver—is a handy way to present a variety of condiments or dipping sauces. It's also a neat way of separating chicken dumplings from the ones filled with shrimp, since they all look alike.

Crabby but Sweet: An Edible Oxymoron

Sweet, succulent crab-meat—each coast has its own: Dungeness and King crabs in the Pacific Northwest; stone crabs along both the Florida Atlantic and Gulf coasts. And natives of the Northeast love their Atlantic blue crabs—hard shelled in winter and soft shelled in summer, a year-round delicacy.

When buying cooked crabmeat, be it fresh, frozen, or canned, purchase the "all-lump" variety. Lump meat is whole pieces of white body meat, whereas flake meat is bits of light and dark meat from both the body and the claws. Lump meat is also the sweetest. Be sure to pick through the meat with your fingers to remove any bits of shell and cartilage.

CRAB EMPANADAS

*E*mpanada is Spanish for "cooked in pastry," but this culinary concept transcends any boundaries and includes everything from French *pâté en croûte* to Russian *pirozhki* to American pot pie. These crab turnovers are elegant and easier than they may at first seem. Both the filling and the pastry can be prepared one day in advance; wrap in plastic and store in the refrigerator. They make lovely lunch fare served with a green salad, but can also be served as bite-size appetizers with cocktails and several dipping sauces.

THE SIDE BOWLS

HOT-AND-SOUR CHOWDER
(page 53)

GREEN SAUCE
(page 259)

THAI DIPPING SAUCE
(page 253)

ROASTED RED PEPPER AND CILANTRO SAUCE
(page 261)

FILLING

1 pound lump crabmeat, picked over for shell and cartilage

½ cup finely diced red bell pepper

½ cup finely chopped scallions, white and green parts

½ cup Spicy Bread Crumbs (page 117)

¼ cup rice vinegar

¼ cup sour cream

4 tablespoons (½ stick) unsalted butter, melted

2 tablespoons dry mustard

PASTRY

3 cups all-purpose flour

½ cup vegetable oil

½ cup ice-cold water

Salt and freshly ground black pepper, to taste

1. Preheat the oven to 400°F.

2. To make the filling, combine the crabmeat, bell pepper, scallions, bread crumbs, vinegar, sour cream, melted butter, and mustard in a large bowl. Stir gently but thoroughly to mix. Set aside.

3. To make the pastry, place 2 cups of the flour in a medium bowl. Add the vegetable oil and the water slowly, stirring. Stir in the remaining cup of flour and add salt and pepper, and stir until a dough forms. Turn the dough out onto a floured surface and knead until smooth and elastic. Using a floured rolling pin, roll the dough out ⅛ inch thick. Cut out 10 rounds with a 4-inch round pastry cutter.

4. Place about ¼ cup of the crabmeat mixture on one side of each pastry round. Fold the pastry over the filling and press the edges of the pastry together with your fingers or the tines of a fork to seal.

5. Arrange the pastries about 2 inches apart on a large baking sheet and bake until golden brown, about 20 minutes.

Serves 10 as a small bowl or 5 as a main bowl

YIN & YANG POT STICKERS

Inherent in everything Chinese—from philosophy to food—is a natural popularity. It is an idea that seeks to achieve harmony and peace through proper balance. When it comes to food, it can apply to color, texture, taste, or preparation. Everyone's heard of, if not tasted, sweet-and-sour pork or hot-and-sour soup. In those dishes, the contrasts are sharp, bitter is matched with sweet, bland with piquant. But, depending on the region, some cooks prefer contrasts that are delicate and subtle. Quick sautés or stir-fries that have a variety of ingredients may be harmonious in preparation, say, slices matched with slices, slivers with slivers, dice with dice.

That said, are you in the mood for fried dumplings but daunted by the calorie content? Chicken or Shrimp Pot Stickers are the perfect solution. By browning these dumplings on the bottom, then finishing them by steaming, you get the best of both worlds—a crispy bottom, with soft filling inside.

The flavor and texture of these pot stickers is so satisfying that you may opt for just a squeeze of lemon juice as a garnish.

Here's an example of a perfect-sized bowl—not too small and not too large—for dumplings and other appetizers.

Sometimes You Feel Like a Nut . . .

One of the delights of biting into the soft wrapper of a shrimp pot sticker is discovering the crunchy texture and mildly sweet flavor of fresh water chestnuts. Despite its name, the water chestnut is not a nut at all. And though the shape of its brownish-black skin closely resembles that of a chestnut, which grows on trees, the water chestnut is a water plant that grows prolifically in flooded fields, marshy beds, and along the edges of ponds and lakes throughout Southeast Asia.

When purchasing fresh water chestnuts, be sure to handle each one, selecting only those with skins that are hard and smooth. You can often find them displayed in their shipping crates in Asian markets, still covered with remnants of the dried brown earth they were plucked from.

▶

Or serve them with a pairing of complementary dipping sauces, such as Hot Chili Oil (page 232) and Sweet Soy Sauce (page 251) or Spicy Peanut Sauce (page 254) and Cilantro Vinaigrette (page 220). Both the chicken and shrimp pot stickers can be prepared in advance and frozen.

CHICKEN POT STICKERS

12 ounces spinach, preferably flat-leaf, stemmed,
    rinsed, blanched and shocked (see box, page 214),
    squeezed dry, and chopped
1 pound skinless, boneless chicken breast, cut into 1-inch chunks
½ cup diced mango
3 tablespoons chopped fresh cilantro leaves
2 tablespoons finely chopped scallion, white and green parts
2 tablespoons finely chopped peeled fresh ginger
2 tablespoons rice vinegar
2 tablespoons mushroom soy sauce or regular soy sauce
2 teaspoons finely chopped lime zest
1 teaspoon Hot Chili Oil (page 232),
    plus 4 tablespoons for frying
1 large egg white
Salt and freshly ground black pepper, to taste
30 gyoza wrappers (see box, facing page)

1. Put the spinach, chicken, mango, cilantro, scallion, ginger, vinegar, soy sauce, lime zest, 1 teaspoon chili oil, egg white, and salt and pepper in a large bowl and stir thoroughly to combine. Transfer the mixture to a food processor and pulse quickly 5 or 6 times to blend evenly and create a smooth consistency. Return to the bowl and refrigerate, covered, at least 1 hour.

2. Make the pot stickers: Lay several gyoza wrappers on a lightly floured work surface. Place 2 teaspoons of cold filling (it's easier to handle when very cold) just off center on each wrapper. Moisten the rim of each wrapper by dabbing your finger in cold water, then running it around the rim on the half of the wrapper that has filling on it. Fold the wrapper over toward the wet rim, and press the edges firmly together to seal in a neat half-moon shape. Repeat with the remaining filling and wrappers.

3. Cook the pot stickers: Heat 2 tablespoons of the remaining chili oil in a medium-heavy skillet over medium-high heat. When it begins to shimmer, add half the pot stickers (be sure not to crowd the pan) and sauté on one side until golden brown, 2 to 3 minutes. Remove the skillet from the heat, slowly add enough water to barely cover the bottom, and return the skillet to the heat. Cover and steam until the pot stickers are resilient to the touch, 5 minutes. Remove from the heat and transfer to a wide serving bowl. Keep warm, covered, in a low oven.

4. Wipe out the skillet, add the remaining oil, and repeat the procedure to cook the remaining dumplings.

5. Pot stickers can be prepared in advance and frozen. Arrange the filled uncooked dumplings on baking sheets and freeze until firm. Transfer to freezer-weight plastic bags, seal, and store in the freezer for up to 1 month. When ready to use them, arrange the frozen pot stickers on a baking sheet and defrost at room temperature. Cook according to the instructions above.

Makes about 30 pot stickers, serving 6 to 8 as a small bowl

Rinse under cold water and peel with a sharp paring knife. Slice the juicy white flesh into thin disks for salads or dice for mixing with other ingredients. Refrigerated in an airtight container, they keep for up to 1 week.

Although water chestnuts are available canned in most supermarkets, we don't recommend using them. They may be crunchy, but they taste nothing like fresh water chestnuts.

GYOZA WRAPPERS

These dough wrappers, made from flour, salt, boiling water, and sometimes egg, are ideal for moist cooking methods (like steaming) but are not a good choice for baking, since they contain no fat and will crack. Although the dough is simple to make, rolling and cutting out 3-inch rounds is labor intensive. Packages of gyoza wrappers are readily available in most markets in either the refrigerator section or in the Asian produce area. The wrappers, sealed airtight, freeze well.

SHRIMP POT STICKERS

1 pound spinach, preferably flat-leaf, stemmed, rinsed,
    blanched and shocked (see box, page 214),
    squeezed dry, and chopped
1 pound small shrimp, peeled, deveined, and chopped
4 scallions, white and green parts, chopped
½ cup fresh water chestnuts, peeled and chopped,
    or ½ cup chopped peeled tart apple
½ cup chopped stemmed shiitake mushrooms
3 tablespoons finely chopped peeled fresh ginger
3 tablespoons soy sauce
4 teaspoons finely grated lemon zest
1 tablespoon Asian sesame oil
1 large egg white
Salt and freshly ground black pepper, to taste
30 gyoza wrappers (see box, page 161)
4 tablespoons Hot Chili Oil (page 232)

1. Put the spinach, shrimp, scallions, water chestnuts, mushrooms, ginger, soy sauce, lemon zest, sesame oil, egg white, and salt and pepper in a large bowl and stir thoroughly to combine. Transfer the mixture to a food processor and pulse quickly 5 or 6 times to blend evenly. Remove while still chunky, return to the bowl, and refrigerate, covered, for at least 1 hour.

2. Make the pot stickers: Fill and form according to the directions in step 2, on pages 160 to161.

3. Cook the pot stickers according to the directions in steps 3 and 4 on page 161.

Makes about 30 pot stickers, serving 6 to 8 as a small bowl

RICOTTA AND SPINACH DUMPLINGS

You can't get much easier than this; these light dumplings are so quick to prepare they might be compared to the premade frozen version we grew up with—in terms of time and effort, that is. These star in our Corn Soup (page 49) and will enhance almost any stew. They also stand on their own with punchy Tomato-Garlic Vinaigrette (page 226) as a main bowl.

I cup ricotta cheese, preferably fresh

3 large eggs plus 2 large egg whites

½ teaspoon five-spice powder

½ cup all-purpose flour

½ cup fresh bread crumbs

I tablespoon baking powder

8 ounces fresh spinach, blanched and shocked (page 214), squeezed dry, and chopped

Salt and freshly ground black pepper, to taste

A large, stark white, ceramic bowl, such as this one from Italy, makes a dramatic presentation for rustic cheese and spinach dumplings.

I. Combine the ricotta, eggs and egg whites, and five-spice powder in a medium bowl. Beat thoroughly with a wire whisk to blend. Stir in the flour, bread crumbs, baking powder, and chopped spinach until well combined.

2. Bring a large saucepan of salted water to a boil over high heat, then reduce the heat to medium-low so that the water just simmers.

3. Meanwhile, form dumplings with the ricotta mixture, a heaping tablespoonful at a time. Drop them as formed into the simmering water and cook, 6 at a time, until firm, about 3 minutes. Remove with a slotted spoon and serve immediately.

Makes about 18 dumplings, serving 4 to 6 as a main bowl

SHRIMP QUESADILLAS

These are known at Lola Bowla as those "crunchy little sandwiches." Adam Barnett, a talented young cook, created them as fodder for the kitchen staff. They were so good, they ended up on a Bowla menu. Thank you, Adam.

¼ cup **Hot Chili Oil (page 232)**

2 medium red onions, cut into small dice

4 fresh poblano chilies, stemmed, seeded, and cut into small dice

2 fresh jalapeño peppers, stemmed, seeded, and cut into thin rounds

2 teaspoons pure chili powder

½ cup fresh lime juice

½ cup dry white wine

4 tablespoons (packed) dark brown sugar

1½ pounds medium shrimp, peeled, deveined, and cut into medium dice

12 flour tortillas (6 inches each)

1 cup grated **Manchego cheese (see page 165)** or another white melting cheese, such as white **Cheddar** (about 4 ounces)

Salt and freshly ground black pepper, to taste

1. Heat the oil in a medium nonreactive skillet over medium heat. Add the onions, poblanos, jalapeños, and chili powder, stir to coat with the chili powder, and sauté until the onions are translucent, about 5 minutes.

2. Add the lime juice, wine, and sugar and cook, stirring constantly, until the liquids are absorbed, about 10 minutes. Add the shrimp and cook, stirring constantly, for 3 minutes. Remove from the heat and season with salt and pepper. Transfer to a bowl to cool.

Serve quesadillas, cut into quarters, in shallow bowls with a dollop of Avocado Wasabi (page 260) or Sour Crema (page 263) to one side.

3. Preheat the oven to 350°F.

4. Arrange 6 tortillas on a large baking sheet and sprinkle with half the cheese. Spread ¼ cup of the shrimp mixture on each tortilla, then sprinkle with the remaining cheese. Top with the remaining tortillas.

5. Place the baking sheet in the oven and bake until the quesadillas are heated through and the tortillas are crisp, 5 to 7 minutes. Remove from the oven and place a cool baking sheet on top to flatten the quesadillas.

6. Quarter each quesadilla and serve while still warm.

Serves 6 as a main bowl, 12 as a small bowl

THAI DIPPING SAUCE
(page 253)

CILANTRO VINAIGRETTE
(page 220)

AVOCADO WASABI
(page 260)

PUMPKIN SEED SAUCE
(page 256)

SOUR CREMA
(page 263)

HALF MOON OVER MANCHEGO

Top a tortilla with Manchego cheese and a mixture of green olives, vegetables, peppers, and spice, then fold it over, and you've got yourself a turnover that can be prepared hours in advance. Cook on an outdoor grill for smoky flavor, slice into finger food, place in a large shallow serving bowl, and serve with a Mango Margarita (page 296) or two at your next summer barbecue. They also make a great luncheon entrée accompanied by a fresh green salad. Either way, we guarantee success.

Manchego, a rich, full-flavored yet mellow Spanish cheese, was once made solely from the milk of Manchego sheep that grazed the plains of La Mancha. Its dense texture makes it popular for quick snacks; it's also an excellent melting cheese.

¼ cup **Hot Chili Oil** (page 232)

½ cup **diced peeled chayote or yellow summer squash**
   (¼-inch pieces)

½ cup **diced red onion (¼-inch pieces)**

½ cup **diced red bell pepper (¼-inch pieces)**

½ cup **diced fresh poblano chili (¼-inch pieces)**

½ cup **green olives, pitted and minced**

2 tablespoons **fresh lime juice**

Salt and freshly ground black pepper, to taste

10 **flour tortillas (6 inches each)**

½ cup **Basil Paste** (page 131)

1 cup **Boniato, Carrot, and Jalapeño Purée**
   (recipe follows)

2 cups **grated Manchego cheese or another**
   white melting cheese (about 8 ounces)

1. Heat the oil in a medium skillet over medium heat. Add the chayote, onion, bell pepper, poblano, and olives and sauté until the vegetables are tender, about 8 minutes. Remove from the heat and add the lime juice and salt and pepper. Set aside to cool.

2. Preheat the oven to 325°F.

3. Lay the tortillas on a flat surface and spread with the Basil Paste, then top with the boniato purée. Sprinkle with half the cheese. Spread the cooled vegetable mixture on one half of each tortilla, dividing it evenly, and sprinkle it with the remaining cheese. Fold the tortillas over to form half-moon shapes. Press the edges firmly to seal.

4. Arrange the half moons on a large baking sheet and bake until heated through, about 8 minutes.

5. Remove from the oven and place a cool baking sheet on top of the quesadillas to flatten them. Cool for about 10 minutes. If serving as an appetizer, quarter each half moon and serve.

Serves 10 as a small bowl

BONIATO, CARROT, AND JALAPEÑO PURÉE

Boniato, a sweet potato from South America, tastes very much like yam, only it's not quite as sweet and is white in color. The carrot and potatoes blend beautifully, and the addition of coconut milk balances the heat of the jalapeño peppers. This vegetable purée is especially satisfying served alongside Stewed Short Ribs (page 76) or Seared Steak Salad with Roasted Tomatoes (page 196), as well as making a tasty filling for tortillas.

3 medium boniatos or sweet potatoes, peeled and quartered

1 medium carrot, peeled and chopped

1 medium Idaho potato, peeled and quartered

1 can (13½ ounces) unsweetened coconut milk

1 cup water

1 tablespoon olive oil

3 fresh jalapeño peppers, stemmed, seeded, and finely diced

1 large red bell pepper, roasted and peeled (see box, page 18), puréed

2 tablespoons unsalted butter

¼ cup finely chopped scallions, white and green parts

Salt and freshly ground black pepper, to taste

1. Combine the boniato, carrot, potatoes, coconut milk, and water to cover in a medium saucepan and bring to a boil over medium heat. Reduce the heat to low, cover, and simmer until the vegetables are very tender, about 20 minutes. Drain. While still hot, pass the mixture through a food mill into large bowl. Set aside.

2. Heat the olive oil in a small skillet over medium heat. Add the jalapeños and sauté for about 3 minutes. Remove from the heat and add them to the puréed vegetables with the red pepper purée and butter. Stir until thoroughly mixed. Fold in the scallions and season with salt and pepper.

Makes about 3 cups

Charming three-legged ceramic bowls like this one come in deep colors that contrast dramatically with the gorgeous color of this boniato purée.

THE GIFT OF CABBAGE

If you grew up on cabbage rolls stuffed with ground beef and caramelized onion and stewed in a sweet tomato sauce, you will relish this vegetarian interpretation. The satisfaction obtained from these warm little bundles cannot be denied. They are soul-comforting to the maker and partaker alike.

GINGER DRESSING
(page 228)

JAPANESE MISO SAUCE
(page 253)

TOASTED MUSTARD SEED AND BALSAMIC DRIZZLE
(page 257)

SHERRY AND GARLIC SOY SAUCE
(page 262)

3 tablespoons peanut oil

I leek, white part only, rinsed, patted dry, and julienned

½ cup fresh shiitake mushrooms, stemmed and thinly sliced

½ cup grated peeled daikon radish

½ cup grated peeled carrot

¼ cup minced peeled fresh ginger

2 tablespoons fermented black beans, rinsed and drained

I teaspoon black mustard seeds, toasted (see box, page 137)

I teaspoon ground coriander

3 tablespoons rice vinegar

½ teaspoon Asian sesame oil

Salt, to taste

8 large Savoy cabbage or kale leaves

I. Heat the peanut oil in a large skillet over medium heat. Add the leek, mushrooms, daikon, carrot, ginger, black beans, mustard seeds, and coriander and cook, stirring frequently, until the vegetables are tender and the mixture is fragrant, about 8 minutes. Remove from the heat and stir in the vinegar and sesame oil.

2. Bring a large pot of salted water to a boil. Have ready a bowl of ice water. Drop the cabbage leaves into the boiling water for 2 minutes. Remove and plunge the leaves into the ice water. Drain well, then pat dry on paper towels.

3. Place the leaves on a flat surface, with the stem ends facing you. In the center of each leaf, place about ¼ cup of the vegetable mixture. Turn the stem end up over the filling, then tuck in the top and sides and roll up. Repeat the process with the remaining leaves.

4. Place the rolls, seam side down in one layer in the top of a steamer set over simmering water. Cover and steam until the cabbage is tender and the rolls are heated through, about 10 minutes. Serve in wide bowls with one or more of the side bowls.

Serves 4 as a main bowl, 8 as a small bowl

Serve two luscious cabbage rolls to each diner in wide-rimmed soup bowls, with small dressing and sauce bowls alongside.

PICADILLO BUNS

Picadillo is a spicy chopped meat preparation originally from Spain that is typically served with rice and beans. Or it can be used as a filling, as it is here. The type of bun taking the picadillo filling is traditional to China, where it would be steamed, but we prefer to bake them for the added flavor. So, here's a Chinese-style bun with a Spanish-style filling that's baked, not steamed.

As to making the dough, you can vary the amount of sugar according to your taste. And know that two risings make for a lighter dough, as does a longer rising in a cool place: Let the dough rise, refrigerated, overnight if you have the time. For moister buns, you can also mist the oven.

169

1 package active dry yeast

⅓ cup sugar, or to taste

½ cup warm water (110° to 115°F)

2 cups all-purpose flour

¼ cup beaten egg

5 tablespoons peanut oil

2 tablespoons Cilantro Oil (page 230)

¾ cup Picadillo (page 78), drained if too saucy

1 large egg beaten with 1 tablespoon milk,
  for eggwash

1. Dissolve the yeast and sugar in the warm water in a large bowl. With a wire whisk, beat in the egg and oils, then stir in the flour. Turn the dough out onto a lightly floured work surface and knead for 15 minutes, until soft and pillowy.

2. Put the dough in a greased bowl and cover with a damp cloth. Let rise in a warm place (75° to 80°F) for about 2 hours, until the dough doubles in size.

3. Meanwhile, grease a baking sheet.

4. Punch the dough down, remove it from the bowl, and knead several times. Roll the dough into a rope about 12 inches long. Divide the rope into 6 even pieces and roll each piece into a ball. Using your fingers, press a hollow, the size of a walnut, in the center of each ball. Place 2 tablespoons of picadillo in each hollow and press the dough up and over the filling. Pinch to seal. Place the buns, seam side down, on the baking sheet and let rise in a warm place for 1 hour.

5. Preheat the oven to 350°F.

6. Brush each bun with eggwash and bake until golden brown, 15 to 20 minutes. Serve warm. Or cool and reheat in a preheated low oven.

Makes 6 buns, serving 6 as a small bowl

Serve these Chinese-Spanish Picadillo Buns in a Mediterranean-style bowl for a really unexpected cultural partnership.

SQUID STUFFED WITH SHRIMP AND GINGER

The distinctive tubular shape of squid bodies makes them a perfect vehicle for our full-flavored, juicy, ginger-spiked stuffing. Before filling the bodies, you can test the seasoning in the stuffing by poaching a teaspoonful of it in a half cup of simmering water: too mild, add more spice; too hot, add more bread crumbs to temper the heat.

Squid shrinks when cooked, so fill the bodies three-quarters full. This seafood bowl deserves a selection of delectable, different-tasting sauces (see The Side Bowls).

8 large squid, bodies only, cleaned (see box, page 90)

1 pound medium shrimp, peeled, deveined, and minced

1 cup thinly sliced stemmed fresh shiitake mushrooms

5 scallions, white and green parts, chopped

½ cup fresh bread crumbs

6 tablespoons Thai Dipping Sauce (page 253)

3 shallots, chopped

3 tablespoons fresh lime juice

2 large egg whites

3 cloves garlic, finely chopped

2 tablespoons finely chopped peeled fresh ginger

½ teaspoon red curry paste (available at Indian or Asian markets)

¼ teaspoon sugar

¼ cup vegetable oil

Salt and freshly ground black pepper, to taste

1. Pat the squid bodies dry inside and out.

2. Combine the shrimp, mushrooms, scallions, bread crumbs, dipping sauce, shallots, lime juice, egg whites, garlic, curry paste, and sugar in a large bowl. Mix well with your hands, then

THE SIDE BOWLS

SWEET-AND-SOUR RED PEPPER DRIZZLE
(page 119)

LEMONETTE
(page 219)

APRICOT AND APPLE CHUTNEY
(page 266)

FIERY RED CURRY SAUCE
(page 124)

transfer the mixture to a food processor and pulse for 3 seconds. Return to the bowl and refrigerate, covered, 30 minutes.

3. Preheat the oven to 375°F.

4. Stuff the shrimp mixture into the squid bodies, packing it tightly but only three quarters full. Remove any air pockets. Close the opening on each squid with a toothpick.

5. Heat the oil in a large ovenproof skillet. Add the stuffed squid in one layer and brown on all sides, 1 minute per side. Season with salt and pepper.

6. Place the skillet in the oven and bake the squid for 15 minutes. Test for doneness with a toothpick. Stick the pick into the middle of one of the squid. If the juice runs clear and the toothpick feels warm to the touch, the squid is ready. Transfer to a cooling rack and cool for 5 to 10 minutes, then slice.

Serves 4 as a main bowl, 8 as a small bowl

MANGO AND RUM-CURED SALMON ROLLS

Whether it's brunch or dinner, cured salmon is a popular choice on many a menu because it's the perfect foil for the liveliest of flavors. Use it as a wrap, or serve it with a non-oil-based vinaigrette over greens in the summer when you desire something light. It also makes great party fare, prepared as it is here as an hors d'oeuvre. Just make the rolls up a few hours ahead and refrigerate, covered, until serving. Assemble the rolls in a large shallow pasta bowl and drizzle with both Cilantro and Mango Vinaigrettes for an exciting presentation.

½ cup fresh bread crumbs

1 teaspoon finely chopped fresh rosemary

1 teaspoon chopped fresh thyme

1 teaspoon salt

½ teaspoon shichimi togarashi (page 115)

24 thin slices **Rum-Cured Salmon** (recipe follows)

2 large ripe mangoes, peeled, pitted, and cut into ⅛-inch dice

1. Combine the bread crumbs, rosemary, thyme, salt, and *shichimi togarashi* spice blend in a small bowl and stir to mix.

2. Lay the salmon slices on a flat surface and sprinkle a thin layer of the crumb mixture over each slice. Place about 1 tablespoon of diced mango in the middle of each slice, roll up, place seam side down in the bowls of your choice, and serve.

Makes 24 rolls, serving 12 as a small bowl

Rum-Cured Salmon

This rendition of gravlax, Swedish cured fresh fish, can be served in a number of ways, in sandwiches, in noodle salads, and in hors d'oeuvres. (See the preceding recipe for one of our favorites.) Or simply arrange slices of it on a bed of peppery greens that have been tossed with Lemonette (page 219).

You want to be sure to purchase the very freshest fish you can from a reliable market and marinate it the same day. Overmarinating can be likened to overcooking: the fish will be rubbery and dry—something to avoid.

1 cup (lightly packed) chopped fresh cilantro

½ cup sugar

¼ cup salt

¼ cup finely chopped peeled fresh ginger

3 tablespoons Sichuan peppercorns, cracked

1 very fresh salmon fillet, 3 inches thick
    (about 2 pounds total weight)

½ cup dark rum

THE SIDE BOWLS

COOL HAND CUKE SOUP
(page 43)

MINT OIL
(page 231)

LEMONETTE
(page 219)

CILANTRO VINAIGRETTE
(page 220)

MANGO VINAIGRETTE
(page 221)

MUSTARD-POTATO CREAM VINAIGRETTE
(page 223)

1. Combine the cilantro, sugar, salt, ginger, and peppercorns in a medium bowl.

2. Place the salmon in a large glass baking dish, skin side down. Drizzle the rum over the salmon, then press the cilantro mixture evenly over the flesh.

3. Lay a piece of plastic wrap over the salmon, covering it completely. Set a second, smaller baking dish or heavy platter directly on top of the salmon and place a 4-pound weight on top of that. Refrigerate for no less than 18 hours but no more than 24 hours to cure.

4. When ready to serve the salmon, scrape off the curing mixture. Using a sharp knife, cut into thin slices on the diagonal. Store wrapped in plastic wrap in the refrigerator for up to 1 week.

Serves 4 to 6 as a small bowl

CHEESE-STUFFED POBLANOS

The addition of a stuffed pepper to a chowder or broth can instantly transform it into a meal, an idea that works especially well with Roasted Red Pepper Broth (page 24). To diversify your meal further, you might add some roasted chicken to the menu.

The poblano is a large fresh chili pepper that is often used for stuffing. The color of the poblano ranges from green to almost black, and the smaller ones are usually hotter than the large. These poblanos can be stuffed up to one day ahead. Cover tightly and refrigerate, then let them come to room temperature before heating.

8 large fresh poblano chilies

3 pounds boniatos (available at Latin American and specialty
     markets) or sweet potatoes, peeled and chopped

2 cans (13½ ounces each) unsweetened coconut milk

2 cups water

2 tablespoons olive oil

2 cups diced red onions

Salt and freshly ground black pepper, to taste

4 cups grated Manchego cheese (about 1 pound) or
     another white melting cheese

½ cup finely chopped fresh rosemary

1. Roast the poblanos over an open flame, turning with tongs
until the skin is blackened on all sides, 10 to 15 minutes. Place the
poblanos in a bowl and set aside, covered with plastic wrap, to
loosen the skin, 10 minutes. Peel away the blackened skin on all
sides. Make a slit from the top of each poblano to the base, leaving
the stem intact. Carefully remove the seeds from the cavities.

2. Combine the boniatos with the coconut milk and water in a
large saucepan. Simmer over medium heat until very tender,
about 15 minutes.

3. Meanwhile, heat the olive oil in a skillet over medium-high
heat. Add the onions and sauté until softened, 3 to 5 minutes.
Season with salt and pepper and remove from the heat.

4. Drain the boniatos and, while still hot, pass them through a
food mill into a large bowl. Fold in the sautéed onions, cheese,
and rosemary. Set the filling aside.

5. Preheat the oven to 375°F. Grease a baking sheet.

6. Spoon ¼ cup filling into each poblano. Reshape the poblanos,
place slit side up on the prepared baking sheet, and bake,
uncovered, until heated through, about 10 minutes. Serve hot.

Serves 8 as a main bowl, 16 as a small bowl

THE SIDE BOWLS

**ROASTED RED PEPPER
BROTH**
(*page 24*)

**MOJO-MARINATED
CHICKEN**
(*page 80*)

PUMPKIN SEED SAUCE
(*page 256*)

DREAMY CREAMY CORN
(*page 264*)

CRISPY THAI MUSHROOM ROLL

Thai-style rolls are often deep-fried, but not this one—it's baked. Baking the tissue-thin phyllo-wrapped roll achieves the same appealing crispy texture as frying does, but without the fat. And because this is one long roll, you can cut it into serving sizes as desired. If it's more convenient, prebake the roll ahead of time—cook it halfway—then finish it minutes before serving.

Serve as a crunchy side to a bowl of smooth, puréed Roasted Garlic and Boniato Soup (page 66) or Cool Hand Cuke Soup (page 43). Or, place several warm pieces of this next to a cool green salad.

8 ounces dried rice stick noodles

1 cup wild mushrooms (such as chanterelle, morel, shiitake, or porcini), stemmed and thinly sliced

½ cup minced scallions, white and green parts

¼ cup minced lemongrass bottoms

¼ cup Sweet Soy Sauce (page 251), plus additional for serving, if desired

¼ cup fresh lime juice

4 shallots, minced

5 sheets phyllo pastry

¼ cup olive oil

½ cup (lightly packed) fresh cilantro leaves

Salt and freshly ground black pepper, to taste

Shichimi togarashi (see box, page 115), to taste

1. Put the rice sticks in a bowl and add very hot water to cover. Soak until softened, about 20 minutes. Drain, cut the noodles in half with scissors or a knife, and set aside.

2. Preheat the oven to 375°F.

So many shallow, rectangular serving dishes have eye-catching designs and glazes that we always find room for them on the table. Over the years, we both have collected them in all sizes.

3. Combine the noodles in a large bowl with the mushrooms, scallions, lemongrass, soy sauce, lime juice, and shallots. Using your hands, toss to mix thoroughly. Set the filling aside.

4. Place 1 sheet of the phyllo on a flat surface with a short side facing you. Brush the sheet lightly with some of the olive oil, then sprinkle it with about 1½ tablespoons of the cilantro and a dusting of salt and the *shichimi togarashi* spice blend. Working quickly, repeat the procedure with the remaining phyllo sheets, stacking them on top of the first sheet.

5. Spread all of the noodle filling mixture in a 1-inch-wide band over the short end of the pastry near you, leaving a 1-inch border on the end and on both sides. Fold the side edges in over the filling, then roll the pastry tightly up from the bottom into a log. Brush the top of the roll with the remaining olive oil and season with salt and *shichimi togarashi*.

6. Place the roll, seam side down, on an ungreased baking sheet and bake until crispy and golden brown, about 15 minutes. Remove the pan from the oven and let the roll cool slightly, then cut the roll crosswise into 8 pieces for a soup accompaniment or into quarters for a main bowl.

Serves 4 as main bowl, 8 as a small bowl

THE SIDE BOWLS

LIMETTE
(page 219)

TAMARIND GLAZE
(page 210)

Ribs, Skewers, Fritters, and a Side of Mashed

ASIAN BABY BACK RIBS

These ribs are a definite crowd-pleaser. When paired with scallion scrambled eggs for brunch they'll fly out of the kitchen. If you want to serve these for dinner, they are especially succulent with Mango and Coconut Rice (see page 147).

**SAFFRON AND WASABI
MASHED POTATOES**
(page 190)

SESAME NOODLEHEAD
(page 133)

NOT-SO-FRIED RICE
(page 145)

CRISPY LEEKS
(see box, page 77)

4 pounds pork baby back ribs

Salt and freshly ground black pepper, to taste

¼ cup olive oil

1 cup dry sherry

1 cup hoisin sauce

½ cup soy sauce

¼ cup honey

1 tablespoon chili paste

¼ cup star anise, cracked

10 cloves garlic, chopped

**Sesame seeds, toasted (see box, page 137),
for garnish (optional)**

1. Preheat the oven to 450°F.

2. Season the ribs with salt and pepper. Heat the olive oil in a large skillet over high heat. When the oil begins to smoke, carefully add the ribs, in batches, and brown for about 4 minutes on each side. Transfer the ribs as they are done to a large roasting pan, arranging them in one layer.

3. Combine the remaining ingredients except for the sesame seeds in a medium bowl, then pour the mixture over the ribs. Cover the pan with aluminum foil and roast until the ribs are tender, about 1 hour.

4. Transfer the ribs to a cutting board and cut into one- or two-rib sections. Divide among 6 or 8 bowls and garnish with the sesame seeds, if desired.

5. Strain the sauce remaining in the pan and serve separately to drizzle over the ribs.

Serves 6 to 8 as a main bowl, 12 as a small bowl

GRILLED CHICKEN SKEWERS

One of the delights of eating street food in China and Thailand is that many delicacies come on easy-to-handle (and easy-to-keep-your-fingers-clean) bamboo sticks. They're a wonderful invention, useful for grilling all kinds of foods, from delicate pieces of fruit to sturdy chunks of lamb. Beyond the aesthetic virtues of the bamboo itself, the slightly charred ends of the skewers lend a natural appeal.

Plan to serve these chicken skewers with your favorite dipping sauces and bowls of sticky rice at your next get-together. While you preheat the grill, remember to soak the skewers in water for at least 10 minutes to prevent them from burning. This recipe can be halved, if desired.

**2 pounds skinless, boneless chicken breasts,
    cut into 1-inch-wide strips
2 cups Pineapple-Sake Marinade (recipe follows)
Thirty 6-inch wooden skewers
Salt and freshly ground black pepper, to taste**

1. Place the chicken strips in a large nonreactive bowl. Toss with the marinade and refrigerate, covered, for 1 hour.

2. About 30 minutes before you're ready to cook, preheat a grill to high and place a rack 8 to 10 inches from the heat. Or 15 minutes before cooking, preheat the broiler.

3. Meanwhile, place the wooden skewers in a shallow dish and add water to cover. Let soak for a least 10 minutes, then drain.

4. Drain the chicken over a medium saucepan, reserving the marinade, and thread 1 strip on each of the skewers. Season with salt and pepper.

Little Stick Variations

Why limit yourself to function when you can have flavor, too? To imbue morsels of food with a particular taste, choose from among the following skewer possibilities. Whichever type of "stick" you choose, however, be sure to soak it in water for 10 minutes or more before using.

• Lemongrass sticks peeled to desired thinness

• Sugarcane sticks cut to desired length and peeled or whittled to desired thickness

• Sturdy rosemary branches with excess leaves removed

• Licorice bark with the ends whittled to sharp points; order licorice bark from specialty spice companies

CHOPPED SCALLIONS

CHOPPED PEANUTS

LIME WEDGES

GRILLED PINEAPPLE

THAI DIPPING SAUCE
(page 253)

SPICY PEANUT SAUCE
(page 254)

5. Bring the marinade to a boil over medium heat. Reduce the heat to low and simmer, uncovered, until reduced by half, about 20 minutes.

6. When ready to cook, oil the grill rack and grill (or broil) the chicken skewers until cooked through, about 8 minutes, turning once, and brushing with marinade. Season to taste with pepper.

Makes about 30 skewers, serving 8 as a small bowl

PINEAPPLE-SAKE MARINADE

A delicious combination of contrasting tastes—sweet pineapple juice, salty soy sauce, and hot red pepper flakes—makes this an excellent choice for marinating chicken or squid. Used as a sauce, this also adds zing to Not-So-Fried Rice (page 145).

Be sure to remember that after using this as a marinade, it can be transformed easily into a sauce. Bring it to a boil, then reduce it by half. Drizzle over what you have just marinated and enjoy!

> **2 cups pineapple juice**
> **1½ cup sake**
> **½ cup light soy sauce**
> **6 tablespoons sugar**
> **6 tablespoons Asian sesame oil**
> **½ teaspoon crushed red pepper flakes**

1. Combine all the ingredients in a small saucepan and cook over medium heat, stirring constantly, until the sugar is dissolved, 2 to 3 minutes. Reduce the heat to low and simmer, uncovered, for 45 minutes.

2. Remove from the heat and cool. Use immediately, or transfer to an airtight container and refrigerate for up to 1 month.

Makes about 2 cups

"ANOTHER SAKE?" NO NEED TO ASK

If each country had a national drink, sake would certainly be Japan's. Once the drink of Shinto gods, today this ancient, fermented rice beverage is universal in appeal. Neither a wine (it is not made from fermented fruit sugars, nor is it aged) nor a beer (although it is made from a grain), this clear, fragrant alcohol is in a class of its own. There are a number of different grades of sake, but all the making of good sake requires is high-quality rice and pure water. Sake is excellent for marinating meats and poultry, as it offers both sweetness and tenderizing properties, and when you do prepare food with it, it is all right to select an inexpensive brand.

Drinking sake calls for a lot of sipping and shmoozing. As the host, you must be a cup and mind reader, a common courtesy dictated by Japanese etiquette. Since sake is often served in small porcelain cups that hold only a couple of sips, always keep your eyes on your companion's cup and always be ready to refill it. (This means, too, that when you are not host but guest you need never ask for more.)

When drinking sake, be sure to lift your cup when being served the dry, sweet, clear alcohol and to acknowledge the filling. And unless you are unable to bear another sip, *never* decline the serving.

GRILLED SHRIMP ON SUGARCANE

Not only are these Vietnamese-inspired, shrimp-molded skewers sensational in flavor, they are fun to eat too, because they're on a stick. Any chopped shellfish can be substituted in this mixture, although shrimp is the custom. Nothing, however, can replace the sugarcane. Savor every last taste of it by chewing on the cane after you've eaten the shrimp.

Enjoy eating these as an appetizer, with several different bowls of dipping sauces. Or serve these as an exotic decorative accompaniment by spiking individual bowls of Shanghai Noodles (page 129) with a sugarcane spear.

HOT-AND-SOUR BROTH
(page 14)

TOMATO SOY SAUCE
(page 252)

NOT-SO-FRIED RICE
(page 145)

TAMARIND GLAZE
(page 210)

About Sugarcane

The tall, tropical grass known as sugarcane looms everywhere in Vietnam and is sold in a variety of forms—in long batons, to be cut, peeled, and split into skewers for grilling shrimp and meat; in short, peeled pieces, for snacking; in thick caramel syrups, brown bricks, and refined granules for cooking. The cane is even sold as juice, extracted fresh at street markets, for drinking.

In the United States, fresh sugarcane may not be so easy to find. And when you do find it, usually in specialty food markets, the stalks have been cut, boiled (to make them edible), and packaged. In this form, they are meant to be eaten as a snack or used as a garnish. However, sometimes it is possible to find fresh sugarcane in Latin markets. Happy hunting—it's worth the search.

3 pieces (each 10 inches long) fresh sugarcane
1 pound medium shrimp, peeled, deveined, and chopped
1 pound spinach, stemmed, rinsed, blanched and shocked (page 214), squeezed dry, and chopped
½ cup chopped fresh cilantro leaves
¼ cup chopped peeled fresh ginger
¼ cup Sweet Soy Sauce (page 251)
¼ cup fresh lime juice
3 tablespoons grated lime zest
1 tablespoon pure chili powder, preferably ancho chili powder
1 large egg
2 fresh Kaffir lime leaves, minced
Salt and freshly ground black pepper, to taste

1. Preheat the broiler and oil a large baking sheet.

2. Using a sharp knife, cut each piece of sugarcane lengthwise into quarters for a total of 12. Peel and sharpen the ends.

3. Combine the remaining ingredients in a large bowl and stir thoroughly to combine.

4. Rub your hands with vegetable oil, then mold about ½ cup of the shrimp mixture in a sausage shape around the middle of each sugarcane stick. Leave the stick ends bare. Repeat with the remaining shrimp mixture and sticks. (You may have leftover sticks.)

5. Arrange the shrimp sticks on the prepared baking sheet and broil 5 to 6 inches from the heat, turning every few minutes, until cooked through, about 15 minutes. Place attractively in a wide bowl and serve.

Serves 6 to 12 as a small bowl

CHILI-MARINATED GRILLED SHRIMP

Although created especially for prawns and large shrimp, the chili marinade gives great color and taste to lobster, fish, and scallops. The annatto oil imparts little flavor but is the secret ingredient responsible for the vibrant orange-red color. You'll want to purchase jumbo shrimp (approximately 10 per pound) for grilling. And we like to skewer them. For tastier, juicier shrimp, we also cook them in their shells—and take care not to let them overcook.

¼ **cup tamarind concentrate**

¼ **cup rice wine vinegar**

3 tablespoons Annatto Oil (page 232)

2 tablespoons Sweet Soy Sauce (page 251)

2 tablespoons chili paste

2 tablespoons nam pla (Asian fish sauce)

2 pounds jumbo shrimp, in shells

12 metal skewers

Skewers of shrimp in a duck? Why not? Lean them perpendicular to the head, shrimp-end down.

1. Combine the tamarind concentrate, vinegar, annatto oil, soy sauce, and *nam pla* in a glass or stainless-steel bowl. Add the shrimp, stir to coat, and marinate, covered, in the refrigerator for 1 hour.

2. Preheat a grill to high and place the rack 5 to 6 inches from the heat.

3. Thread 2 shrimp on each skewer. When ready to cook, oil the grill rack and grill the shrimp, turning them every couple of minutes, until the shells are slightly charred and the meat is opaque, 5 to 8 minutes. Serve immediately.

Serves 4 to 6 as a main bowl, 8 to 10 as a small bowl

SHRIMP AND YUCA FRITTERS

Yuca, also known as cassava or manioc, is a root of Brazilian origin. Like the potato, yuca is suitable for boiling, frying, or sautéing; because it is extremely starchy and sticky, it stands up particularly well to frying. You'll find yuca at any market with a Latin clientele and also in larger supermarkets. These fritters take on a golden-brown hue and are crisp to the bite, but remain moist on the inside.

THE SIDE BOWLS

CHA-CHA CHILI BROTH
(page 8)

TAMARIND BROTH
(page 18)

SPICY TOMATO GLAZE
(page 263)

SPICY CILANTRO SOY PASTE
(page 239)

3 tablespoons nam pla (Asian fish sauce)

I tablespoon soy sauce

I tablespoon olive oil

2 cloves garlic, chopped

8 ounces medium shrimp, preferably rock shrimp, peeled, deveined, and chopped

I pound piece yuca (cassava), peeled

I medium onion

3 tablespoons minced fresh jalapeño pepper

I tablespoon curry powder, preferably homemade (page 10)

½ cup all-purpose flour

I large egg, beaten

Salt and freshly ground black pepper, to taste

1½ cups vegetable oil, for deep-frying

1. Combine the *nam pla*, soy sauce, olive oil, and garlic in a medium bowl. Add the shrimp, stir well to mix, and let stand for 30 minutes, covered, in the refrigerator.

2. Coarsely grate the yuca and onion into a large bowl. Stir in the jalapeño and curry powder. Add the flour, egg, and salt and pepper and stir just enough to combine. Using a slotted spoon, remove the shrimp from the marinade and stir them into the batter. Discard the marinade.

3. Heat the vegetable oil in a large heavy skillet over medium heat until it is very hot but not smoking. Spoon a heaping tablespoonful of the batter into the skillet and press down slightly to form a patty. Continue to add batter, pressing it into patties, without overcrowding the pan; cook until golden brown on both sides, about 3 minutes per side. As the fritters are done, transfer them with a slotted spoon to paper towels to drain. Serve immediately. Or keep warm in a preheated low oven.

Makes about 30 fritters, serving 6 to 8 as a small bowl

CHICKPEA FRITTERS

Too often we reach for all-purpose flour, forgetting the many different varieties of flour available—rice, chestnut, almond, and chickpea, to name a few. In this Indian-style recipe, the nutty flavor of chickpea flour gives these crispy fritters their basic character.

A unique contribution to White Bean and Mushroom Soup (page 62), these bite-size fritters are also delicious as a snack or hors d'oeuvre served with Tamarind Glaze (page 210) as a dipping sauce.

1¼ **cups chickpea flour**

1 **tablespoon curry powder, preferably homemade (page 10)**

2 **teaspoons baking powder**

1 **teaspoon ground turmeric**

½ **teaspoon salt**

½ **teaspoon imported sweet paprika**

2 **large eggs, separated**

¼ **cup milk**

1 **cup coarsely grated zucchini**

½ **cup coarsely grated onion**

2 **fresh jalapeño peppers, stemmed, seeded, and chopped**

4 **cups vegetable oil, for deep-frying**

Line the bottom of a mesh basket with a piece of parchment paper and pile in a stack of fritters.

185

PUMPKIN SEED SAUCE
(page 256)

PISTACHIO YOGURT SAUCE
(page 255)

CURRIED CORN BROTH
(page 15)

CARROT CARDAMOM SOUP
(page 46)

COOL HAND CUKE SOUP
(page 43)

1. Combine the flour, curry powder, baking powder, turmeric, salt, and paprika in a large bowl.

2. Beat the egg yolks and milk together in a small bowl. Add the egg mixture to the flour mixture with the zucchini, onion, jalapeños, and salt and stir well to combine.

3. Beat the egg whites in a small bowl with a wire whisk until stiff peaks form. Fold the whites into the zucchini mixture with a rubber spatula until just combined. Do not overmix.

4. Heat the oil in a deep heavy saucepan to 350°F on a deep-fat thermometer. Carefully drop the chickpea batter, by heaping tablespoonfuls, into the hot oil and deep-fry them until browned on all sides, about 3 minutes. Do not crowd the pan. Transfer with a slotted spoon to paper towels to drain. Serve immediately or keep warm in a preheated low oven while making the remaining fritters. Let the oil cool, then discard.

Makes about 24 fritters, serving 6 as a small bowl

MY LITTLE CHICKPEA

In Italy, chickpea flour is used to make cakes, or fritters. The French use it to make *panisses,* or chickpea fries. In India, they turn it into *sev,* a crunchy fried noodle that is a popular street snack.

Once you discover the sweet earthy rewards of chickpea flour, which is sold as besan or gram flour at Indian markets, it will hit the top of your favorites list. It's certainly among the most flavorful flours we've ever tasted, and we use it every chance we can—from dusting soft-shell crabs before a quick sauté to enhance their crispness and flavor to making crêpelike pancakes and filling them with goat cheese and greens, or layering them with seared foie gras and finishing with a drizzle of pomegranate syrup for an out-of-this-world appetizer.

THREE-ONION POTATO CAKES

When you're looking for something really hearty to eat with a brothy soup or stew, try these potato cakes. If you were lucky enough to grow up with an aunt who specialized in *latkes*—potato pancakes beloved Jewish-style—you know what we're talking about. For those who don't, let these be an introduction, with a little twist. Traditional potato pancakes are made from freshly grated potatoes, but we like using our mashed recipe, instead. Try rolling them into balls, sauté them quickly, then drop them gently into a bowl of Latin Chicken Soup with Noodles (page 54); the potato thickens the broth. A hearty, homey meal.

3 tablespoons Annatto Oil (page 232)

1 cup diced red onion

4 cups Mashed Potatoes (page 189)

½ cup Crispy Shallots (see box, page 77)

1 tablespoon chopped fresh thyme

Salt and freshly ground black pepper, to taste

½ cup chopped scallions, white and green part

½ cup all-purpose flour

½ cup cornmeal

¼ cup olive oil

For a little variation, spread four shallow, ovenproof bowls like this one with 1 cup of the mashed potato mixture (step 1), sprinkle each with some of the cornmeal mixture (step 3), and gratinée under the broiler just before serving.

1. Heat the Annatto Oil in a large saucepan over medium heat until it begins to sizzle, about 3 minutes. Add the red onion and sauté until translucent, about 5 minutes. Add the potatoes, fried shallots, thyme, and salt and pepper and beat them in with a spatula until thoroughly combined. Remove from the heat, stir in the chopped scallions, and cool.

2. Preheat the oven to 350°F.

3. Combine the flour and cornmeal with salt and pepper in a shallow dish. Form the cooled potato mixture into eight 3- to 4-inch pancakes. Dip each into the flour mixture to coat both sides, then shake gently to remove any excess coating.

4. Heat the oil in a large skillet with a heatproof handle over medium heat until hot but not smoking. Add the potato cakes in one layer and sauté until golden brown, about 2 minutes per side.

5. Transfer the skillet to the oven and bake the pancakes, uncovered, until crisp and cooked through, about 20 minutes. Transfer to a flat surface with paper towels to drain. Serve immediately while still hot.

Serves 8 as a small bowl

ZUCCHINI PANCAKES

GREEN THUMB GAZPACHO
(*page 41*)

MANGO VINAIGRETTE
(*page 221*)

MUSTARD-POTATO CREAM VINAIGRETTE
(*page 223*)

In this favorite Passover specialty, Jewish cooks substitute matzo meal for the bread crumbs. These crisp pancakes are so good, you'll enjoy eating them any time of year, as an accompaniment to many a different bowl of soup or stew. Serve with Apricot and Apple Chutney (page 266) as a sweet counterpoint to each bite.

5 cups coarsely grated zucchini (about 1¼ pounds)
1 large onion, coarsely grated
1½ cups bread crumbs or matzo meal
4 large eggs, beaten
2 tablespoons fresh lemon juice
½ cup olive oil or vegetable oil
Salt and freshly ground black pepper, to taste

1. Combine the zucchini and onion in a large bowl. Add the matzo meal, eggs, and lemon juice and mix well.

2. Heat the olive oil in a large heavy skillet over medium heat until hot but not smoking. Drop the batter, ½ cup at a time, carefully into the hot oil. Flatten with a metal spatula to form pancakes that are approximately 4 inches in diameter and ½ inch thick. Do not crowd the pan. Cook until golden brown all over, 2 to 3 minutes per side.

3. Remove the pancakes as they are done to paper towels to drain. Make pancakes with the remaining batter in the same manner.

4. Serve immediately, or keep warm in a preheated low oven.

Makes 12 to 14 pancakes, serving 4 to 6 as a small bowl

MASHED POTATOES

There are few simpler, more satisfying foods than this. For those of us who count fat calories, time to close your eyes and enjoy. The extra calories here are well worth it. And hey, how often do you eat real mashed potatoes? A bowl of these will warm your soul.

These can be prepared an hour ahead of time, covered, and held in the top of a double boiler over barely simmering water. For variation in color and flavor, blend several tablespoons of Olive and Basil Paste (page 240) into the potatoes just before serving.

CRISPY SHALLOTS
(see box, page 77)

CHOPPED CHIVES

    4 pounds Idaho potatoes, peeled and cut into 1-inch cubes
    Salt, to taste
    1½ cups heavy (or whipping) cream
    ¾ cup (1½ sticks) unsalted butter, in pieces

1. Combine the potatoes and water to cover in a large saucepan. Salt the water. Bring to a boil over medium-high heat, then reduce the heat to medium-low and cook, covered, until the potatoes are tender when pierced with a fork, 15 to 20 minutes.

2. Meanwhile, combine the cream and butter in a small saucepan and heat over medium-low heat until the butter melts. Remove from the heat.

3. Drain the potatoes and pass through a food mill into a large bowl, adding some of the warm cream mixture, if necessary, to help mill them.

4. When all the potatoes are mashed, add the remaining cream mixture. Stir in gently but thoroughly. Season with salt, and serve in deep bowls.

Makes 8 cups, serving 8 as a small bowl

Saffron and Wasabi Mashed Potatoes

Here, the quintessential American classic is spiced with Japanese wasabi (a pungently sharp type of horseradish) and Spanish saffron. You may think it a strange combination. But once you taste it, you'll agree that it satisfies even the most primal cravings for mashed potatoes. Serve with Roasted Pork Loin with Honey-Hoisin Marinade (page 79).

¼ cup warm water

2 tablespoons wasabi powder (Japanese horseradish)

½ cup milk

1 teaspoon saffron threads, crushed

3 tablespoons Garlic Paste (page 61)

4 cups Mashed Potatoes (page 189)

2 tablespoons unsalted butter, softened

2 tablespoons chopped fresh chives or green part of scallions

Salt and freshly ground black pepper, to taste

¼ cup Crispy Shallots (see box, page 77), for garnish

1. In a small bowl, combine the warm water and the wasabi and stir until smooth.

2. Bring the milk to a boil in a small saucepan over medium heat, stirring occasionally. Reduce the heat to low, stir in the saffron, and simmer for 5 minutes. Transfer to a large saucepan.

3. Add the Garlic Paste and potatoes and whip with a wire whisk or fork until light and fluffy. Remove from the heat and fold in the wasabi paste, butter, and chives until blended. Season with salt and pepper. Serve in deep bowls, garnishing each serving with Fried Shallots.

Serves 4 to 6 as a small bowl

Here's a great big, heavy, homey piece of Americana cookware. There's no better way to serve up everyone's favorite comfort food: mashed potatoes.

A BITTER HERB THAT BRIGHTENS TASTE

The Asian cousin of horseradish, wasabi made itself known to the American palate, in large part, because of sushi, which it traditionally accompanies as a condiment. In Avocado Wasabi (page 260), we use the powdered root for both its spunky flavor and its pale green color. Powdered wasabi and wasabi paste can be bought in Asian markets. Store as you would a dried herb, in a cool, dark place.

ROASTED EGGPLANT PURÉE

Japanese eggplants, or the Asian variety, are sweeter and have a creamier texture than the large, pear-shaped ones commonly found in grocery stores. Their skins are also much thinner, so if some skin ends up in this mixture, don't fret; it simply adds more flavor.

This is great on grilled flatbreads and vegetables, with root vegetable chips, on sandwiches, and even in soups.

8 Japanese eggplants (about 7 ounces each)
½ cup (tightly packed) fresh basil leaves
¼ cup fresh lemon juice
3 tablespoons Kalamata olives, pitted
1 tablespoon Garlic Paste (page 61)
1 tablespoon capers, drained
Salt and freshly ground black pepper, to taste

1. Preheat the oven to 400°F.

2. Place the eggplants on a baking sheet and roast until soft throughout, about 20 minutes. Remove from the oven and cool.

3. Halve the cooled eggplants lengthwise and scrape out the pulp. Transfer the pulp to a food processor, add the basil, lemon juice, olives, Garlic Paste, and capers, and process until smooth. Season with salt and pepper. Use immediately, or transfer to an airtight container and store in the refrigerator for up to 3 days.

Makes about 3 cups

Chapter 6

SALAD BOWLS

Salads

Salad Dressings

More than Greens

It wasn't so long ago that green salads were pretty much limited to a plate of crisp iceberg lettuce saddled with a swathe of creamy, tart and sweet French dressing. That's not to say that a cool wedge of iceberg with French dressing doesn't have its merits or its place. It's that when it comes to salads, that combination is, literally, just the smallest tip. Happily, these days, large supermarkets carry a full range of greens, both mature and young. Popular bin mates Boston, bibb, and romaine are lined up alongside frisée, mâche, arugula, baby spinach, and sorrel. They even carry mixes of fresh, young, exotic greens called mesclun. Tossed together with an interesting home-made vinaigrette—and in this chapter we offer a full range of them—these flavorful greens are tantalizing and worthy of a prominent position on the dinner table. By the way, don't limit our vinaigrettes just to salads. All can be used to liven up pastas, grilled meats, and seafood, or used as dips for dumplings and doodads.

Good as green salads are, the ones we most enjoy eating are inspired composed salads. Made up of attractively arranged components, some are big, lusty bowls like chili-rubbed Seared Steak with Roasted Tomatoes, which we serve on a bed of peppery arugula. Others feel more delicate—Crab and Potato Salad with Jalapeño Sauce, Thai-Style Summer Lobster and Noodle Salad, and Green Bean and Baby Vegetable Salad—but are main bowls nonetheless.

In this chapter we've also included a selection of infused oils. They are easy to make, keep for a week in the refrigerator, and add haunting flavor to sauces, soups, stews, and of course, vinaigrettes. You will especially appreciate them after a difficult day when you come home to nothing but a few near-forgotten vegetables. Drizzled over steamed anything—from artichokes to zucchini—they help make a delicious bowlful. And, if you have some crusty bread to sop up the remaining oil and juices, you are doubly fortunate.

Salads

SEARED STEAK SALAD WITH ROASTED TOMATOES

Because it's difficult, if not impossible, to get a household oven hot enough to rapidly sear a cut of beef, we've opted to pan-sear the steak stovetop in a heavy, cast-iron skillet over high heat. That way, we achieve a crust that seals in juices until gently released when sliced. The juice of the chili-flavored beef, the plump and sweet tomatoes, and the peppery bite of the arugula all band together to deliver a delicious trio of tastes. Serve in shallow wooden bowls.

Dig out those old wooden salad bowls from the back of the kitchen cabinet and use them for serving contemporary combinations like this one full of peppery heat and cooling crunch.

3 boneless New York strip steaks (12 ounces each;
    about 2 inches thick), trimmed of two thirds of the fat
1 cup Chili Rub (recipe follows)
¼ cup extra virgin olive oil
3 tablespoons chopped fresh thyme leaves
1 tablespoon chopped fresh rosemary leaves
1 tablespoon chopped garlic
2 pounds ripe plum tomatoes, cut crosswise into ¼-inch slices
Salt and freshly ground black pepper, to taste
¼ cup plus 3 tablespoons Parsley and Garlic Oil (page 234)
1 tablespoon red wine vinegar
1 pound arugula, stemmed, rinsed, and patted dry
4 ounces Parmigiano-Reggiano cheese, slivered into shards

1. Rub each steak all over with chili rub. Wrap or cover tightly with plastic wrap and refrigerate for 24 hours.

2. Preheat the oven to 400°F.

3. Combine the olive oil, thyme, rosemary, and garlic in a large bowl. Add the tomato slices and toss gently to coat. Arrange the tomatoes on a baking sheet and sprinkle with salt and pepper. Roast for 20 minutes, remove, and cool.

4. Heat the ¼ cup Parsley and Garlic Oil in a large, heavy cast-iron skillet over high heat. Add the steaks, in 2 batches if necessary, and sear for 4 minutes on each side, 8 minutes total for medium-rare. Do not crowd the pan. Remove from the pan to a plate, season with salt, and let rest for 20 minutes, to seal in the juices. Slice each steak into 1-inch-wide slices. Keep warm.

5. Combine the vinegar and remaining 3 tablespoons Parsley and Garlic Oil in a small bowl and beat with a fork to blend.

6. Combine the arugula with the roasted tomatoes in a large bowl and toss gently but thoroughly. Divide the mixture among 6 serving bowls and drizzle with the parsley vinaigrette. Arrange equal amounts of steak slices over each serving of arugula. Place Parmesan shards attractively over each salad.

Serves 6 as a main bowl

CHILI RUB

The best meat rub ever, this spicy blend helps tenderize meat as it seals in juices. When you're looking for robust homemade flavor, here it is. In fact, it's so good you'll want to use it on fish steaks and poultry, too.

½ **cup fresh lime juice**

6 **tablespoons freshly ground black pepper**

1 **tablespoon imported sweet paprika**

1 **tablespoon cayenne pepper**

1 **tablespoon coriander seeds, toasted (see box, page 137)**
   and ground

8 **cloves garlic, roasted (see box, page 48)**

1 **tablespoon salt**

½ **cup olive oil**

THE SIDE BOWLS

BONIATO, CARROT, AND JALAPEÑO PUREE
(*page 167*)

THREE-ONION POTATO CAKES
(*page 187*)

CREAMY POLENTA
(*page 73*)

WARM POTATO AND WILD MUSHROOM SALAD
(*page 215*)

1. Combine the lime juice, black pepper, paprika, cayenne pepper, coriander seeds, and roasted garlic in a blender or food processor and process until smooth. With the motor running, add the oil in a slow, steady stream and blend until thoroughly incorporated. Use immediately, or transfer to an airtight container and store in the refrigerator for up to 2 weeks.

2. To use, brush the rub over all surfaces of the meat, cover or wrap tightly with plastic wrap, and refrigerate overnight.

Makes about 1¼ cups

FRIED CHICKEN SALAD

Crucial to the success of any fried dish—this one included—is the temperature of the oil that is destined to do the frying. It must be heated until hot and kept hot. So don't overcrowd the pan. Quick frying at the right temperature ensures a crispy coating, helping to reduce the amount of oil absorbed into the chicken and sealing in the juices. The coating gives a wonderfully hot bang, and the Sour Crema drizzle added at the end has a gentle cooling effect.

1 medium head garlic, separated into cloves, cloves peeled
2 pounds skinless, boneless chicken breasts,
   cut into 2-inch strips
¼ cup fresh lemon juice
¼ cup imported sweet paprika
2 tablespoons freshly ground black pepper
1 tablespoon coarse (kosher) salt
2 tablespoons soy sauce
2 tablespoons Tabasco sauce
2 cups vegetable oil, preferably peanut oil
1½ cups all-purpose flour
2 bunches watercress, stemmed, rinsed, and patted dry

**2 Granny Smith apples, peeled, cored, and
cut into ½-inch dice**
1 cucumber, peeled, seeded, and cut into ¼-inch dice
½ cup walnut pieces, toasted (see box, page 137)
¼ cup Lemonette (page 219)
4 tablespoons Sour Crema (page 263)

1. Place the garlic cloves in a blender and purée them. Set aside.

2. Place the chicken in a large glass baking dish, pour the lemon juice over it, and toss thoroughly to coat. Cover with plastic wrap, and refrigerate for 30 minutes.

3. Rub the chicken all over with the puréed garlic, cover again, and refrigerate for 15 minutes.

4. Combine the paprika, pepper, and salt in a small bowl and sprinkle the chicken with the mixture, tossing thoroughly to coat. Add the soy sauce and Tabasco and toss again.

5. Heat the oil over medium heat to 325°F on a deep-fry thermometer in a large deep skillet.

6. Place the flour in a large brown paper bag, add the seasoned chicken, in batches, and shake to coat evenly. Carefully add the chicken, in batches, to the hot oil and fry until crispy golden brown on all sides, about 4 minutes per batch. As the chicken is fried, remove it to a baking sheet lined with paper towels to drain. Keep warm. Be sure to reheat the oil to 325°F before frying another batch.

7. Combine the watercress, apples, cucumber, and walnuts in a large bowl. Add the dressing and toss well.

8. Divide the salad mixture among large serving bowls. Top with the chicken and drizzle with the Sour Crema.

Serves 4 to 6 as a main bowl

Consider using that pasta bowl for salads. Your greens and other crispy and crunchy ingredients will appreciate the room.

SEAFOOD-BY-THE-SEA SALAD

If lazy, hot summer were to choose a complementary partner, it would be sprightly, fresh green cilantro. This refreshing flavor, combined with a tangy lemon dressing, jasmine rice, and a variety of seafood, creates a light yet so very satisfying salad for a sweltering afternoon picnic at the beach.

THE SIDE BOWLS

DICED MANGO
CHOPPED CHIVES

½ cup (tightly packed) fresh cilantro leaves

¼ cup grapeseed oil or another mild-flavored vegetable oil

6 cups cooked jasmine rice

I pound cooked cleaned squid bodies, sliced into rings

8 ounces medium shrimp, peeled, deveined, halved, and cooked

I cup chopped cooked lobster meat

I medium cucumber with peel, seeded and diced

5 scallions, white and green parts, finely chopped

¾ cup orange segments, seeded, if necessary, and chopped

¼ cup fresh lemon juice

2 tablespoons finely chopped lemon zest

Shichimi togarashi (see box, page 115), to taste

Salt and freshly ground black pepper, to taste

3 cups arugula leaves, rinsed, patted dry,
    and cut into thin crosswise strips

I cup Lemonette (page 219)

Lemon wedges, for serving (optional)

I. Combine the cilantro leaves and grapeseed oil in a blender or food processor and process until smooth.

2. Combine the remaining ingredients through the salt and pepper in a large bowl. Add the cilantro purée and toss well to combine. Add the arugula and Lemonette, toss again, and serve in large bowls with chopsticks and lemon wedges, if desired.

Serves 6 as a main bowl

CRUSTACEANS:
CLEANING AND COOKING

LOBSTERS: Lobsters need no advance cleaning, but because bacteria form quickly once they die, it's important that they remain alive until it's time to cook them. We quickly pierce the brain area (vertically through the center space between the eyes) with the sharp point of a chef's knife, immediately driving it through while rocking the blade. This way, the lobster dies immediately.

When cooked properly, the sweet taste and natural tenderness of a lobster are preserved. We've found that boiling them in very little water (2 quarts for 2 lobsters in a 12-quart stockpot) is sufficient. Drop the lobsters into a stockpot of boiling water and cover tightly. A lobster needs to cook about 8 minutes per pound, less if you plan to remove the meat from the shell for cooking with other ingredients. The cooking liquid, which captures the lobster's natural juices, can become the base, or foundation, for a sauce.

SHRIMP: Shrimp can be cooked shelled or unshelled, but either way, they should always be deveined before cooking. Score the full length of the shrimp along its backside, using a sharp paring knife. Remove the shell, if desired, and pull out the dark vein. Poach (never boil) shrimp in simmering broth until just opaque, about 2 to 4 minutes. Or, sauté them in a hot skillet with a little oil and some salt. A couple of minutes does it. The cooked shrimp will have an opaque pinkish color.

SOFT-SHELL CRABS: Soft-shells represent a brief stage in the life cycle of a blue crab; it is the time just after the crab sheds its hard winter coat. When sautéed, the edible, new, thin outer shell that encapsulates the soft, rich interior crisps, and rewards each juicy bite with a burst of the sweet sea that is incredibly delicious.

Buy live crabs and clean them just before cooking. Rinse under cold running water. With a pair of sharp kitchen scissors, cut off the face of each crab ¼ inch behind the eyes and mouth. Discard the face. Pull up the pointed flap on one side of the top shell to expose the gills. Pull out the gills and discard them. Repeat on the other side. Turn the crab over; twist off and discard the "apron," or tail flap, on the bottom. Rinse and pat the crabs dry. Now heat up that skillet, because the crabs are ready to cook.

Although it isn't necessary to reserve bowls with fish designs for serving seafood, wide, shallow ones do add a little something to a seafood salad.

CRAB AND POTATO SALAD WITH JALAPEÑO SAUCE

Here we took an American classic—potato salad—and had some fun with it. By adding lump crabmeat and lots of sprightly flavors, we turned an accompaniment into a fabulous entrée. Red Bliss potatoes are sweet and delicate and a perfect match for the crab.

Quick and easy to assemble, this summer combination can be prepared in advance, tossed together at the last minute, and arranged in a wide platter-type bowl on a bed of arugula.

1 pound small red-skinned potatoes,
    preferably Red Bliss, scrubbed

Salt, to taste

1 pound lump crabmeat, picked over for cartilage

1 cucumber, seeded and cut into small dice

1 yellow or red bell pepper, stemmed, seeded,
    and cut into small dice

½ cup diced ripe tomato

2 medium shallots, minced

2 fresh jalapeño peppers, stemmed, seeded,
    and minced

3 tablespoons chopped fresh chives

½ cup fresh lime juice

2 tablespoons Dijon mustard

1 tablespoon ground coriander

1 teaspoon grated peeled fresh ginger

½ teaspoon crushed red pepper flakes

1 cup Jalapeño Sauce (recipe follows)

1 pound arugula, stemmed, rinsed, and
    patted dry

Lemon and lime wedges, for serving

We always save the most attractive shells from oysters, clams, and scallops—they make great vessels for little tastes of seafood or other bite-size appetizers. You can also buy an array of different kinds of serving shells.

1. Put the potatoes in a large pot of cold salted water and bring to a boil. Boil gently until you can pierce the potatoes easily with the tip of a knife. Drain and set aside until cool enough to handle.

2. Cut the potatoes, with the skin on, into ½-inch slices. Combine in a stainless-steel or glass bowl with the crab, cucumber, bell pepper, tomato, shallots, jalapeños, and chives.

3. Combine the lime juice, mustard, coriander, ginger, pepper flakes, and salt to taste in a small nonreactive bowl and beat with a fork to blend. Pour over the potato-crabmeat mixture and toss gently but thoroughly to coat.

4. Divide the arugula among 6 serving bowls and top with the potato-crabmeat salad. Drizzle Jalapeño Sauce decoratively over each portion and serve with lemon and lime wedges.

Serves 6 as a main bowl, 10 to 12 as a small bowl

JALAPEÑO SAUCE

Jalapeños come in green and red varieties. Unripe green jalapeños are hot, whereas the ripened red ones are sweeter and milder. Either will work here. Let your color palette determine your choice. We like to fill squeeze bottles with one of each and drizzle narrow crossing streams over a wide bowl of Crab and Potato Salad. The sauce holds well when refrigerated for up to 4 days.

> **2 large egg yolks (see Note)**
> **¼ cup rice vinegar**
> **2 fresh jalapeño peppers, stemmed, seeded, and chopped**
> **3 tablespoons chopped fresh Italian (flat-leaf) parsley leaves**
> **2 tablespoons fresh lime juice**
> **1½ tablespoons Dijon mustard**
> **½ teaspoon five-spice powder**
> **¾ cup olive oil**
> **Salt and freshly ground black pepper, to taste**

CRISPY LEEKS
(see box, page 77)

CHOPPED CILANTRO

Combine the egg yolks, vinegar, jalapeños, parsley, lime juice, mustard, and five-spice powder in a blender or food processor and pulse off and on until smooth. With the motor running, add the olive oil in a slow, steady stream and blend in thoroughly. Season with salt and pepper. Use immediately, or transfer to an airtight container and store in the refrigerator for up to 4 days.

Makes about 1½ cups

Note: The sauce here is made with uncooked egg yolks. Use the freshest available refrigerated eggs to avoid any risk of salmonella. If you are unsure about the safety of your raw eggs, it is best not to make the sauce.

CRISP SOFT-SHELL CRAB AND CUCUMBER SALAD

Soft-shell Atlantic blue crabs, available May through September, are so tender and sweet when cooked that you can eat the whole thing. Sauté them quickly to give the shells a crispy texture, then feature them in this bright-flavored combination, punctuated by a duo of dressings and a generous sprinkling of pine nuts.

Attractive bowls at each place setting hold additional salad toppings or dressings.

¼ **cup olive oil**

5 **cloves garlic, minced**

8 **live soft-shell crabs, cleaned (see box, page 201)**

Salt and freshly ground black pepper, to taste

2 **cucumbers, peeled, seeded, and cut into ¼-inch dice**

12 **ounces mâche (lamb's lettuce) or flat-leaf spinach leaves, rinsed and patted dry**

½ **cup chopped ripe tomato**

1 **small red onion, thinly sliced**

2 **scallions, white and green parts, chopped**

½ cup **Lemonette (page 219)**

¼ cup **Ginger Dressing (page 228)**

¼ cup **pine nuts, toasted (see box, page 137)**
and chopped

1. Heat the olive oil with the garlic in a large skillet over medium heat. When the garlic is lightly browned and fragrant, add the crabs, top side down, and sauté until the shells are crispy and turn a reddish color, about 3 minutes. With tongs, turn the crabs over and sauté until done, another 3 minutes. Remove the crabs to paper towels to drain. Season with salt and pepper.

2. Combine the cucumbers, mâche, tomato, red onion, and scallions in a medium bowl. Add the Lemonette and toss well. Season, if necessary, with salt and pepper.

3. Divide the salad among 4 serving bowls and arrange 2 soft-shell crabs on top of each serving. Drizzle the dressing over the crabs and sprinkle with the toasted pine nuts.

Serves 4 as a main bowl, 8 as a small bowl

THAI-STYLE SUMMER LOBSTER AND NOODLE SALAD

T hai cuisine offers an enormous range of salads. Most of them contain basil but few contain oil, which makes them light and especially appealing in the summer. Sweet, succulent fresh Maine lobster, quickly poached in the shell and immediately removed, is the best way to go for this light irresistible salad.

The Great White Root

The daikon radish is as common to Chinese and Japanese cuisine as the potato is to American. In fact, Asians go through as many pounds of this foot-long vegetable as we do potatoes. The two roots have almost the same number of uses, except that the daikon can be eaten raw.

After discovering daikon in China some years ago, we came to love its juicy white flesh, which when cooked, gives a sweet, refreshing taste to stews, stir-fries, pan-fried radish cakes, and more. We use it raw and shredded for toppings or sliced into disks to replace crackers in an hors d'oeuvre bowl.

Daikons are available year-round at Asian markets and many supermarkets. When shopping for it, look for a root that is firm and solid, not flabby and flexible, which would indicate that the daikon is old.

12 ounces soba noodles

½ cup Thai Dipping Sauce (page 253)

½ cup Tomato Soy Sauce (page 252)

2 tablespoons chili paste

1 tablespoons Basil Paste (page 131)

1 tablespoon finely chopped lemongrass bottoms

8 ounces fresh sprouts, preferably daikon

1 cup chopped cooked lobster

1 small ripe tomato, seeded and cut into small dice

½ cup fresh corn kernels, blanched and shocked (page 214)

½ cup snow peas, cut into ⅛-inch slices on the diagonal

¼ cup chopped fresh chives

Salt and freshly ground black pepper, to taste

8 to 10 ounces arugula, rinsed and patted dry

¼ cup Limette (page 219)

2 tablespoons white sesame seeds, toasted (see box, page 137)

1. Bring a medium pot of salted water to a boil. Add the noodles and cook, stirring, until soft, 5 to 6 minutes. Drain the noodles in a colander, rinse under cold water, drain again, and set aside.

2. Combine the dipping sauce, soy sauce, chili and basil pastes, and lemongrass in a large nonreactive bowl. Stir well to blend.

3. Add the noodles, sprouts, lobster, tomato, corn, snow peas, and chives. Season with salt and pepper and toss well to mix.

4. Combine the arugula with the Limette in a medium bowl and toss gently but thoroughly to coat.

5. Divide the arugula among 4 serving bowls and top with the noodle salad. Sprinkle sesame seeds over each portion and serve.

Serves 4 to 6 as a main bowl, 8 to 10 as a small bowl

SHRIMP, AVOCADO, AND BLACK BEAN SALAD

Dainty as a shrimp is, it is anything but skimpy on flavor. Our favorites are the pink-and-whites from the Gulf of Mexico; they are sweet to the taste and crisp to the bite. Shrimp range from small to large in size, so be sure to count 31 to 35 per pound for medium and 15 to 17 for large. Selection of shrimp size for this salad may vary, depending on whether you serve it as a small bowl or as a main bowl.

2 tablespoons olive oil

1 teaspoon minced garlic

½ teaspoon fresh thyme leaves

Leaves from ½ sprig fresh rosemary

4 ripe plum tomatoes, cut crosswise into ¼-inch slices

Salt and freshly ground black pepper, to taste

1 ripe avocado, cut into ½-inch dice

¼ cup **Limette (page 219)**

1 pound medium shrimp, peeled and deveined

1 cup cooked black beans

1 small tomatillo, husks removed and diced

2 yellow bell peppers, stemmed, seeded, and cut into ¼-inch dice

1 shallot, minced

½ cup **Cilantro Vinaigrette (page 220)**

2 bunches arugula, stemmed, rinsed, and patted dry

Lime wedges, for serving

1. Preheat the oven to 400°F.

2. Combine the olive oil, garlic, thyme, and rosemary in a medium bowl. Add the tomato slices and toss gently to coat. Arrange the tomato slices on a baking sheet and sprinkle with salt and pepper. Roast for 20 minutes. Remove and cool.

THE SIDE BOWLS

HALF MOON OVER MANCHEGO
(page 165)

ZUCCHINI PANCAKES
(page 188)

3. Toss the avocado with the Limette in a small bowl. Cover tightly with plastic wrap and refrigerate until needed.

4. Meanwhile, combine the shrimp with lightly salted water to cover in a medium saucepan. Bring to a simmer over medium heat and simmer just until the shrimp turn opaque, about 3 minutes. Do not allow the water to come to a boil. Drain and rinse under lukewarm running water.

5. Combine the roasted tomato slices, shrimp, black beans, avocado, tomatillo, peppers, and shallot with the Cilantro Vinaigrette in a large nonreactive bowl and toss gently. Season with salt and pepper and toss again.

6. In another bowl toss the arugula with the rest of the Limette and salt and pepper. Divide the arugula evenly among 6 bowls and top each serving with shrimp salad. Serve with wedges of lime.

Serves 6 as a small bowl, 4 as a main bowl with large shrimp

GRILLED SQUID WITH TAMARIND GLAZE ON SPINACH SALAD

The trick to cooking squid is either to cook it quickly, 1 to 2 minutes, as in sautéing, frying, or grilling, or to cook it for a long, long time, as in stewing for an hour or more. Anything in between usually results in a texture similar to rubber. Here we use Pineapple-Sake Marinade to ensure tenderness before we grill the squid. Because squid shrinks when cooked, it's a good idea to score each side lightly with the tip of a sharp knife before sautéing or grilling.

1½ pounds medium squid bodies, cleaned and scored
   (see box, page 90)

1½ cups Pineapple-Sake Marinade (page 180)

1 pound fresh spinach, preferably flat-leaf, stemmed,
   rinsed, and patted dry

1 medium red onion, thinly sliced

2 large ripe mangoes, peeled, pitted,
   and cut into ½-inch dice

½ cup peanuts, toasted (see box, page 137)
   and chopped

½ cup Limette (page 219)

Salt and freshly ground black pepper, to taste

½ cup Tamarind Glaze (recipe follows)

This may look like one of those hopeless wedding gifts that is hard to store, serves no real purpose, and is, for one reason or another, unreturnable. But, in fact, it makes a delightful presentation for seafood salads. Aunt Shirley will be pleased to see how beautifully you've put her treasured present to use!

1. Place the squid bodies on a flat surface and cut each open lengthwise along one side. Transfer to a large nonreactive bowl. Add the marinade, cover, and marinate in the refrigerator for 30 minutes.

2. Meanwhile, preheat the grill to high. Or preheat the broiler.

3. Drain the squid. Oil the grill rack, place the squid on the rack, and quickly grill about 30 seconds on each side. (Or broil the squid on the rack of a broiler pan about 3 inches from the heat for about the same amount of time.) Remove the squid from the grill and set aside.

4. Combine the spinach, onion, mangoes, and peanuts in a large nonreactive bowl. Add the Limette and toss well. Season with salt and pepper.

5. Divide the spinach salad among 6 serving bowls. Top each serving with squid and drizzle with Tamarind Glaze.

Serves 6 as a main bowl, 10 as a small bowl

TAMARIND GLAZE

Tamarind pods can be nearly impossible to find where we live and shop, so we use the liquid concentrate that is available in jars or plastic containers at Asian and Indian markets. Tamarind adds a tangy taste to food, in much the same way as citrus juice does. This glaze freezes well, so if you don't need the entire recipe, simply freeze what is left over for another time.

When using glazes, it's best to apply them during the last moments of cooking or immediately after cooking, since the sugar in the glaze can easily burn.

> 1 cup tamarind concentrate
> ½ cup rice vinegar
> ½ cup (packed) dark brown sugar
> ¼ cup olive oil
> 2 tablespoons nam pla (Asian fish sauce)
> 1 tablespoon chopped peeled fresh ginger

1. Combine all the ingredients in a small saucepan and bring to a boil over medium heat. Reduce the heat to low and simmer, uncovered, until thickened, about 20 minutes. Remove from the heat and cool.

2. Process the mixture in a blender or food processor until smooth. Use immediately, or transfer to an airtight container and store in the refrigerator for up to 2 weeks or freeze for up to 2 months.

Makes about 1¾ cups

Present extra Tamarind Glaze at the table in fanciful, small dipping bowls.

HALIBUT CEVICHE SALAD

Ceviche figures prominently in the cuisines throughout the countries of Latin America. While there are many variations on this preparation, some things always remain the same: Impeccably fresh seafood is marinated in an acid, such as lemon or lime juice, along with onion, an herb of choice, and hot spice. Because the acid "cooks" the fish, you never need to turn on the stove. Once the halibut has marinated, it will be firm to the touch and turn an opaque white, just as it would if cooked by a hot method. For starters, try our creation as is, serving it with crisp flatbreads. Then let your culinary imagination play, adding fruits, vegetables, or flavored oils.

2 pounds very fresh top-quality skinless halibut fillets

½ cup fresh lime juice

½ cup tomato juice

¼ cup rice vinegar

¼ cup extra virgin olive oil

**2 tablespoons Thai Dipping Sauce
   (page 253)**

**½ teaspoon curry powder, preferably homemade
   (page 10)**

**4 fresh jalapeño peppers, stemmed and
   chopped with seeds**

3 cloves garlic, chopped

Salt and freshly ground black pepper, to taste

1 small red onion, cut in half and thinly sliced

**1 pound fresh spinach, preferably flat-leaf, stemmed,
   rinsed, and patted dry**

¼ cup Limette (page 219)

1. With a very sharp knife, cut the halibut into 1-by-1-by-½-inch pieces. Place the pieces in a large stainless-steel or glass bowl and refrigerate, covered, while you prepare the marinade.

If the Fish Ain't Fresh, Forget About It!

It couldn't be truer that freshness is first and foremost when it comes to fish. There are no exceptions. If the fish or the shellfish does not appear, feel, and smell perfectly fresh, don't buy it. We never have our hearts set on any one kind of fish until we get to the market and see what's available. If you are preparing a recipe that calls for a particular fish and are unsure about how to make substitutions, your fish merchant should be able to suggest an alternative.

The fish you buy should be firm to the touch and should smell fresh, not fishy. The scales should be tight to the skin, the gills bright red, and the eyes clear. Shellfish should be purchased in the shell. Make sure that the shells are tightly closed before buying.

2. Combine the lime juice, tomato juice, vinegar, olive oil, dipping sauce, curry powder, jalapeños, garlic, and salt and pepper in a blender or food processor and process until smooth.

3. Pour the marinade over the halibut, add the sliced red onion, and toss gently but thoroughly to coat. Refrigerate, covered, for 1 hour, stirring once or twice.

4. When ready to serve, combine the spinach and Limette in a medium bowl and toss well.

5. Divide the spinach among 6 serving bowls. Adjust the seasonings in the halibut salad, then, using a slotted spoon, spoon it over the spinach. Serve at once.

Serves 6 as a main bowl, 12 as a small bowl

Whimsical platelike bowls are large enough to hold the full recipe of a salad. This one, with its ceramic frog, is perfect for laying out the translucent pieces of halibut on a bed of spinach.

Green Bean and Baby Vegetable Salad

In the past few years, baby vegetables have enjoyed rave reviews from cooks. Their welcome appearance at the table has guaranteed their availability at better produce or specialty markets. Small as they are, everything from baby beets to baby carrots to baby squash are tender, young, and full of flavor. We've combined them here in an irresistibly colorful celebration of youth!

6 baby turnips, peeled

8 ounces thin green beans

10 thin asparagus spears, cut into 1-inch pieces

8 baby carrots, peeled

1 fennel bulb, trimmed and quartered

6 baby zucchini, quartered lengthwise

6 baby yellow squash, quartered lengthwise

½ cup shelled fava beans

6 small shallots, roasted (see Note)

3 cups spinach leaves, preferably flat-leaf, rinsed, patted dry,
   and cut into thin crosswise strips

4 baby red beets and 4 baby golden beets, roasted and peeled
   (see box, page 23)

8 ounces red currant tomatoes or cherry tomatoes

1 cup Shallot-Parsley Vinaigrette (page 224)

1. Bring a large pot of salted water to a boil over high heat and blanch and shock (see box, page 214) each type of vegetable individually, starting with the turnips and ending with the fava beans (do not blanch and shock the shallots, spinach, beets, or tomatoes). As each vegetable is blanched, remove it immediately with a slotted spoon to a bowl of ice water. Then drain and set aside. If not serving immediately, place each type of vegetable in a separate container and set aside.

2. When ready to serve, place the spinach in a large bowl and arrange the vegetables, including the beets, decoratively on top. Heat the vinaigrette in a small nonreactive saucepan over medium heat just to warm it through. Spoon the warm vinaigrette over the salad and serve immediately.

Serves 4 as a main bowl, 8 as a small bowl

Note: Roast shallots as you would garlic (see box, page 48).

Serve out helpings of a baby vegetable salad into cheerfully decorated toddler bowls.

BLANCH AND SHOCK YOUR VEGETABLES

When vegetables and herbs are briefly submerged in boiling water, or blanched, then removed to cold water, it is the icy plunge that shocks or suddenly stops the cooking process. Without an ice bath, even quickly cooked vegetables may turn flaccid and dull. The two-step process is invaluable for precooking just about any vegetable, depending on your purpose.

Blanched and shocked vegetables can be stored in airtight containers in the refrigerator. Add to stews just before serving or use them to make blended oils.

Since blanching and shocking can be done for different purposes, here are some examples of what and why you want to do this:

• To heighten the flavor and intensify the color of tender vegetables, such as peas or asparagus.

• To shorten the cooking time of hardy root vegetables, such as carrots and turnips.

• To set or intensify the color of herbs and leafy greens, such as cilantro.

• To eliminate the sometimes undesirable earthy taste of bean sprouts and snow peas.

• To help rid a vegetable—Brussels sprouts or endive—of its bitterness.

No matter why you're doing it, the way you do it remains the same. The only thing that varies is the blanching time, which will range from a couple of seconds for herbs, leafy greens, and tender vegetables to a minute or two for root vegetables, such as carrots or parsnips, cut into 1- or 2-inch pieces. Tender vegetables, such as summer squash, zucchini, and green beans take less than 1 minute. Because every vegetable has a different cooking time, depending on size and variation of cut, each should be blanched separately. However, you can use the same water for all.

1. Bring water to a boil in a large saucepan over high heat. Have a bowl of ice water ready on the counter.

2. Add herbs to the boiling water for about 2 seconds; vegetables for up to 2 minutes. Remove with a slotted spoon, drain, then plunge into the bowl of ice water. Drain again after 1 minute or less. Be sure to squeeze out all the remaining liquid from the herbs or leafy greens.

Before you get started, make sure the bowl in which you are shocking your vegetables is deep and wide enough to hold plenty of ice water and all the vegetables, too.

WARM POTATO AND WILD MUSHROOM SALAD

Fresh shiitake mushrooms are easy to find in most super-markets. As the seasons change, you may have access to other varieties of mushroom. Try as many as you like to alter the earthy, savory flavor and texture of this salad. For a really elegant presentation and taste sensation, serve this on a bed of lamb's lettuce (mâche) as directed below, then top each serving with a teaspoonful of osetra caviar.

2 bay leaves

4 large Idaho potatoes, peeled and cut into
   uniform medium dice (about 4 cups)

¼ cup finely chopped shallots

4 cloves garlic, roasted (see box, page 48) and
   finely chopped

¼ cup sherry wine vinegar

¼ cup grapeseed oil or other bland vegetable oil

1 tablespoon fresh lemon juice

1 teaspoon honey

1 teaspoon finely chopped fresh thyme leaves

1 cup fresh shiitake mushrooms, stemmed and
   very thinly sliced

¼ cup chopped fresh chives

Salt and freshly ground black pepper, to taste

3 to 4½ cups lamb's lettuce (mâche)

2 to 3 ounces aged goat cheese, shaved
   (optional)

Choose earthy bowls with bright glazes to serve salads with earthy colors and flavors.

1. Bring a medium saucepan of salted water with the bay leaves to a boil over high heat. Add the potatoes, reduce the heat to medium, and cover. Cook until tender, 5 to 10 minutes. Drain the potatoes and return to the pan to cool while you prepare the dressing.

215

2. Combine the shallots, garlic, vinegar, oil, lemon juice, honey, and thyme in a small bowl and beat with a fork to blend. Add the dressing and the sliced wild mushrooms to the potatoes in the pan and toss gently but thoroughly to combine.

3. Set the pan over medium-low heat and heat the mixture just until warmed through, about 3 minutes. Remove from the heat and gently stir in the chives. Remove the bay leaves and season with salt and pepper.

4. Divide the lettuce among individual serving bowls. Top with potato salad and drizzle any pan juices over top of each serving. Garnish with the goat cheese shavings, if desired.

Serves 4 to 6 as a main bowl, 8 to 10 as a small bowl

GRILLED RATATOUILLE SALAD WITH SHERRY-SHALLOT VINAIGRETTE

In this summer ratatouille, each vegetable maintains a distinctive character, each with its own vivid color and bright flavor—red tomatoes, green beans, charred and sweetened eggplant, onion, to name a few. The delicately sweet and mild-flavored chayote, also known as mirliton, especially benefits from grilling, which imparts a gentle smoky taste to the vegetables.

> 2 medium chayotes or yellow summer squash,
>   cut crosswise into ¼-inch slices
> 2 medium red onions, cut crosswise into ½-inch slices
> 1 large zucchini, cut lengthwise into ¼-inch slices
> 1 medium eggplant, cut lengthwise into ¼-inch slices

¼ **cup olive oil**

Salt and freshly ground black pepper, to taste

2 large ripe tomatoes, seeded and cut into medium dice

1 cup fresh green beans, blanched and shocked
    (see box, page 214), cut into 1-inch pieces

½ **cup Kalamata olives, pitted and chopped**

½ **cup Sherry-Shallot Vinaigrette (page 225)**

2 cloves garlic, minced

8 ounces red oak-leaf lettuce, rinsed and patted dry

8 ounces fresh spinach, preferably flat-leaf,
    rinsed and patted dry

3 ounces frisée, rinsed and patted dry

1 tablespoon minced fresh thyme leaves

1 bunch fresh chives, finely chopped

1. Preheat a grill to medium-low.

2. Lightly brush the chayotes, onions, zucchini, and eggplant slices with the olive oil. Season with salt and pepper. Arrange the slices on the grill and grill for 1 minute on each side. Do not overcook. Remove from the grill and cool.

3. Cut the cooled vegetables into medium dice and place them in a large bowl with the tomatoes, green beans, olives, and half of the vinaigrette. Toss gently but thoroughly to combine. Cover and let the vegetables marinate for about 30 minutes. Season, if necessary, with salt and pepper.

4. Combine the lettuce, spinach, and frisée with the remaining vinaigrette in another large bowl and toss gently but thoroughly to coat. Add the thyme and season with salt and pepper.

5. Divide the greens among individual serving bowls. Top with the grilled vegetable salad and sprinkle with the chives.

Serves 4 to 6 as a main bowl

Few of us make soufflés as often as we do salads—and most of us don't make soufflés at all. But the traditional inexpensive soufflé dish makes an unusual and successful salad server.

Spinach Salad With Warm Pecan-Garlic Vinaigrette

Eat Your Spinach!

If you are a spinach fan, there's only one thing you have to know to truly enjoy it: Unless it's canned, frozen, or hydroponically grown, spinach comes to us full of grit. And unless thoroughly rinsed, this healthy, hearty, sometimes celebrated vegetable will bring your mouth to a teeth-grinding halt. To prevent this unpleasantness, plunge stemmed fresh spinach leaves into a bowl of cold water and swirl them around to loosen the grit, allowing it to sink to the bottom. Lift out the spinach, drain and rinse the bowl, and do it all over again until there's no evidence of grit at the bottom of the bowl. Drain the spinach, pat it dry, and it's ready to use.

This is one delicious salad. The heat of a warm vinaigrette wilts the spinach leaves gently, allowing the spinach to maintain an ever-so-slight crispness. Add a crumbling of firm, rich-flavored Stilton and you've got an ideal marriage.

> 4 cloves garlic, roasted (see box, page 48)
> ½ cup chopped pecans, toasted (see box, page 137)
> 1½ tablespoons sugar
> ⅛ cup red wine vinegar
> ½ cup olive oil
> Salt and freshly ground black pepper, to taste
> 1 pound fresh spinach, preferably flat-leaf, stemmed, rinsed, and patted dry
> ½ cup crumbled Stilton cheese or another good-quality blue cheese

1. Combine the garlic, pecans, and sugar in a blender or food processor and process until smooth. Add the vinegar. With the motor running, add the olive oil in a slow, steady stream and blend until thoroughly incorporated. Season with salt and pepper. Transfer the vinaigrette to a small nonreactive saucepan and heat over medium heat just to warm through.

2. Meanwhile, arrange the spinach leaves in a large bowl. Spoon the warm vinaigrette over the spinach, sprinkle the Stilton on top, and toss gently but thoroughly to combine. Serve at once.

Serves 6 as a small bowl

Salad Dressings

LEMONETTE

Grapeseed oil is a clear, cholesterol-free, clean-tasting oil that adds no flavor. When combined with other fresh-tasting ingredients as it is here or as it is in Limette (below), Cilantro Vinaigrette (page 220), and Mango Vinaigrette (page 21), it produces a memorably refreshing dressing. Serve with any combination of mixed greens.

> ½ **cup fresh lemon juice**
> I **tablespoon rice vinegar**
> ½ **cup grapeseed oil (see headnote)**
> **Salt and freshly ground black pepper, to taste**

Combine the lemon juice and vinegar in a small nonreactive bowl and beat with a wire whisk to blend. Whisk in the grapeseed oil in a slow, steady stream. Season with salt and pepper. Use immediately, or transfer to an airtight container and store in the refrigerator for up to 1 week.

Makes about I cup

LIMETTE

The tartness of the lime juice in this dressing is held in check by the sweetness of the mirin (Japanese rice wine). If mirin isn't available, substitute sugar.

> ¼ **cup fresh lime juice**
> 2 **tablespoons rice vinegar**
> 2 **tablespoons mirin, or substitute I tablespoon sugar**
> ½ **cup grapeseed oil (see Lemonette headnote, above)**
> **Salt and freshly ground black pepper, to taste**

Combine the lime juice, vinegar, and mirin in a small nonreactive bowl and beat with a wire whisk to blend. Whisk in the grapeseed oil in a slow, steady stream. Season with salt and pepper. Use immediately, or transfer to an airtight container and store in the refrigerator for up to 1 week.

Makes I cup

MIRIN, MIRIN, ON THE WALL . . .

Stock a bottle of this syrupy, light yellow rice wine on your pantry shelf. Consumed strictly in cooking, mirin is especially good when a little is combined with other ingredients and used to glaze fish. We find ourselves drizzling mirin in every savory dish that needs a little sweetener and never feel restricted to Japanese-style recipes.

Be careful not to confuse mirin with sake or rice vinegar. Although each is made from sticky rice, the latter is vinegar. And if you don't have mirin, don't substitute sake sweetened with sugar; simply use sugar alone: I teaspoon sugar replaces I tablespoon mirin. Purchase mirin at Japanese food stores or liquor stores.

CILANTRO VINAIGRETTE

A cilantro lover's dream, this vinaigrette is a light tribute to summer. The grapeseed oil imparts no flavor, while the vinegar punches up the taste of the refreshing herb. A simple salad of julienned cucumber and chopped tomato benefits greatly from a drizzle of this. For a heartier dose, use it as a marinade for a thick piece of snapper or bass before grilling it over a charcoal or wood fire.

¼ **cup (tightly packed) fresh cilantro leaves**

½ **cup grapeseed oil (see Lemonette headnote, page 219)**

⅛ **cup rice vinegar**

Salt and freshly ground black pepper, to taste

1. Combine the cilantro and ¼ cup of the grapeseed oil in a blender or food processor and process until smooth.

2. Combine the remaining ¼ cup oil and the vinegar in a medium bowl and beat with a wire whisk to blend thoroughly. Whisk in the cilantro purée. Season with salt and pepper. Use immediately, or transfer to an airtight container and store in the refrigerator for 2 to 3 days.

Makes about ¾ cup

MANGO VINAIGRETTE

A fruit, the mango can also be served unripe as a vegetable. Here we enjoy its delectable, exceedingly juicy ripe sweetness with little embellishment. The smooth flesh of the mango gives this vinaigrette a silken quality. Brush on fish or chicken or drizzle generously over Chili-Marinated Grilled Shrimp (page 183) as soon as they come off the grill. Or serve as a dip for spicy empanadas.

2 ripe mangoes, peeled, pitted, and chopped (see box, page 222)
⅛ cup fresh lemon juice
⅛ cup cider vinegar
1½ tablespoons (packed) light brown sugar
½ tablespoon chopped peeled fresh ginger
Pinch ground cinnamon
⅛ cup grapeseed oil (see Lemonette headnote, page 219)

Combine the mangoes, lemon juice, vinegar, ginger, brown sugar, and cinnamon in a blender or food processor and process until smooth. With the motor running, add the oil in a slow, steady stream and blend in thoroughly. Use immediately, or transfer to an airtight container and store in the refrigerator for up to 1 week.

Makes about 1 cup

MAKING THE MOST OF MANGOES

The exotic mango has been adored for centuries, but nowhere has it been celebrated more than in India, its land of origin, where more than 2,500 years ago, Buddha is touted to have been the original mango lover.

Today mango trees grow around the world in temperate climates. Although mangoes are cultivated in California and Florida, the U.S. imports most of its supply from Mexico, the West Indies, and South America, not only because they are cheaper, but also because they are available year-round.

Any way you choose to enjoy this succulent fruit—raw or cooked, ripe or unripe—you must first peel away its tough, thin skin. Then its intensely juicy flesh must be carved away from the long, tongue-shaped pit.

To peel and slice a mango: Hold the mango lengthwise in the palm of one hand and, with a sharp paring knife or peeler, carefully peel off half the skin. Then cut the flesh in lengthwise slices, at an angle to form wedges, down to the pit; cutting in wedges releases the pit from the flesh. Repeat the process on the other half of the mango. Continue to slice, or dice, or eat as desired.

PORCINI VINAIGRETTE

This vinaigrette is unbelievably versatile. It's fabulous used warm on tossed greens or spooned over ravioli. Chilled, it's great on salad or drizzled over a main course. No matter how you serve it, be sure to have some crusty bread on hand to sop up any leftover dressing at the bottom of the bowl.

I cup Vegetable Stock for Mediterranean Bowls (page 29)

½ cup red wine vinegar

½ cup dry white wine

¼ cup Porcini Garlic Paste (page 242)

I stalk lemongrass, bottom finely chopped

2 shallots, chopped

I teaspoon coriander seeds, toasted (see box, page 137) and ground

½ cup extra virgin olive oil

Salt and freshly ground black pepper, to taste

1. Combine the stock, vinegar, wine, and Porcini Garlic Paste in a small nonreactive saucepan and bring to a boil over medium heat. Cook, uncovered, until reduced by half, about 20 minutes. Remove from the heat and cool.

2. Combine the reduced stock mixture, lemongrass, shallots, and coriander seeds in a blender or food processor and process until smooth. With the motor running, add the olive oil in a slow, steady stream and blend in thoroughly. Season with salt and pepper. Use immediately, or transfer to an airtight container and store in the refrigerator for up to 2 weeks.

Makes about 1½ cups

Pour or spoon this almost meaty-tasting vinaigrette from a gravy boat.

MUSTARD-POTATO CREAM VINAIGRETTE

How do you create an interesting recipe? Take a simple, common ingredient, like vinegar, and use it in an uncommon way. Here vinegar combines with puréed creamed potatoes to become a one-of-a-kind vinaigrette that can be used as a dressing or as a sauce. For another twist, try roasting (instead of boiling) potatoes and/or cauliflower, carrots, and parsnips, then toss them with this unusual vinaigrette, and serve warm or cold.

¾ **pound Idaho potatoes, peeled and cut into ½-inch dice**

½ **cup milk**

¼ **cup heavy (or whipping) cream**

2 **tablespoons prepared horseradish**

1½ **tablespoons Dijon mustard**

1 **tablespoon mustard oil**

2 **tablespoons sherry wine vinegar**

Salt and freshly ground black pepper, to taste

1. Combine the potatoes, milk, cream, horseradish, mustard, and mustard oil in a medium saucepan and bring to a boil over medium heat. Reduce the heat to low, cover, and simmer 15 minutes. Remove from the heat and cool.

2. Combine the potato mixture and vinegar in a blender or food processor and process until smooth. Season with salt and pepper. If necessary, add water to thin. Use immediately, or transfer to an airtight container and store in the refrigerator for up to 1 week.

Makes about 2 cups

Shallot-Parsley Vinaigrette

Multi-purposed and beautiful, too, this bright green vinaigrette is splendid warm or at room temperature. It is delicious on poached fish or shellfish, or try it on your favorite pasta. It's lighter than most store-bought vinaigrettes because, proportionately, it is made with less oil.

2 cups Vegetable Stock for Mediterranean Bowls (page 29)
½ cup dry white wine
1 bunch fresh Italian (flat-leaf) parsley, stemmed and roughly chopped
3 shallots, chopped
1 teaspoon coriander seeds, toasted (see box, page 137) and ground
½ cup extra virgin olive oil
Juice of 1 lemon, or to taste
Salt and freshly ground black pepper, to taste

1. Combine the vegetable stock and wine in a medium nonreactive saucepan and bring to a boil over medium heat. Cook, uncovered, until reduced by half, about 20 minutes. Remove from the heat and cool.

2. Combine the reduced stock mixture, shallots, and coriander seeds in a blender or food processor and process until smooth. With the motor running, add the olive oil in a slow, steady stream and blend in thoroughly. Season with lemon juice and salt and pepper. Use immediately, or transfer to an airtight container and store in the refrigerator for 2 to 3 days.

Makes 1¾ cups

SHERRY-SHALLOT VINAIGRETTE

U sing an imported sherry vinegar determines the success of this recipe. It is what makes this vinaigrette so very good. We highly recommend a Spanish import. Since Spain is where sherry originated, Spanish sherry vinegar is the best. You'll find it at specialty food markets. Keep the bottle refrigerated to ensure a long shelf life.

Use this vinaigrette on any salad and as a dipping sauce for grilled vegetables. It's so enticing you won't be able to leave a trace on your plate.

¼ **cup sherry wine vinegar, preferably Spanish**
2 **tablespoons honey**
1 **shallot, minced**
½ **teaspoon freshly ground black pepper**
½ **cup extra virgin olive oil**
Salt, to taste

Adorable little square-shape bowls are easy to stack and store and come in handy for holding portion-size dipping sauces.

Combine the vinegar, honey, shallot, and pepper in a small nonreactive bowl and beat with a wire whisk to blend. Whisk in the olive oil in a slow, steady stream. Season with salt. Use immediately, or store in an airtight container in the refrigerator for up to 1 week.

Makes about 1 cup

TOMATO-GARLIC VINAIGRETTE

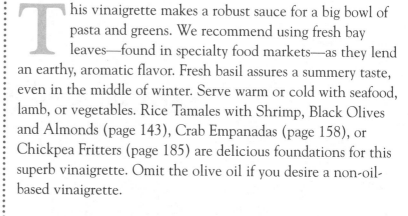

This vinaigrette makes a robust sauce for a big bowl of pasta and greens. We recommend using fresh bay leaves—found in specialty food markets—as they lend an earthy, aromatic flavor. Fresh basil assures a summery taste, even in the middle of winter. Serve warm or cold with seafood, lamb, or vegetables. Rice Tamales with Shrimp, Black Olives and Almonds (page 143), Crab Empanadas (page 158), or Chickpea Fritters (page 185) are delicious foundations for this superb vinaigrette. Omit the olive oil if you desire a non-oil-based vinaigrette.

You can never have enough small serving bowls. They're so useful for dips, sauces, and extra dressing.

**4 large fresh ripe tomatoes, peeled, seeded,
    and diced, or one 28-ounce can whole tomatoes,
    drained and seeded**
½ cup cloves garlic, roasted (see box, page 48)
¼ cup red wine vinegar
10 fresh basil leaves
3 bay leaves, preferably fresh
½ cup extra virgin olive oil
Salt, to taste

1. Combine the tomatoes, roasted garlic, vinegar, basil leaves, and bay leaves in a large nonreactive saucepan and cook, uncovered, over medium heat for 30 minutes, stirring occasionally. Remove from the heat and cool. Remove the bay leaves.

2. Transfer the tomato-garlic mixture to a blender or food processor and process until smooth. With the motor running, add the olive oil in a slow, steady stream and blend in thoroughly. Season with salt. Use immediately, or transfer to an airtight container and store in the refrigerator for up to 1 week.

Makes about 2¼ cups

EGGLESS CAESAR DRESSING

Italian chef Caesar Cardini was credited with the creation of the original Caesar dressing. Once voted the greatest recipe to originate from the Americas in fifty years, it might be argued that to omit the eggs would be to commit a culinary sin. We believe that with recent increased concern over salmonella poisoning from raw eggs, it makes good sense to leave them out. Were Cardini to be unhappy about that omission, he probably wouldn't be in favor of the addition of anchovies, either. But we like them, as they contribute richer flavor. The choice is yours.

¼ **cup cloves garlic, roasted (see box, page 48)**
¼ **cup Dijon mustard**
¼ **cup fresh lemon juice**
4 imported canned anchovies, drained (optional)
¾ **cup extra virgin olive oil**
¼ **cup cold water, or as necessary**
Salt and freshly ground black pepper, to taste

1. Combine the garlic, mustard, lemon juice, and anchovies, if using, in a blender or food processor and process until smooth. With the motor running, add the olive oil in a slow, steady stream and blend until thoroughly incorporated.

2. Slowly add cold water as necessary to thin the dressing to the desired consistency. Season with salt and pepper.

3. Use immediately, or transfer to an airtight container and store in the refrigerator for up to 2 weeks.

Makes about 1½ cups

Anchovies: The Fish People Love to Hate

These delicious tiny, silvery fish often come salt-cured and canned in oil. Many people don't like them, finding the bottled or canned fillets too fishy and too salty. However, when heated, they dissolve almost entirely, leaving behind a pleasant salty taste. Once opened, anchovies can be refrigerated for up to 2 months in an airtight container, and you'll have them on hand for pastas, soups, and salads. To reduce their saltiness, soak in cool water for about 30 minutes, then dry on paper towels. Use sparingly to flavor.

GINGER DRESSING

All too often what could have been a palate-pleasing salad is shortchanged by a less than enticing dressing. Dress a green salad in a remarkable blend of flavors such as these and you will have guests reaching for more. This dressing enhances any combination of greens. It also makes a snappy dipping sauce for grilled seafood. The recipe can be halved, if desired.

> 1 medium carrot, peeled and coarsely chopped
> ¼ cup chopped onion
> ¼ cup rice vinegar
> ¼ cup soy sauce
> 1½ tablespoons chopped peeled fresh ginger
> 1 tablespoon chopped peeled lemon pulp
> 1 tablespoon ketchup
> ¼ teaspoon shichimi togarashi (see box, page 115)
> ¼ cup water
> ½ cup grapeseed oil (see Lemonette headnote, page 219)

The edging on these charming side servers makes them stand out next to plainer main bowls.

1. Combine the carrot, onion, vinegar, soy sauce, ginger, lemon pulp, ketchup, and spice mix in a blender or food processor and process until smooth. Add the water and process to blend. With the motor running, add the grapeseed oil in a slow, steady stream and blend until thoroughly incorporated. Use immediately, or transfer to an airtight container and store in the refrigerator for up to 1 week.

2. Just before using, whisk the dressing to blend the ingredients.

Makes about 2½ cups

STRIKING OIL:
A SELECTION OF INFUSED OILS

Remember standing in a specialty food market admiring those tall, glamorous, glimmering bottles of flavored oil? Most likely you didn't buy one because it was expensive and you weren't sure what it would taste like or whether you'd even like the taste; whether you'd use it up or even use it at all; or end up relegating it to a kitchen shelf or countertop as decor by default.

Suffer the question—to buy or not to buy?—no more. Make your own subtly flavored oil at a fraction of the cost. Choose the flavors you like the best, the quantities you are sure to use, the bottles you have on hand—decorative, practical, or both—and a technique that suits your needs.

There are two ways of infusing oil, with heat and without. Both are easy to do. While you decide on the type of oil to infuse (keep in mind that a neutral-tasting oil will accentuate the infusion's own distinct flavor), the herb, spice, or fruit that is going to flavor that oil determines the method of infusion. For example, the flavor of a high-quality, freshly chopped herb or freshly ground spice is best extracted by the cold method—allowing it to sit lightly covered with oil in a glass or stainless-steel container for 2 to 3 days. But there are always exceptions. Some ingredients, such as fresh ginger, dried chili peppers, and annatto seeds, need gentle heat to bring out their flavors and colors. Cardamom, coriander, cumin, and fennel seeds, to mention a handful of others, become bitter when steeped in hot oil. Fresh, delicate herbs, such as basil, dill, and cilantro, always come out best when first blanched and shocked to enhance and hold color before infusing via the cold method. Still other heartier herbs, such as rosemary, oregano, and thyme, impart fuller flavor when heated slowly in oil in a heavy-bottomed pot to 140°F for 10 minutes, transferred to a bowl to cool, and allowed to sit for a day before using.

Don't be shy about using a serving bowl as a workbowl as well. Having an attractive piece at your side to hold chopped herbs can make the preparation more pleasant.

BASIL OIL

On a hot summer night, when the thought of cooking dinner is too much to bear, let this oil rescue you. Just cut a big juicy beef-steak tomato into wedges, place them in a medium-deep bowl, drizzle with this aromatic oil, grab a chunk of bread, pour a glass of chilled white wine, and retire to the patio.

This oil can also be used on any variety of greens and pastas or in a marinade. It's best when fresh, so use quickly.

2 cups (tightly packed) fresh basil leaves
1 cup (tightly packed) Italian (flat-leaf) parsley leaves
1½ cups olive oil

1. Have a bowl of ice water ready on the counter.

2. Bring a large saucepan of water to a boil over high heat. Add the herbs to the boiling water and blanch several seconds only. Drain immediately, then plunge into the ice water. Drain well again, and squeeze out all the liquid.

3. Process the herbs and oil in a blender until smooth. Strain, if desired, through a fine sieve. Store in a tightly capped clean jar in the refrigerator for up to 1 week.

Makes about 2½ cups

CILANTRO OIL

Blanching and shocking the herbs here significantly brightens the color they impart to the oil. Now it offers not only lively flavor but stunning visual effect as well. We like this drizzled on fish, such as salmon or halibut, and on chicken. This recipe can be halved, if desired.

1 cup (tightly packed) fresh cilantro leaves
½ cup (tightly packed) fresh Italian (flat-leaf) parsley leaves
2 cups olive oil

A lipped bowl makes it easy to drizzle infused oil over your salad or into a soup.

1. Have a bowl of ice water ready on the counter.

2. Bring a large saucepan of water to a boil over high heat. Add the herbs to the boiling water and blanch for several seconds only. Drain, then plunge into the ice water. Drain well again, and squeeze out all the liquid.

3. Process the herbs and oil in a blender until smooth. Store in a tightly capped clean jar in the refrigerator for up to 1 week. Use this oil unstrained.

Makes 3 cups

MINT OIL

We use grapeseed oil here because of its mild, neutral flavor and do not recommend substituting any other oil in this recipe. The result is a versatile blend that performs as well on fruit and vegetable salads as it does on desserts—yes, desserts, such as Wine-Poached Pears (page 293) and Mango Ginger Ice Cream (page 280). Grapeseed oil is available in supermarkets.

> **½ cup (tightly packed) fresh mint leaves**
> **2 cups grapeseed oil**

1. Have a bowl of ice water ready on the counter.

2. Bring a large saucepan of water to a boil over high heat. Add the mint to the boiling water and blanch several seconds only. Drain immediately, then plunge into the ice water. Drain well again, and squeeze out all the liquid.

3. Process the mint and oil in a blender until smooth. Strain, if desired, through a fine sieve. Store in a tightly capped clean jar in the refrigerator for up to 1 week.

Makes about 2 cups

A small bowl with decorative handles makes a nice way to pass around a flavorful oil or dressing at the table.

ANNATTO OIL

We use this light oil to perk up the color rather than the flavor of a dish. See what it does for our Chili-Marinated Grilled Shrimp (page 183), and take it from there.

I tablespoon annatto (achiote) seeds
I cup light olive or other light vegetable oil

I. Heat the oil in a heavy skillet over medium heat. Add the annatto seeds, turn off the heat, and allow them to steep until their color is a vibrant red, about 2 hours.

2. Strain the oil through a fine mesh strainer, and store in a tightly capped clean jar in the refrigerator for up to 1 week.

Makes I cup

HOT CHILI OIL

Some Love It Hot

Vary the intensity of this oil by choosing different pepper combinations. We like dried ancho chilies for their mildly hot character. For flaming-hot oil, though, substitute dried cayenne or habanero peppers.

When your desire for spicy food overpowers the wishes of the other diners at your table, don't fret. This oil can be placed tableside for added heat whenever and wherever desired. Drizzled, it satisfies even the fiercest of fire-eating palates. It's also excellent for cooking, stir-frying in particular, but stand clear of the smoke; hot-pepper-infused oil fumes can be irritating to the eyes and throat.

3 dried ancho chilies
I tablespoon crushed red pepper flakes
2 cloves garlic, crushed
2 cups olive oil

I. Steep the ancho chilies in hot water to cover in a small bowl until soft, about 40 minutes.

2. Drain the chilies and squeeze dry. Transfer to a food processor, add the red pepper flakes, and process until smooth.

3. Combine the puréed chilies, garlic, and olive oil in a small saucepan. Heat over medium heat until the oil begins to ripple. Remove from the heat and cool. Strain the cooled oil through damp coffee filters, changing the filter each time until the oil is clear. Store in a tightly capped clean jar in the refrigerator for up to 1 month.

Makes 2 cups

YELLOW CURRY OIL

This oil adds great roasted curry flavor when drizzled over grilled meats or fish. Or use on bread—instead of butter. It also makes a tasty vinaigrette when mixed with cider vinegar. Simpler still, toss rice noodles with this, then garnish with chopped chives. This recipe can be halved, if desired.

> **2 cups olive oil**
> **¼ cup curry powder, preferably homemade (page 10)**
> **1 teaspoon ground turmeric**
> **1 teaspoon five-spice powder**
> **1 teaspoon black peppercorns**
> **2 shallots, finely minced**

1. Heat ¼ cup of the olive oil in a small heavy saucepan over medium heat. Add the spices and shallots and reduce the heat to low. Sauté for 2 minutes. Add the remaining oil, bring to a simmer, and simmer, uncovered, for 15 minutes. Remove from the heat and cool.

2. Strain the cooled oil through a damp coffee filter into a clean jar. Cap tightly and store in the refrigerator for up to 3 months.

Makes about 2 cups

Little potlike bowls are versatile enough to use as serving pieces for sauces and oils.

The handy plate under this covered bowl makes a good resting place for a small spoon or ladle that travels with a dressing as it is passed around the table.

GARLIC OIL

We consider this oil a pantry essential, as good drizzled on breads and over pastas as it is in salads and stuffings. Or use it in place of olive oil for sautéing.

1 cup peeled cloves garlic
2 cups olive oil

Combine the garlic and oil in a small heavy saucepan and heat over low-to-medium heat just until the garlic browns slightly. Turn off the heat and let the garlic steep in the warm oil for 1 hour. Strain the oil through a damp coffee filter into a tightly capped clean jar and store in the refrigerator for up to 1 month.

Makes about 2 cups

PARSLEY AND GARLIC OIL

Use this as a dressing over a mixed green salad, as a marinade for grilled shrimp or vegetables, or as a flavoring in soups and stews. Or use as a dip alongside bowls of steamed shellfish.

1 cup olive oil
1 cup fresh Italian (flat-leaf) parsley leaves, finely chopped
1 cup rinsed and dried chopped arugula leaves
8 cloves garlic, roasted (see box, page 48) and chopped
6 scallions, green part only, finely chopped
1 teaspoon salt
½ teaspoon freshly ground black pepper

1. Combine the olive oil, parsley, arugula, garlic, and scallions in a medium bowl. Let stand at room temperature for 2 to 3 hours.

2. If not using immediately, store in a tightly capped clean jar in the refrigerator for up to 3 days. Season with the salt and pepper before using. Use this oil unstrained.

Makes about 2 cups

Chapter 7

GREAT LITTLE BOWLS OF FIRE AND SPICE

Pastes, Rubs, Seasonings & Sauces

When we were growing up in America our parents had in their kitchens what was affectionately regarded as the spice rack. Some of the more familiar "spices" decoratively displayed in that rack were, in fact, dried herbs—oregano, basil, dill, parsley. Nestled alongside small glass bottles of these dried herbs were ground cinnamon, nutmeg, cream of tartar, garlic powder, onion powder, and last but not least, Accent—that magical glistening flavor enhancer we later discovered was monosodium glutamate (MSG). Progress meant never having to spend time chopping fresh green herbs or wipe eyes made watery by pungent onions.

But, this is precisely what both of us yearn for. The aromatic dried seeds, barks, buds, and berries of spices are considered aromatic because what you smell is what you taste. As émigrés from every ethnic tradition carry out their culinary customs in big cities and small towns all across America, a vast array of spices from around the world have made their way into our markets. Although different cultures lean more heavily toward certain spices and spice blends, we've found plenty of crossover. For example, moist spice blends, called *recados* in Mexico, *kaeng wan* in Thailand, and *harissa* in Morocco, are each ground or pounded to a wet paste and used as rubs to marinate and seal in flavor. Each share in common the use of garlic and chili, but are distinctive in other ways: cloves and cinnamon are common to most Mexican blends, while lemongrass and ginger are basic to Thai curries, and cumin and coriander to Moroccan seasonings.

A paste invariably combines spices and/or herbs, garlic, or ginger with oils, stock, or citrus juice. In short, it is wet and spreadable. Pastes seal in flavor and can tenderize. Because they coat, they frequently form wonderful savory crusts. A dry rub, on the other hand, combines herbs and spices, plus other ingredients, but no liquid. Rubs tend to be more intense in flavor, are not spreadable, and are actually best when patted on or rubbed in. Sprinkling is best for seasonings.

Spices are versatile and should be exploited to their full potential. Just as you would use salt and pepper to season, feel free to use these spice blends—for rubbing on meats, poultry, or fish to seal in natural flavors; in sautés; in crusts; and for infusing oils. Roast your spices to bring out their essential oils, to round out their flavor, and to infuse the air with their exotic aromas. The freshness of any spice is critical to its flavor. When preparing spice blends, grind only what you need and be sure to hold them in airtight containers away from light.

Use the pastes that follow to punch up the flavor of a sauce, as in a dipping sauce for dumplings, or stir a little bit into one of our broths or vinaigrettes. Most of them keep for two weeks, which should be plenty of time for you to find clever ways to enjoy them.

Our selection of sauces, like much of the cooking in this book, is eclectic and ranges from fiery Horseradish Rouille to milder Pumpkin Seed Sauce to sweet Sherry and Garlic Soy Sauce. Each recipe comes with a starter suggestion or two for serving, but again, don't limit yourself to just those.

It's so easy to infuse flavor and complexity into simple preparations with pastes and rubs, seasonings and sauces. Here are our suggestions for trying them; start at the beginning and work your way to the end. One day serve an Indian-inspired Yellow Curry Oil with Chicken Pot Stickers or try our Thai-flavored Cilantro Vinaigrette with Shrimp Quesadillas. Another day, stir the oil into soup and toss a salad with the vinaigrette. And keep going, just like that, experimenting all the way through to the end. Keep a list of all the different sensational flavors—there are a lot of them, and a lot of them you are going to really like. These may be small bowls, but these are not small flavors. For that reason alone, this may be our favorite chapter.

Pastes and Rubs

SPICY CILANTRO SOY PASTE

Wondering how to use this paste? Spread a bit on chicken skewers before grilling, or add a few drops to Dreamy Creamy Corn (page 264). Or, use it to change the very character of Thai Dipping Sauce (page 253) by blending in a spoonful. First mix a dab of the paste into a small amount of the sauce, then, when you're satisfied with the flavor, blend a proportionate amount into the rest of the sauce.

- **I cup (packed) fresh cilantro leaves**
- **¼ cup extra virgin olive oil**
- **2 tablespoons mushroom soy sauce or regular soy sauce**
- **2 tablespoons roasted garlic (see box, page 48)**
- **I fresh serrano or jalapeño pepper, stemmed and seeded**

Combine all the ingredients in a food processor or blender and process until smooth. Use immediately, or transfer to an airtight container and store in the refrigerator for up to 2 weeks. Bring to room temperature before using.

Makes about I cup

GARLIC AND HERB PASTE

Pastes are equally effective used as rubs or as an added flavoring agent. Rely on them when a fast and easy alternative to a full-bodied sauce is desired. Add just a couple of tablespoons to hot chicken stock, then reduce by half, and you have an intensely flavored and delicious sauce for grilled chicken, a dip for vegetables, or a spread for grilled bread.

¼ cup roasted garlic (see box, page 48)

½ cup cilantro leaves, chopped

2 tablespoons chopped fresh basil

2 tablespoons ground coriander

1 tablespoon chopped fresh thyme

Combine all the ingredients in a blender or food processor and process until smooth. Transfer to an airtight container and store in the refrigerator for up to 2 weeks.

Makes about ¾ cup

OLIVE AND BASIL PASTE

Add a tablespoon or two of this paste to some Chicken Stock for Mediterranean bowls, then reduce it by half to a sauce consistency, and you'll have a truly Italian dressing for any kind of pasta. Or spread this as is on toasted bread, then top it with tomatoes and cheese or onions, and you have bruschetta.

1 cup (tightly packed) basil leaves

¾ cup Niçoise olives, pitted

¼ cup capers, rinsed and drained

¼ cup roasted garlic (see box, page 48)

¼ cup fresh lemon juice

½ teaspoon cayenne pepper

¾ cup extra virgin olive oil

Combine the basil, olives, capers, garlic, lemon juice, and cayenne in a blender or food processor and process until smooth. With the motor running, add the olive oil in a slow, steady stream and blend in thoroughly. Use immediately, or transfer to an airtight container and store in the refrigerator for up to 2 weeks. Bring to room temperature before using.

Makes about 1½ cups

OLIVE TIPS

Never ever substitute salted, stuffed cocktail olives for properly brined (like Spanish) or preserved olives (like Kalamata and Niçoise). There are so many good imported olives from the Mediterranean basin and Latin America to choose from that all you need to do is to decide which flavor, size, or color you want. And whether the olive you have in mind is black, green, brown, or purple, it is still an olive, just at a different stage of ripeness: Green olives are always young, whereas dark olives are always mature. If you preserve your olives in oil (or purchase them that way), they will last indefinitely, so why not keep a few of your favorite varieties on hand?

To pit olives packed in brine: Place the olive on your work surface, lay the flat side of a chef's knife over it, and hit the blade with your fist to smash the flesh. The flesh will now separate easily from the pit; just pick it out with your fingers.

To pit olives cured in oil: Simply squeeze the olives with your fingers to force out the pits.

THAI FISH PASTE

This paste is so intensely flavored and concentrated that you'll find that it takes only a small amount to achieve some very big results. That said, it will prove a tremendous addition to Asian-flavored sauces and broths in general, as well as main bowls like our Thai Paella (page 140).

3 tablespoons tomato paste

2 tablespoons dried shrimp (see box, page 29)

2 tablespoons roasted garlic (see box, page 48)

2 tablespoons finely chopped peeled fresh ginger

I tablespoon Sichuan peppercorns

I tablespoon chili paste

I tablespoon Hot Chili Oil (page 232)

I medium shallot, chopped

I stalk fresh lemongrass, bottom only, finely chopped

Combine all the ingredients in a blender or food processor and process to the consistency of paste. Use immediately, or transfer to an airtight container and store in the refrigerator for up to 2 weeks.

Makes about ¾ cup

PORCINI GARLIC PASTE

The smooth, dense texture and strong woodsy flavor of porcini mushrooms are what makes them so desirable. And while you'll almost never find them fresh, you will love the flavor the dried ones deliver once they have been reconstituted in warm water for about 30 minutes.

Spread this robust-tasting paste on toast or use it on a baked potato. The flavor is so rich that only a small amount is needed to create or transform a dish. Toss with pasta for a quick fix, or add this to everyday stew to lend unique aromatic complexity.

> **2 ounces dried porcini**
> **1 cup very hot water**
> **2 tablespoons roasted garlic (see box, page 48)**
> **½ teaspoon crushed red pepper flakes (optional)**
> **¼ cup olive oil**

1. Soak the dried porcini in the hot water until soft, about 30 minutes. Drain, reserving the liquid. Strain the liquid in a fine mesh sieve lined with cheesecloth.

2. Combine the mushrooms, garlic, pepper flakes if using, and 3 tablespoons of the soaking liquid in a blender or food processor and process until smooth. With the motor running, add the olive oil in a slow, steady stream and blend in thoroughly. Use immediately, or transfer to an airtight container and store in the refrigerator for up to 2 weeks. Bring to room temperature before using.

Makes about 1 cup

Odd-shaped porcelain bowls in light colors have just enough depth to hold extra mushroom-garlic paste for those who want more on their pasta.

EARTHY TREASURES

The single most important benefit of dried porcini is that they are available year-round. No other dried mushroom equals porcini. Their earthy, robust intensity enhances the flavor of every savory recipe they are added to. Reconstituted in very hot (not boiling) water, stock, wine, or vinegar, porcini are welcome additions, whole or cut, to risottos, soups, stews, and warm salads, and 1 ounce of dried porcini is enough for six to eight servings of any of these. The soaking liquid has a power of its own; when incorporated into sauces, vinaigrettes, glazes, and soups it enriches and deepens flavor.

To reconstitute porcini: Cover 2 ounces mushrooms with 1 cup hot liquid in a bowl. Soak for 30 minutes. Lift the porcini out of the soaking liquid with a slotted spoon and squeeze out any remaining liquid. Rinse thoroughly under running water to remove any remaining grit. To use the soaking liquid, strain it through a fine mesh sieve lined with cheesecloth. The resulting liquid will have an intense mushroom flavor.

Dried porcini also make a delicious rub when ground to a powder and dusted on fish, meat, or poultry before searing, grilling, or roasting. Stored in an airtight container, dried porcini will keep indefinitely.

GINGER PASTE

Add a spot of this potent paste to a bowl of noodles, or stir a teaspoonful of it into vinaigrette, or swirl a dab into mayonnaise. It is versatile and will prove a handy condiment in your pantry.

The long cooking time—two hours—mellows the intensity of the ginger, which means you can use the paste generously, without fear of its flavor overwhelming other foods.

½ **pound fresh ginger, peeled and cut into 1-inch pieces**
½ **shallot, chopped**
1 **clove garlic**
2 **tablespoons olive oil**

1. Combine the ginger, shallot, and garlic in a medium saucepan. Add water to cover and bring to a boil over medium heat. Reduce the heat to low and simmer, uncovered, until the ginger is soft enough to purée, about 2 hours. Every 20 minutes or so, drain off the water and add fresh boiling water to cover. When the ginger is soft, drain and cool.

2. Transfer the ginger mixture to a food processor and process until smooth. With the motor running, add the olive oil in a slow, steady stream and blend in thoroughly. Use immediately, or transfer to an airtight container and store in the refrigerator for up to 2 weeks.

Makes about ½ cup

YELLOW DUST

Spice rubs are a simple and fast way to dress up an uninspired piece of poultry or seafood or enhance a meat dish. This assertive-tasting rub performs an outstanding job on fresh tuna steaks or beef filet. Cardamom, the most pronounced spice in the blend, is a member of the ginger family and contributes singular spiciness. This recipe makes enough for about three pounds of fish or meat.

> **3 tablespoons black peppercorns**
> **3 tablespoons cumin seeds**
> **1 tablespoon cardamom seeds**
> **1 tablespoon coriander seeds**
> **2 tablespoons ground turmeric**

1. Combine the peppercorns and all the seeds in a dry medium skillet over medium heat and heat, shaking the pan continuously to prevent burning, until the seeds are fragrant and just beginning to smoke, 1 to 2 minutes.

2. Transfer the seeds to a bowl to cool, then grind to a powder in a spice grinder. Add the ground turmeric and blend. Use immediately, or store in an airtight container in a cool, dry place for up to 2 months.

Makes about ½ cup

An Aromatic Rub

This recipe presents a counterbalance of Asian and Mediterranean flavors. Simply massage the blend into the surface of the meat before cooking. It makes enough for about three pounds of pork or poultry.

> **2 tablespoons Sichuan peppercorns**
> **4 star anise**
> **1 tablespoon fennel seeds**
> **½ teaspoon cardamom seeds**
> **¼ cup (packed) dark brown sugar**
> **¼ cup coarse (kosher) salt**
> **1 teaspoon saffron threads**

1. Combine the peppercorns, star anise, fennel seeds, and cardamom seeds in a dry medium skillet over medium heat and heat, shaking the pan continuously to prevent burning, until the spices are fragrant and just beginning to smoke, 1 to 2 minutes.

2. Transfer the mixture to a bowl to cool, then grind to a powder in a spice grinder.

3. Return the mixture to the bowl, add the sugar, salt, and saffron, and stir to mix. Use immediately, or transfer to an airtight container and store in a cool, dry place for up to 2 months.

Makes about ¾ cup

A bowl inside a bowl inside a bowl—nesting conserves storage space.

BODY RUBS

Applying a spice rub before roasting meats, poultry, or seafood can transform an otherwise ordinary meal into something exotic. Spice rubs help keep the integrity of whatever they are coating, both in texture and in flavor, because they do not entirely penetrate the flesh. Of course, the quality and freshness of the spices will deeply affect the end result, so buy the best and store them away from heat and light.

Wet spice rubs, or pastes, are subtler in flavor and are often bound together with oils, garlic, ginger, citrus juices, stock, and ground herbs. They seal in flavor and can form a savory crust, and they also tenderize. Some wet rubs are best when allowed to sit overnight. Dry rubs, on the other hand, are more intense and adhere better to the flesh of what they are applied to. After rubbing on a mixture, allow it to rest, covered and refrigerated, for at least an hour. When applying a dry spice rub, don't just sprinkle on the mixture. Take a small handful and actually pat it on to coat the surface.

Seasonings and Sauces

A PINCH FOR ALL SEASONS

Make a home in your kitchen for this mild, pleasant, versatile spice blend. Allow it to find its way into many of your recipes. It always adds just the right touch of flavor as an alternative to salt and pepper. You'll find that a little goes a long way.

3 tablespoons Sichuan peppercorns

I tablespoon sesame seeds

I teaspoon cumin seeds

I teaspoon fennel seeds

¼ cup coarse (kosher) salt

I teaspoon cayenne pepper

⅛ teaspoon ground cloves

1. Combine the peppercorns, sesame seeds, cumin seeds, and fennel seeds in a dry medium skillet over medium heat and heat, shaking continuously to prevent burning, until the seeds are fragrant and just beginning to smoke, 1 to 2 minutes.

2. Transfer the mixture to a bowl to cool, then grind to a powder in a spice grinder.

3. Transfer the mixture back to the bowl and stir in the salt, cayenne, and cloves. Use immediately, or store in an airtight container in a cool, dry place for up to 2 months.

Makes about ½ cup

CARDAMOM SPICE BLEND

Cardamom is a spice not commonly used in the United States. A member of the ginger family, this warm, sweet spice is traditionally found in Indian cooking, flavoring a wide variety of curries, rice dishes, and Indian-style desserts.

It is best to purchase the pod and grind the seeds yourself; once ground, cardamom begins to lose its essential oils. You can also crush the pods lightly, then add them to hearty stews and lentil or other bean soups. The outer pods will dissolve, but the little black seeds within will pleasantly spice the mix.

**2 tablespoons ground cardamom,
preferably freshly ground**

1 tablespoon ground turmeric

1 tablespoon ancho chili powder

1½ teaspoons ground cinnamon

You can both cool toasted spices and serve them in a thick-walled pottery bowl like this one.

Combine all the spices in a dry medium skillet over medium heat and heat, shaking the pan continuously to prevent burning, until the spices are fragrant and just beginning to smoke, 1 to 2 minutes. Transfer the spices to a bowl to cool. Use immediately, or store in an airtight container in a cool, dry place for up to 2 months.

Makes about ¼ cup

A LITTLE CARDAMOM HISTORY

One of the world's oldest and most expensive spices, after saffron, aromatic cardamom pods have been prized in India for thousands of years. Green cardamom pods, always considered the best, are sometimes bleached white for what some people consider a more esthetically appealing appearance. Brown cardamom, should you come across it, is not true cardamom and should be avoided, as it has a medicinal taste.

The pod itself is not edible. It can, however, be crushed and added to stews and sauces, where it will disintegrate as they cook. It is the dark, sticky, highly aromatic black seeds inside the pod that give off the mellow, lemony-spicy flavor. A dozen or more seeds are contained in each ¼- to ½-inch oval pod. A small number of cardamom seeds add big taste, so go easy, and put them in everything—sweet and savory alike.

*Oyster shells make great spice and topping bowls, especially at a seafood meal.
Use them to serve individual portions of Crispy Shallots (see box, page 77),
Horseradish Rouille (page 251), and chopped scallions.*

PUMPKIN SEED CRUMBS

This crumb mixture makes a particularly good crust for oily fish, such as salmon. But, when sautéing, be careful not to leave the fish crust side down for too long—the crumbs will burn. We suggest the following technique: Always heat an ovenproof skillet first, then add a little oil and allow it to get hot before adding the fish. Pat the flesh side of the salmon with most of the crumb mixture and sear it, crust side down, for about 1 minute, until crusty and golden brown. Turn, and finish cooking in a 350°F oven. When you're ready to serve, sprinkle the remaining crust mix over the fish to decorate and season.

½ cup raw unsalted pumpkin seeds

¼ cup white sesame seeds

2 tablespoons sliced almonds

1 tablespoon coriander seeds

1 tablespoon fennel seeds

1 tablespoon imported sweet paprika

1 tablespoon coarse (kosher) salt

1 teaspoon ground cardamom

1. Combine all the ingredients in a dry large skillet over medium heat and heat, shaking the pan continuously to prevent burning and holding the lid over the skillet to prevent the pumpkin seeds from popping out, until the pumpkin seeds begin to pop, about 1 minute.

2. Transfer the mixture to a bowl to cool, then process in a blender or food processor until finely ground, 2 to 3 minutes. Use immediately, or transfer to an airtight container and store in a cool, dry place for up to 2 months.

Makes about ½ cup

Pepitas

Throughout Mexico, *pepitas*, or pumpkin seeds, are popular fare and a notable ingredient in many dishes. They are especially delicious when roasted and spiced. Here in the United States, pumpkin seeds are enjoyed as snacks—hulled or whole, raw or roasted—but rarely is their charming, unmistakable, almost nutty flavor exploited anywhere else.

We love pumpkin seeds, and we venture with them into the cuisines of all regions of the world: Italian pesto, Japanese cabbage salads, Chinese fried rice, Mediterranean soups, and African chicken stews, to name a few!

CHIPOTLE BUTTER

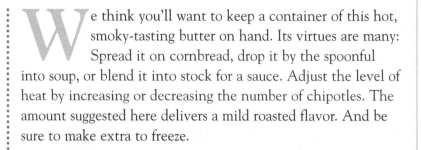

We think you'll want to keep a container of this hot, smoky-tasting butter on hand. Its virtues are many: Spread it on cornbread, drop it by the spoonful into soup, or blend it into stock for a sauce. Adjust the level of heat by increasing or decreasing the number of chipotles. The amount suggested here delivers a mild roasted flavor. And be sure to make extra to freeze.

I cup (2 sticks) unsalted butter, softened and cut into chunks
½ cup honey
¼ cup fresh lime juice
¼ cup water
2 canned chipotle chilies in adobo, drained and chopped

Combine all the ingredients in a blender or food processor and process until smooth and evenly colored. Use immediately, or transfer to an airtight container and store in the refrigerator for up to 1 week or freeze for 1 month.

Makes 2 cups

Serve chipotle butter on the side, allowing diners to add just the right amount to their soup. This compound butter is so good, "just the right amount" is a lot.

ABOUT CHIPOTLES

The chipotle is a dried jalapeño pepper that has been slow-roasted to give it a wonderful smoky flavor. Chipotles, with their deep, rounded, medium heat, are often sold in adobo, a vinegary, extremely hot tomato sauce of Mexican origin. Chipotles packed in adobo are widely available in cans. The sauce is great to use as an addition to marinades, vinaigrettes, and other sauces; in fact, the temptation is to toss some into everything!

If you are using the dried chipotles, place them in a bowl and cover with extremely hot water. Allow them to soften for about 30 minutes, then remove from the water and drain. Split the chipotles open and remove the seeds.

HORSERADISH ROUILLE

ouille, French for "rust," is the name of a flavorful purée made with roasted red peppers, which explains its name and color. This horseradish version supports that translation by producing a fiery red paste. Spread on sandwiches or fish, it provides a tasty accent with a delectable horseradish bite. Or try it whisked into broth, or use it as a dip for poached shrimp.

½ cup coarsely chopped, roasted and peeled red bell peppers
    (see box, page 18)
½ cup fresh bread crumbs
¼ cup chopped peeled fresh horseradish or
    drained prepared horseradish
2½ tablespoons rice vinegar
2 tablespoons roasted garlic (see box, page 48)
1½ tablespoons extra virgin olive oil
Salt, to taste

Combine all the ingredients in a blender or food processor and process until smooth. Use immediately, or transfer to an airtight container and store in the refrigerator for up to 2 weeks.

Makes about 1 cup

SWEET SOY SAUCE

good amount of sugar balances the natural saltiness of soy sauce here. If you prefer, the chili paste can be omitted, but it does punch up the flavor and contributes just the right bite. This makes a tasty dipping sauce for Chicken or Shrimp Pot Stickers (page 160 and 162) and Grilled Shrimp on Sugarcane (page 181).

2 cups regular or light soy sauce

I cup sugar

I tablespoon chili paste

Combine all the ingredients in a small heavy saucepan and bring to a boil over medium heat, stirring to dissolve the sugar. Reduce the heat to low and simmer, uncovered, until reduced and thickened, about 25 minutes. Use immediately, or cool, then transfer to a clean airtight container and store in the refrigerator for up to 1 month.

Makes about I cup

TOMATO SOY SAUCE

This sauce is great tossed into a rice salad. But, if you're in a dipping frame of mind, try it with Chicken or Shrimp Pot Stickers (pages 160 and 162) or just about anything savory on a stick. This recipe can be halved, if desired.

Here's a pretty and traditional-looking dipping sauce bowl that will work well as a side bowl for chutneys and our Dreamy Creamy Corn (page 264)—and as a dessert bowl for ice cream, too.

2 cups tomato juice

½ cup soy sauce

¼ cup rice vinegar

2 tablespoons Hot Chili Oil (page 232)

3 tablespoons blond miso paste (see box, page 28)

Combine all the ingredients in a blender or food processor and process until smooth. Use immediately, or transfer to a clean airtight container and store in the refrigerator for up to 2 weeks.

Makes about 3 cups

JAPANESE MISO SAUCE

Miso has two attributes in common with America's passion for peanut butter—its consistency and its popularity with Japanese people everywhere. Here we use light miso, which is mild and slightly sweet tasting. Serve it with foods that stand up to its distinctive flavor. Toss the sauce with steamed asparagus and sesame seeds for a great spring salad. Or serve it as a sauce with grilled salmon or sea bass.

¼ cup blond miso paste (see box, page 28)

¼ cup rice vinegar

2 tablespoons mirin, sweet sherry, or sweet vermouth

2 tablespoons fresh lime juice

1 tablespoon wasabi powder (Japanese horseradish)

¼ teaspoon shichimi togarashi (see box, page 115)

⅛ teaspoon Asian sesame oil

Combine all the ingredients in a blender or food processor and process until smooth. (Add a small amount of water if you desire a thinner consistency.) Use immediately, or transfer to a clean, tightly capped jar and store in the refrigerator for up to 1 month.

Makes about ¾ cup

THAI DIPPING SAUCE

This recipe contains the basic ingredients of most Thai cooking, and it's packed with flavor. If you want it spicy, add a few drops of Hot Chili Oil (page 232). For visual appeal, float chopped scallion or sesame seeds on top. And for a tasty marinade for chicken, scallops, or vegetables on the grill, just add a splash of Cilantro Oil (page 230).

2 cups water

½ cup sugar

¼ cup rice vinegar

5 cloves garlic, lightly crushed

3 fresh jalapeño peppers, stemmed and coarsely chopped

¾ cup fresh lime juice

¼ cup nam pla (Asian fish sauce)

1. Combine the water, sugar, and vinegar in a medium nonreactive saucepan and bring to a boil over medium heat, stirring until the sugar is dissolved. Transfer to a heatproof bowl and cool.

2. Add the garlic, jalapeños, lime juice, and *nam pla* and refrigerate, covered, for 1 to 2 hours. Strain before using. Store in a clean airtight container in the refrigerator for up to 1 week.

Makes about 3 cups

SPICY PEANUT SAUCE

This intriguing sauce with its rich complexity of exotic flavors comes together remarkably quickly and easily, making it a definite mainstay of your culinary cache. Serve as a dipping sauce for Chickpea Fritters (page 185), Shrimp and Yuca Fritters (page 184), Chili-Marinated Shrimp (page 183), or Grilled Chicken Skewers (page 179). Or simply use it as a spread on a piece of crisp flatbread. This recipe can be halved, if desired.

1½ cups unsalted raw peanuts, coarsely chopped

3 tablespoons honey

3 tablespoons rice vinegar

2 tablespoons nam pla (Asian fish sauce)

2 tablespoons mushroom soy sauce or regular soy sauce

2 tablespoons chopped peeled fresh ginger

1 tablespoon Asian sesame oil

1 teaspoon **Garlic Paste (page 61)**

1 teaspoon **chili paste**

½ cup **Chicken Stock for Asian Bowls (page 5)** or **water**

3 tablespoons **fresh lime juice**

1. Preheat the oven to 375°F.

2. Spread the peanuts in a jelly-roll pan and roast in the oven until they turn a toasty-brown color, about 4 minutes. Check frequently and shake the pan to avoid burning. Remove and cool in the pan.

3. Combine the honey, vinegar, *nam pla*, soy sauce, ginger, sesame oil, Garlic Paste, and chili paste in a food processor or blender and process until smooth. Add the peanuts and pulse until the consistency of chunky peanut butter. Add the chicken stock or water and lime juice and process just to blend; avoid overprocessing the peanuts. Use immediately, or store in a clean, tightly capped jar in the refrigerator for up to 1 week.

Makes about 2 cups

PISTACHIO YOGURT SAUCE

The highly scented and flavor-rich combination of toasted and ground spices and nuts bound together by water is commonly known in India as *masala*. It is often used in preparations that are served with yogurt, which provides a cooling, palate-refreshing sensation.

There are many variations of masala. Here we blend the nut mixture with the yogurt, and recommend using a Middle Eastern yogurt called *labneh*, available in specialty food markets, for its tangier, richer consistency. Serve with grilled fish, particularly monkfish.

See the box on page 137 for toasting nuts and seeds.

¼ cup shelled pistachios, toasted

2 tablespoons almonds, toasted

2 tablespoons sesame seeds, toasted

I tablespoon black mustard seeds, toasted

2 tablespoons water

I tablespoon chopped peeled fresh ginger

1½ teaspoons Garlic Paste (page 61)

Pinch ground cinnamon

Pinch coriander seeds, toasted and ground

Pinch ground allspice

Pinch saffron threads

I cup labneh or plain yogurt

2 tablespoons fresh lime juice

I tablespoon rice vinegar

Salt, to taste

1. Combine the pistachios, almonds, sesame seeds, and mustard seeds in a food processor. Add the 2 tablespoons water and process to a paste consistency.

2. Add the ginger, Garlic Paste, cinnamon, coriander, allspice, and saffron and process for 1 minute. Add the yogurt, lime juice, and vinegar and pulse 5 or 6 times until blended. Season with salt. Use immediately, or transfer to a clean airtight container and store in the refrigerator for up to 1 week.

Makes about 1½ cups

PUMPKIN SEED SAUCE

Sometimes it's hard to believe that so little effort can result in such outstanding flavor, but that is just the case with this sauce. Use as a sauce for dumplings or seafood and poultry dishes, and feel free to serve it hot, cold, or at room temperature.

¼ **cup raw unsalted pumpkin seeds, toasted (page 137)**

¼ **cup chopped fresh cilantro leaves**

¼ **cup rice vinegar**

2 **tablespoons freshly grated Parmesan cheese**

¼ **teaspoon ground cumin**

½ **cup water**

Salt and freshly ground black pepper, to taste

Combine the pumpkin seeds, cilantro, vinegar, Parmesan, and cumin in a blender or food processor and process until smooth. Add the water and process to blend. Season with salt and pepper. Use immediately, or transfer to a clean, tightly capped jar and store in the refrigerator for up to 1 week.

Makes about 1 cup

This lovely little bowl works nicely for side sauces as well as for broth. The slightly scalloped edge doesn't make sipping difficult and the rounded shape is comforting.

TOASTED MUSTARD SEED AND BALSAMIC DRIZZLE

A light hand is required when drizzling this potent vinaigrette on roasted vegetables, sautéed greens, or fruit salad. If you reduce the balsamic vinegar too much, or it becomes too thick, just add warm water to thin it. Know that in this dressing the balsamic vinegar sits on the bottom of the bowl while the oil floats on top; be sure to spoon from the bottom for the appropriate flavor balance.

¾ **cup balsamic vinegar**

3 **tablespoons Dijon mustard**

2 **tablespoons honey**

¾ **cup extra virgin olive oil**

5 **tablespoons dark or yellow mustard seeds, toasted (see box, page 137)**

Salt and freshly ground black pepper, to taste

1. Bring the vinegar to a simmer in a small heavy nonreactive skillet over medium heat until it is reduced by about one third and achieves a syrupy consistency, 5 to 8 minutes. Remove from the heat and transfer to a medium bowl to cool.

2. Beat the mustard and honey with a wire whisk into the cooled vinegar. Add the olive oil in a slow, steady stream and stir to blend. Add the mustard seeds and season with salt and pepper. Stir again. Use immediately, or transfer to a clean, tightly capped jar and store in the refrigerator for up to 2 weeks. Bring to room temperature before using.

Makes about 1¾ cups

WOULD THE REAL BALSAMIC VINEGAR PLEASE STAND UP?

Bottle No. 1: Red wine vinegar with caramel added for color and sweetness

Bottle No. 2: The concentrated sweet juice of aged white grapes

The truth is, most Americans have never tasted real balsamic vinegar! That's right, Bottle No. 2 is the real thing. Following a centuries-old Italian tradition, true balsamic vinegar is aged for decades in a succession of barrels, each made from a different wood. True balsamic vinegar, which comes from the province of Modena, can be as expensive as a very fine wine, and it is so precious that it is sold by the ounce in perfume-sized bottles labeled with the official established appellation, *Aceto Balsamico Tradizionale di Modena*. A deep, rich, translucent brown color, smooth syrupy texture, balanced sweet and pungent flavor, and pleasantly intense aroma give balsamic vinegar its unique character.

All the other so-called "balsamic" vinegars are imposters. Although they may be imported from Italy, they are merely commercial red wine vinegars with extra color and flavor added. But don't feel cheated—this is what we use, too. In fact, unless you intend to sip minute amounts of the real stuff after a satisfying meal or drizzle a few drops over strawberries for an extravagant dessert, save your money. For most culinary purposes, commercially sold balsamic vinegars are fine. True balsamic vinegar is rarely used for cooking since heat destroys its subtle qualities, and it is used only sparingly, in combination with red wine vinegar, in salad dressings.

GREEN SAUCE

This easy-to-make sauce has a cool, herb-filled flavor, and the cooked egg yolk in it adds a rich creaminess. Great on empanadas or poached salmon.

¼ cup (tightly packed) fresh Italian (flat-leaf) parsley leaves

¼ cup (tightly packed) fresh cilantro leaves

1 fresh tomatillo, husk removed and chopped

1½ cloves garlic, roasted (see box, page 48)

1 hard-cooked egg yolk

2 tablespoons fresh lime juice

½ teaspoon dry mustard

⅓ cup olive oil

Salt and freshly ground black pepper, to taste

1. Have a bowl of ice water ready on the counter.

2. Bring a large saucepan of water to a boil over high heat. Add the herbs to the boiling water and blanch several seconds. Drain immediately, then plunge into the ice water. Drain well again, and squeeze out all the liquid.

3. Combine the herbs, tomatillo, garlic, egg yolk, lime juice, and mustard in a blender or food processor and process until smooth. With the motor running, add the olive oil in a slow, steady stream and blend in thoroughly. Season with salt and pepper. Use immediately, or transfer to a clean airtight container and store in the refrigerator for up to 3 days. Bring to room temperature before using.

Makes about 1 cup

A handled sauce server makes a beautiful presentation for this creamy Green Sauce.

POURABLE PESTO

During the summer months, basil grows abundantly, and that is the perfect time to make plenty of this pesto and freeze some of it for future use. What you don't freeze, keep refrigerated in a squeeze bottle for drizzling on sliced farm-fresh tomatoes or warm potato salad. Or simply use it as a colorful and aromatic garnish to finish a bowl just before serving.

I cup (tightly packed) fresh basil leaves, blanched and shocked
   (see box, page 214)
¼ cup fresh lemon juice
3 tablespoons Garlic Paste (page 61)
2 tablespoons freshly grated Parmesan cheese
I tablespoon dry mustard
¾ cup walnut oil
¼ cup olive oil
Salt and freshly ground black pepper, to taste

Combine the basil, lemon juice, Garlic Paste, Parmesan, and mustard in a blender or food processor and process until smooth. With the motor running, add the oils in a slow, steady stream and blend in thoroughly. Season with salt and pepper. Transfer to an airtight container and store in the refrigerator for up to 1 week or freeze for 3 months. Thaw in the refrigerator overnight. Bring to room temperature before using.

Makes about 1½ cups

AVOCADO WASABI

The sharp fiery flavor of wasabi, also known as Japanese horseradish, is tempered here by the satiny texture and buttery, almost nutlike, flavor of avocado. Mild rice vinegar provides a hint of sweet tang and helps prevent discoloration of the bright green avocado. Serve chilled, with chips, fritters, or shrimp skewers. Or dollop into soups, such as gazpacho, or onto simple tomato and lettuce salads.

I ripe avocado, peeled, pitted, and cut into chunks
2 tablespoons rice vinegar
1½ tablespoons wasabi powder
    (Japanese horseradish)
Salt, to taste

Combine the avocado, vinegar, and wasabi in a blender or food processor and process until smooth. Season with salt. Using a rubber spatula, scrape the sauce into an airtight container and store in the refrigerator for up to 1 week.

Makes about 1 cup

ROASTED RED PEPPER AND CILANTRO SAUCE

Warm or chilled, this sauce serves as a tantalizing toss for warm egg noodles. Add freshly cut vegetables and voilà—your repast is complete!

½ cup chopped, roasted and peeled red bell peppers
    (see box, page 18)
¼ cup (tightly packed) fresh cilantro leaves
¼ cup Tomato-Garlic Vinaigrette
    (page 226)
¼ cup cold water
2 tablespoons ketchup
2 tablespoons red wine vinegar
½ fresh jalapeño pepper, stemmed and seeded
Salt, to taste

Combine all the ingredients in a blender or food processor and process until smooth. Use immediately, or transfer to an airtight container and store in the refrigerator for up to 1 week.

Makes about 1½ cups

SHERRY AND GARLIC SOY SAUCE

The provocative taste of this dipping sauce will have you searching for doodads to dip. It can be equally successful used as a glaze on pork (brush on just after cooking) or on Rum-Cured Salmon (page 173) just before it's arranged on a bowl of crisp green salad.

> ¾ **cup soy sauce**
> ¼ **cup dry sherry**
> ¼ **cup hoisin sauce**
> ¼ **cup honey**
> ¼ **cup sugar**
> **5 star anise, cracked**
> **4 cloves garlic, roasted (see box, page 48)**
> **1 cinnamon stick (3 inches)**

1. Combine all the ingredients in a medium nonreactive saucepan and bring to a boil over medium heat. Reduce the heat to low and simmer, uncovered, until reduced by half, about 30 minutes. Remove from the heat and strain the sauce through a fine-mesh sieve into a small heatproof bowl. Cool.

2. Use immediately, or transfer to an airtight container and store in the refrigerator for up to 1 month.

Makes about ¾ cup

SOUR CREMA

This sauce has a great cooling effect on spicy dishes and serves as a refreshing contrast to fiery Fried Chicken Salad, for example. It is also a terrific accompaniment to Latin-style bean and rice dishes, such as our Rice Tamales with Shrimp, Black Olives, and Almonds (page 143), and a delicious topping for empanadas. You can drizzle or drop a dollop into a bowl of soup or onto a salad, too.

I cup sour cream

¼ cup red wine vinegar

2 tablespoons fresh lime juice

2 tablespoons imported sweet paprika

I teaspoon ground cumin

¼ teaspoon cayenne pepper

Salt and freshly ground black pepper, to taste

Combine the sour cream, vinegar, lime juice, paprika, cumin, and cayenne in a small nonreactive bowl and stir until thoroughly blended. Season with salt and pepper. Use immediately, or transfer to a clean, tightly capped jar and store in the refrigerator for up to 1 week.

Makes about 1½ cups

SPICY TOMATO GLAZE

When a piece of plain grilled fish just won't do, this glaze offers the solution. Just a mere brushstroke of this complex, deeply flavored glaze will transform mild-tasting cod or halibut into something exotic.

1 tablespoon Garlic Paste (page 61)

2 shallots, chopped

½ teaspoon crushed red pepper flakes

¼ cup balsamic vinegar

1 cup chopped fresh tomatoes, or canned, drained

¼ cup dry red wine

¼ cup ketchup

¼ cup mirin, sweet sherry, or sweet vermouth

1 ancho chili, toasted, seeded, soaked, and drained

Salt and freshly ground black pepper, to taste

1. Bring the Garlic Paste, shallots, red pepper flakes, and balsamic vinegar to a boil in a medium nonreactive saucepan over medium heat. Reduce the heat to low and simmer until syrupy, about 10 minutes.

2. Add the remaining ingredients and continue to simmer until reduced by half, about 15 to 20 minutes. Remove from the heat and cool.

3. Transfer the mixture to a blender or food processor and process until smooth. Use immediately, or transfer to an airtight container and store in the refrigerator for up to 2 weeks.

Makes about 1 cup

DREAMY CREAMY CORN

Every once in a while, the rules for healthy-heart eating beg to be stretched to include something worthy of mealtime dreaming. This comforting recipe would have to be considered one of those rule stretchers. Use it as sauce for Mojo-Marinated Chicken (page 80), Cheese-Stuffed Poblanos (page 174), grilled shrimp or fish, or steamed greens. Thinned with stock, it becomes a soup. And, with the addition of fresh fava beans, it becomes a satisfying succotash.

5 tablespoons extra virgin olive oil

2 medium red onions, cut into medium dice

3 fresh serrano chilies or jalapeño peppers,
    stemmed, seeded, and chopped

4 cups yellow or white corn kernels (7 to 8 ears),
    fresh from the cob

3 cups heavy cream

I bunch chives or scallions (green part only),
    finely chopped

Salt, to taste

Freshly ground Sichuan peppercorns, to taste

I. Heat the olive oil in a medium saucepan over medium heat. Add the onions and chilies and sauté until softened, about 5 minutes. Reduce the heat to low and add half of the corn. Cook for 10 minutes, stirring occasionally.

2. Meanwhile, bring a medium saucepan of water to a boil, add the 2 remaining cups of corn, and blanch for 2 minutes. Drain, rinse under cold running water, and set aside.

3. Add the cream to the corn and onion mixture and bring to a boil over medium heat. Reduce the heat to low and simmer, uncovered, for 15 minutes. Remove from the heat. Transfer to a food processor and process until smooth. Transfer the purée to the saucepan and bring to a simmer over low heat. Add the reserved blanched corn and stir to combine. Add the chives and season with salt and Sichuan pepper.

Makes about 4 cups

A Southwestern-style sauce in a Santa Fe-style bowl makes sense, especially if the bowl has a handle for easy passing. Diners seem to never take enough the first time round.

APRICOT AND APPLE CHUTNEY

Chutney is easy to make, tastes great with savory food, and is a good way to use up fruit that might otherwise go to waste. The variations are endless. Raw or cooked, chunky or smooth, hot or mild, chutneys are made from four basic ingredients: fruits or vegetables, sugar, vinegar, and spice.

This chutney perks up anything grilled—Mojo-Marinated Chicken (page 80), Crisp Soft-Shell Crab and Cucumber Salad (page 204), even a hot dog!

1½ tablespoons Hot Chili Oil (page 232)
1 tart green apple, peeled, cored, and cut into ½-inch dice
½ medium red onion, cut into ½-inch dice
½ cup dried unsweetened apricots, cut into ½-inch dice
1 tablespoon minced peeled fresh ginger
2 cloves garlic, minced
½ teaspoon minced serrano chili, stemmed and seeded
¼ cup (packed) light brown sugar
¼ cup cider vinegar
¼ cup fresh orange juice
1 tablespoon fresh lime juice

1. Heat the oil in a large nonreactive sauté pan over medium heat. Add the apple, onion, apricots, ginger, garlic, and serrano and sauté until the onion is translucent, about 10 minutes.

2. Add the sugar, vinegar, and orange juice and bring to a boil, stirring to dissolve the sugar. Reduce the heat to low and simmer for 4 minutes. Remove from the heat and cool.

3. Stir in the lime juice. Use immediately, or transfer to an airtight container and store in the refrigerator for up to 1 week. Serve either warm or cold.

Makes about 1 cup

SWEET BOWLS & A FEW SIPS

READY FOR DESSERT

Desserts that really stick in our minds are the ones that conjure up warm, loving, clichéd-but-real memories: our mothers spending hours in the kitchen baking apple and pumpkin pies with aromas so inviting they kept us indoors. Their painstaking efforts to please every waiting mouth might have meant preparing at least three different kinds of rice pudding—one with fruit, one without, and one with a creamy layer of custard that sat on the top. And when they baked cookies, neither of us could resist eating too many before they cooled off, knowing full well there was the inevitable stomachache to follow.

Our takes on desserts as kids have not changed much. We still like ice cream a lot, only now it might be raspberry or a variation on chocolate that we make with bittersweet chocolate chunks and caramel. Cookies still figure prominently in our lives, only now they are Pecan Lace Cookies or Almond Meringue Cookies or Cinnamon Rugelach with Chocolate-Raisin-Nut Filling, which we freely admit to loving for breakfast as well. And although stewed fruit didn't seem too appealing back then (it was more of an adult dessert), now nothing sounds more comforting than a bowl of warm baked apple and maple syrup.

All of the desserts and the few drinks that follow are sophisticated in one way or another but easy to make. Needless to say, but we'll repeat it anyway, each deserves a great bowl for serving. We leave that judgment call up to you, but share some thoughts on a few not-so-obvious options. Don't rule out café au lait cups for pieces of cake slathered with Cognac Caramel Sauce, or Japanese rice bowls for Mango Ginger Ice Cream, or even clear glass fish bowls for sipping icy beverages like our Watermelon Freeze.

269

Sweet Bowls

ALMOND BISCOTTI

F inally, the perfect biscotti—crunchy *and* chewy—the ideal accompaniment to ice cream or cappuccino. For serious crunch, the way we like it, bake them 45 minutes; for softer, cakier biscotti, bake them 30 to 35 minutes.

2¼ cups all-purpose flour

2 teaspoons baking powder

I teaspoon ground cinnamon

½ teaspoon salt

I cup granulated sugar

I cup (packed) dark brown sugar

4 large eggs

½ cup vegetable oil

2 tablespoons water

3 cups (13 to 14 ounces) almonds

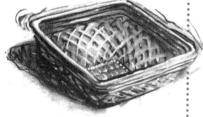

At the end of your meal or for a snack, serve biscotti piled high in a shallow bowl. This beauty with a woven basket pattern is a piece of Depression glass and was a yard sale find.

I. Place an oven rack in the center of the oven and another rack directly below it. Preheat the oven to 350°F. Line 2 baking sheets with parchment paper or aluminum foil.

2. Combine the flour, baking powder, cinnamon, and salt in a medium bowl and whisk to combine. Set aside.

3. Combine the sugars, 2 of the eggs, the oil, and water in a large bowl and beat with an electric mixer at medium speed until smooth and well blended. With the mixer at low speed, or using a rubber spatula, stir in the flour mixture until just combined. Do not overmix.

4. Turn the dough out onto a well-floured board. Flour your hands, then work the almonds into the dough. Divide the dough in half. Roll each piece into a ball and flatten slightly into a log. Place one loaf on each prepared baking sheet.

5. Lightly whisk the remaining 2 eggs in a small bowl and brush over the loaves. Place each baking sheet on a shelf in the oven and bake until the tops of the loaves are cracked and golden, 30 to 35 minutes for softer biscotti, 40 to 45 minutes, for crunchier. Halfway through the baking time, rotate the baking sheets, moving the top sheet to the bottom rack and vice versa.

6. Transfer the loaves to wire racks to cool, leaving the oven on. Using a sharp knife, cut the cooled loaves into 12 slices each. Return the cookies to the baking sheets, cut side down, and bake for an additional 10 to 15 minutes. Transfer to racks to cool completely. Store in airtight containers for up to 2 weeks.

Makes at least 2 dozen cookies

ALMOND MERINGUE COOKIES

These are exceptional. Don't pass up making them because you think the recipe is too difficult; you just have to remember a few pointers: For best results in making meringue, use a heavy-duty stand mixer fitted with the whip attachment. Be sure that the mixer bowl and beaters are grease free; otherwise the egg whites will not form soft peaks. Don't overbeat the egg whites because they'll become too dry and actually separate. (You'll know when it happens—the whites will look like soap suds.)

A wonderful alternative to serving these as an accompaniment to ice cream is to layer them with pastry cream or whipped cream and fresh berries, or with lemon curd or chocolate ganache. Place in individual shallow bowls, then sprinkle with powdered sugar for an elegant dessert.

1 cup unblanched whole or slivered almonds

1¼ cups sugar

1 tablespoon cornstarch

9 large egg whites, at room temperature

Pinch of salt

1. Place an oven rack in the center of the oven and another directly below it. Preheat the oven to 275°F. Butter 2 large baking sheets and dust with flour, tapping off the excess. With a 3-inch round cookie cutter, trace 6 circles, 1 inch apart, in the flour on each baking sheet.

2. Combine the almonds, ¼ cup of the sugar, and the cornstarch in a food processor and process until finely ground, about 2 minutes.

3. In a large grease-free bowl, using a stand mixer fitted with the wire whip attachment, begin to beat the egg whites with the salt on a medium-to-high setting until they form soft peaks. With the mixer running, slowly add the remaining sugar and beat until the meringue is stiff and shiny, about 10 minutes. Use a rubber spatula to gently fold the ground almond mixture, one third at a time, into the meringue.

4. Fit a pastry bag with a large plain tip and fill it with the meringue mixture. Starting from the center of each circle and working your way out, pipe concentric circles to fill each tracing. (The unbaked cookies should look like spirals.) Place one baking sheet on the top rack of the oven and the other below and bake until the meringues are dry and slightly golden, about 2 hours, rotating the baking sheets from top to bottom shelf after 1 hour.

5. Remove the baking sheets from the oven to wire racks to cool completely. If not using immediately, store the cookies in an airtight container at room temperature for up to 2 weeks.

Makes 1 dozen 3-inch cookies

Use a wide, delicate, platelike bowl to serve delicate cookies. Arrange them attractively before bringing them to the table.

PECAN LACE COOKIES

The thin, airy texture of these crunchy cookies reminds us of lovely lace, and they add a graceful touch to any bowl of ice cream. They are outrageously addictive and, as luck would have it, easy to prepare!

1½ cups (packed) dark brown sugar

½ cup water

½ cup (1 stick) unsalted butter, in pieces

1 teaspoon pure vanilla extract

1 cup all-purpose four, sifted

1 cup finely chopped pecans

1. Place an oven rack in the center of the oven and another directly above and below it. Preheat the oven to 350°F. Butter 3 large baking sheets well and dust with flour, tapping off the excess.

2. Combine ½ cup of the sugar and the water in a medium saucepan and bring to a boil over medium heat. Remove from the heat, add the butter and vanilla, and let the mixture stand until the butter melts. Stir in the remaining 1 cup sugar, whisk in the flour, then stir in the pecans.

3. Drop the batter by generous teaspoonfuls onto the prepared baking sheets, leaving 2 inches in between. (There should be approximately 12 cookies per sheet.) Place all 3 baking sheets in the oven (top shelf, middle shelf, and oven bottom). Bake 9 to 10 minutes, rotating the top and bottom baking sheets once after the first 5 minutes. Remove the cookies from the baking sheets while they are still warm, before they have a chance to harden, to wire racks to cool. Store the cookies in layers in airtight containers.

Makes about 3 dozen cookies

A French tureen makes a surprise serving dish for cookies. Arrange them early in the day; the lid will keep the cookies fresh and there will be no chance of any slipping to the floor when you take dessert to the table.

CINNAMON RUGELACH WITH CHOCOLATE-RAISIN-NUT FILLING

Chocolate Throb

Chocolate consumption in the United States amounts to about 11 pounds per person per year. It's so good, some people think chocolate is addictive. And it may actually be because it contains theobromine, a natural chemical that is closely related to caffeine and has a similar stimulating effect.

True cinnamon aficionados, will appreciate these morsels even more when served with Cinnamon Espresso Ice Cream (page 281).

A readily available semisweet chocolate like Baker's works well here. Or you can indulge yourself with a brand containing a higher butterfat content. Just remember that this act of fancy will result in added calories!

CREAM CHEESE DOUGH

1 cup (2 sticks) unsalted butter, softened

8 ounces cream cheese, softened

3 tablespoons sugar

⅛ teaspoon salt

2 cups all-purpose flour

CHOCOLATE-RAISIN-NUT FILLING

¾ cup sugar

¾ cup raisins

1 tablespoon ground cinnamon

3 ounces semisweet chocolate, coarsely chopped

1½ cups walnut or pecan pieces

CINNAMON TOPPING

¼ cup sugar

2 tablespoons ground cinnamon

½ cup (1 stick) unsalted butter, melted

1. Place an oven rack in the center of the oven and another directly below it. Preheat the oven to 350°F. Line 2 baking sheets with parchment paper or aluminum foil.

2. Prepare the dough: Combine the butter, cream cheese, sugar, and salt in a large bowl and beat with an electric mixer at medium speed until smooth and well blended. Add the flour and beat at low speed until just incorporated. Do not overmix. Gather the dough into a log shape and cut into three equal pieces. Shape each piece into a ball and flatten slightly, to make a disk. Wrap the disks in plastic wrap and refrigerate to firm them up, 1 to 2 hours.

3. Meanwhile, prepare the filling: Combine the sugar, raisins, and cinnamon in a food processor and process until the raisins are finely chopped, about 30 seconds. Add the chocolate and nuts and pulse until the nuts are coarsely chopped, 6 to 7 seconds. (For a less-textured filling, pulse the nut mixture until finely chopped, about 30 seconds.) Set aside.

4. Prepare the topping: Combine the sugar and cinnamon in a small bowl, stirring to mix well. Set aside.

5. Remove one dough disk at a time from the refrigerator. Place the dough between two large sheets of clean plastic wrap and roll it into a 9-inch circle. Using a large sharp knife, divide the circle, like a pie, into 12 equal wedges. Brush the wedges with some of the melted butter. Place 1 heaping teaspoon of the filling mixture on the wide end of each triangle and roll each up as tightly as possible, from the wide end to the point, making a crescent shape. Make cookies with the remaining dough and filling in the same manner.

6. Place the cookies, point side down and about 1 inch apart, on the prepared baking sheets. Brush lightly with butter and sprinkle the tops with the cinnamon sugar. Place each baking sheet on a shelf in the oven and bake until the cookies are

Use your imagination— as well as available bowls— when serving little sweets. We've always believed that dog bowls were too cute to be reserved only for the family pooch. Keep a supply on hand (for human use only) and you'll find them showing up on your table for all manner of foods.

golden brown, 25 to 30 minutes, switching the shelves the baking sheets are on after 15 minutes.

7. Remove the baking sheets to wire racks and let the pastries cool completely. Store the pastries in an airtight container for up to 1 week.

Makes 3 dozen

For a traditional elegant cookie presentation, nothing beats a plain white shallow platter-style bowl.

SOMETIMES LOOKS ARE EVERYTHING: THE WALNUT

The Chinese believe that the way a walnut looks has meaning. Because the wrinkled bilateral shape of the actual walnut resembles the human brain's two cerebral hemispheres, the Chinese have long considered walnuts to be brain food. Whether or not walnuts have any direct benefit on the brain, they may actually be healthful in other ways. Even though they're high in fat, the fat in a walnut is the good kind—the type that does not clog arteries—and walnuts are said to contain a cholesterol-lowering substance known as linolenic acid.

The truth is, we've never needed a good reason to eat nuts of any kind, especially walnuts, which have a rich meaty texture. They also have an assertive taste that can be intensified by toasting them, making them wonderful with everything from soup to . . . well, dessert!

When baking or cooking with walnuts—all nuts, in fact—it's worth the effort to buy them whole and shell them yourself. Nuts keep best in their shells, where they are protected from light and heat, conditions that cause the fat in them to turn rancid over time. However, if you opt to purchase shelled nuts, choose fresh-smelling, plump, well-formed ones that feel firm when squeezed. Store shelled nuts in an airtight container in a cool, dry place or in the freezer.

PINEAPPLE UPSIDE-DOWN CAKE WITH TANGY VANILLA SAUCE

Ripe, fresh pineapple and a little grated fresh ginger spice up an old-time favorite. Although canned pineapple will do, this cake delivers an especially mouth-puckering kiss of sweetness and tartness when its caramelized fresh fruit combines with a spoonful or two of Tangy Vanilla Sauce, our favorite accompaniment. Serve individual portions in tropical fruit shaped bowls.

¾ cup (1½ sticks) unsalted butter, softened

½ cup (packed) dark brown sugar

½ fresh pineapple, peeled, quartered lengthwise, cored, and sliced, or 1 can (20 ounces) unsweetened pineapple rings, drained

¾ cup granulated sugar

3 large egg yolks

1 teaspoon pure vanilla extract

½ cup sour cream

1 tablespoon finely grated peeled fresh ginger

1½ cups all-purpose flour

¾ teaspoon baking powder

¼ teaspoon baking soda

¼ teaspoon salt

Tangy Vanilla Sauce (recipe follows)

1. Melt 4 tablespoons of the butter in a 9-inch cast-iron skillet or a heavy, flameproof, 9-inch round cake pan over medium heat. Stir in the brown sugar until it dissolves, about 2 minutes. Remove from the heat.

2. Arrange the pineapple in concentric circles in the butter-

An Exquisite Fruit

English-speaking people call it "pineapple," but it originally derived from a Spanish word meaning "exquisite fruit." Tangy, sweet, and succulent, this tropical fruit wears a craggy, mosaiclike coat of diamond shapes, and atop its oblong body is a head of spiny, rigid green leaves. Fresh pineapple that is ready to eat should have a bright color and perfumy fragrance and be a little tender when pressed with your finger. Without these characteristics, the fruit is probably not ripe, and an unripe pineapple will never reach the same degree of sweetness as one allowed to ripen on the plant.

sugar mixture without overlapping, cutting pieces to fit any unfilled spaces. Set aside.

3. Preheat the oven to 350°F.

4. Using an electric mixer at medium speed, beat the remaining ½ cup butter and the granulated sugar in a large bowl until light. Beat in the egg yolks and vanilla until blended thoroughly. Beat in the sour cream and ginger until combined.

5. Combine the flour, baking powder, baking soda, and salt in a medium bowl. Add to the butter mixture and beat until just combined and smooth, about 30 seconds. (The batter will be fairly stiff.) Do not overbeat. Pour the batter evenly over the pineapple in the skillet and spread it gently with a rubber spatula to cover the fruit.

6. Bake the cake until it is golden brown on top and springs back when touched lightly with a finger, 35 to 45 minutes.

7. Remove the skillet from the oven and place a serving plate larger than the circumference of the skillet on top. Invert the skillet and plate to unmold the cake, waiting about 30 seconds before removing the skillet. If any pineapple sticks to the skillet, release it with a rubber spatula and place it back on the cake.

8. Serve warm, in bowls, accompanied by the vanilla sauce.

Serves 8 to 10

Delicate compote dishes make lovely dessert bowls—fruit desserts, ice cream, even small portions of cake with sweet sauce spooned over, all seem to taste better when they come from a compote.

TANGY VANILLA SAUCE

It doesn't get easier than this—a deceptively tantalizing treat of a dessert sauce that can be prepared in a pinch. Although it is designed especially for the Pineapple Upside-Down Cake, you might also try it as a sauce or as a dip for fresh strawberries, or dollop it on a sparkling glass bowl of blueberries or other fresh fruit.

2 cups sour cream

6 tablespoons (packed) light brown sugar

2 teaspoons pure vanilla extract

Combine all the ingredients in a small bowl and stir until blended and smooth. Use immediately, or transfer to an airtight container and store in the refrigerator for up to 3 days.

Makes about 2 cups

RASPBERRY ICE CREAM

The slight tartness of this ice cream is beautifully balanced when it is accompanied by cloudlike yet crunchy Almond Meringue Cookies (page 271) and topped with smooth Honeyed Crema (page 294). For a stunning presentation, use sleek bowl-like goblets, and alternate layers of the ice cream with crumbled cookies. Freeze until ready to serve, then drizzle with the crema.

1½ cups (12 ounces) ripe, absolutely fresh raspberries, or 1 package (10 ounces) loose-pack unsweetened frozen raspberries, thawed

¾ cup plus 2 tablespoons sugar

2 cups half-and-half

1 tablespoon Chambord, crème de cassis, or other berry liqueur of choice

1 teaspoon fresh lemon juice

1. Combine the raspberries and sugar in a food processor and process to a thick purée, about 1 minute.

2. To eliminate the seeds, strain the purée through a fine-meshed sieve into a medium stainless-steel or glass bowl, pressing with a rubber spatula to push through as much of the fruit and liquid as possible. Discard the seeds.

3. Stir in the half-and-half, liqueur, and lemon juice. Cover tightly with plastic wrap and refrigerate for 24 hours.

4. Freeze the chilled mixture in an ice cream maker according to the manufacturer's instructions.

Makes about 1 quart, serving 4 to 6

MANGO GINGER ICE CREAM

Crisp Pecan Lace Cookies (page 273) are the perfect foil for this rich mango ice cream, a smooth rich custard spiked with bits of crystallized ginger.

    9 large egg yolks
    ½ cup plus 2 tablespoons sugar
    1½ cups whole milk
    1½ cups heavy (or whipping) cream
    2 medium ripe mangoes
    1 teaspoon lemon juice
    ¼ cup coarsely chopped crystallized ginger

1. Combine the egg yolks and ¼ cup of the sugar in a medium bowl and whisk until thick and pale in color, 3 to 4 minutes. Set aside.

2. Combine the milk, cream, and ¼ cup of the sugar in a large heavy saucepan and bring to a gentle boil over medium heat, stirring occasionally with a wooden spoon. Reduce the heat to low.

3. Gradually whisk 2 cups of the hot cream mixture into the beaten yolk mixture, then immediately pour the mixture into the cream mixture in the saucepan. Cook over low or medium-low heat, stirring constantly with the wooden spoon until the custard is thick enough to coat the spoon. Do not allow the custard to boil or it will curdle. (If it should, whisk the mixture rapidly. Any bits of cooked yolk remaining will be strained out in step 4.)

4. Remove the custard from the heat and strain it through a fine-meshed sieve into a medium stainless-steel or glass bowl. Place the bowl in the refrigerator and chill, stirring occasionally, until the custard is cool, about 10 minutes. When cooled, cover tightly and return to the refrigerator for at least 6 hours, or overnight.

5. Peel the mangoes, then cut the flesh away from the pits directly into the bowl of a food processor. Add the lemon juice and the remaining 2 tablespoons sugar and process to a smooth purée. Transfer to a large bowl and store, covered, in the refrigerator until ready to use.

6. Freeze the chilled custard in an ice cream maker according to the manufacturer's instructions, adding the chilled mango purée and the chopped crystallized ginger for the final 2 minutes of churning.

Makes about 1½ quarts, serving 6 to 8

CINNAMON ESPRESSO ICE CREAM

Cinnamon sticks and fragrant espresso beans are what give this frozen dessert its spicy depth of flavor. Serve in chilled earthenware bowls with Cinnamon Rugelach with Chocolate-Raisin-Nut Filling (page 274) or Almond Biscotti (page 270) for a completely satisfying finale to any bowlfood meal.

2 cups heavy (or whipping) cream

2 cups whole milk

6 fresh cinnamon sticks (3 inches each),
  broken in half

½ cup espresso beans, coarsely crushed

¾ cup sugar

8 large egg yolks

⅛ teaspoon salt

2 tablespoons Kahlúa or other
  coffee-flavored liqueur

Stemmed Margarita or Martini glasses make great bowls for serving ice cream. Take your time, and if any melts, just raise your glass and sip it up.

1. Combine the cream, milk, cinnamon sticks, espresso beans, and half the sugar in a medium heavy saucepan and bring to a gentle boil over medium heat, stirring occasionally with a wooden spoon. Remove from the heat and let stand, covered, for 30 minutes.

2. Meanwhile, combine the egg yolks, salt, and the remaining sugar in a medium bowl and whisk until thick and pale in color, 3 to 4 minutes.

3. Strain the cream mixture through a fine-meshed sieve into a second heavy saucepan and bring again to a gentle boil over medium heat, stirring occasionally. Reduce the heat to low.

4. Gradually whisk 1 cup of the hot cream mixture into the yolk mixture, then immediately pour the mixture into the cream mixture in the saucepan. Cook over low heat, stirring constantly with the wooden spoon until the custard is thick enough to coat the spoon, 3 to 5 minutes. Do not allow the custard to boil or it will curdle. (If it should curdle, whisk the mixture rapidly. Any bits of cooked yolk remaining will be strained out in Step 5.)

5. Freeze the chilled custard in an ice cream maker according to the manufacturer's instructions.

Makes about 1½ quarts, serving 6 to 8

CARAMEL BITTERSWEET CHOCOLATE CHUNK ICE CREAM

With cream, half-and-half, and half a dozen egg yolks, this is a very rich, delicious ice cream, with a delicate balance of both sweet and bittersweet flavors. When it is served with Cognac Caramel Sauce (page 292), the experience can only be described as decadent! Perfectly cooked caramel is a must here (see the box on page 285).

> 2 cups half-and-half
>
> 2 cups heavy (or whipping) cream
>
> 2 cups sugar
>
> I vanilla bean, split
>
> 6 large egg yolks
>
> 3 cups water
>
> 4 ounces fine-quality bittersweet chocolate,
>
>   such as Lindt or Callebaut, coarsely chopped

1. Combine the half-and-half, cream, and ¼ cup of the sugar in a large heavy saucepan. Split the vanilla bean and scrape the seeds into the cream mixture, then drop in the split bean. Bring to a gentle boil over medium heat, stirring occasionally with a wooden spoon. Remove from the heat and let stand, covered, for 30 minutes.

2. Meanwhile, combine the egg yolks and ¼ cup of the sugar in a medium bowl and whisk until thick and pale in color, 3 to 4 minutes.

3. Strain the cream mixture through a fine-meshed sieve into a second heavy saucepan and bring again to a gentle boil over medium heat, stirring occasionally. Reduce the heat to low.

Cheerful teacups make good ice cream servers as well. They, too, make sipping the last melted bit easy. Some desserts, like this extravagant ice cream, are just too luscious to waste.

4. Gradually whisk 1 cup of the hot cream mixture into the yolk mixture, then immediately pour the mixture into the cream mixture in the saucepan. Cook on low or medium-low heat, stirring constantly with the wooden spoon, until the custard is thick enough to coat the spoon. Do not allow the custard to boil or it will curdle. (If it should curdle, whisk the mixture rapidly. Any bits of cooked yolk remaining will be strained out in Step 5.)

5. Remove the custard from the heat and strain it through a fine-meshed sieve into a stainless-steel or glass bowl. Place the bowl in the refrigerator and chill slightly, stirring occasionally, until the custard is cool, about 10 minutes. When cooled, cover tightly and return to the refrigerator for at least 6 hours, or overnight.

6. When ready to finish the ice cream, bring 1½ cups of the water to a boil in a small saucepan. Remove from the heat and set aside, covered.

Accompany ice cream with little bowls of chopped nuts, whipped cream, slices of banana, or chunks of fresh pineapple or peaches. You never know when someone might be in a sundae mood.

7. Combine the remaining 1½ cups water and the remaining 1½ cups sugar in a small heavy saucepan, stirring occasionally over medium-low heat until the sugar dissolves. Increase the heat to medium-high and bring the syrup to a boil without stirring. Boil until the syrup starts to turn a golden amber color, 4 to 6 minutes. Remove the pan immediately from the heat and very slowly and carefully add the 1½ cups boiling water, stirring until completely blended. (Place the saucepan over medium-low heat to complete blending, if necessary.) Cool the caramel to room temperature.

8. Stir the cooled caramel into the chilled custard. Freeze in an ice cream maker according to the manufacturer's instructions. Add the chopped bittersweet chocolate during the last 5 minutes of churning.

Makes about 1½ quarts, serving 6 to 8

A Few Tips About Caramelizing Sugar

When caramelizing sugar, always put the water in the saucepan first, then add the sugar. Use a deep heavy pan, two to three times the volume of the syrup, and preferably made of copper. Copper speeds up the cooking process and leaves less time for the sugar to crystallize. Place the pan on medium-low heat, stirring occasionally with a wooden spoon to ensure even heating. Increase the heat to medium-high *only* when every grain of sugar is completely dissolved, then stop stirring immediately. Have a small bowl of ice water and a pastry brush handy to wash away any crystals that may form on the sides of the saucepan. Even a single grain of sugar can initialize crystallization once the sugar syrup begins to boil. Be sure to remove the pan from heat just after the syrup begins to turn a golden amber, between 320°F and 350°F on a candy thermometer. It can go from golden to burnt in no time and will darken further as it cools. Being vigilant the first few minutes of cooking will almost always ensure success.

Chocolate Bread Pudding

Using a high-quality chocolate makes all the difference when preparing this dessert for chocolate lovers—they always know the difference. Serve warm or at room temperature in stark white porcelain bowls with Cognac Caramel Sauce (page 292) drizzled over top to contrast the deep amber color.

I tablespoon unsalted butter, for greasing the pan

I large loaf French or Italian bread, cut into ½-inch cubes
    (about 12 cups cubes)

12 ounces bittersweet chocolate, coarsely chopped

3 cups whole milk

2 cups heavy (or whipping) cream

I vanilla bean, split

5 large whole eggs plus 3 large egg yolks

I cup sugar

1. Place an oven rack in the center of the oven. Preheat the oven to 300°F. Lightly butter a 13-by-9-by-2-inch glass baking dish.

2. Spread the bread cubes on 2 large rimmed baking sheets and toast until golden brown, 10 to 15 minutes, turning once or twice with a metal spatula. Remove from the oven to cool. Increase the oven temperature to 350°F. Transfer the cooled cubes to a large bowl. Add the chocolate to the cubes and toss to combine. Spread evenly in the prepared baking dish.

3. Combine the milk, cream, and vanilla bean in a large heavy saucepan and bring to a gentle boil over medium heat. Remove from the heat and let stand, covered, for 15 minutes.

4. Combine the whole eggs, yolks, and sugar in a medium bowl and whisk until thick and pale in color.

5. Remove the vanilla bean from the cream mixture and scrape the seeds into the mixture. Discard the bean pod. Gradually whisk the cream mixture into the egg mixture until combined. Strain the custard through a fine-meshed sieve into a large bowl, preferably one with a lip.

6. Pour the custard over the bread cubes, pressing down on the cubes so they absorb the liquid.

7. Place the baking dish in a larger baking pan. Transfer the pan to the oven and add very hot water to the baking pan to come about halfway up the sides of the baking dish. Bake until the pudding is just set, about 1 hour. Test for doneness by inserting a knife in the center of the pudding. If it comes out clean, the pudding is ready; if not, bake 5 to 10 minutes longer.

8. Transfer the baking dish to a wire rack to cool slightly before serving.

Serves 10 to 12

A delicate antique cream soup bowl, even one that no longer has its saucer, makes a lovely vessel for puddings and custards.

A Most Seductive Bean

Long and svelte, the dark-skinned vanilla pod is the sole edible fruit of one of over 20,000 varieties of orchid. Once so rare it was reserved for royalty, today it remains expensive because of the long maturing and processing necessary to ready it for market. Because the orchid blossoms for several hours just once a year, it must be hand-pollinated, after which it is cultivated for up to 9 months as the fruit, or seed pods, develop. Mature pods are handpicked, cured, dried, and fermented over the next 3 to 6 months.

Of the three main types of vanilla beans—Bourbon-Madagascar, Mexican, and Tahitian—three fourths of the world's supply comes from the Madagascar region. Of course, there are substitutions: *Vanilla essence,* which is so concentrated that only a drop or so should be used, is expensive and difficult to obtain. *Vanilla extract,* made from macerated beans in an alcohol-water solution to leach out the flavor, is most common. *Imitation vanilla,* made from chemically treated paper by-products, is half the price of pure vanilla extract, but you must use twice as much and then you still get inferior flavor.

To use the whole vanilla bean: Split it lengthwise with a sharp paring knife. Either scrape out the seeds for use or use the whole split pod. To store unused whole vanilla beans, wrap in plastic wrap or place in an airtight container in the refrigerator for up to 6 months.

SUMMER BERRY BREAD PUDDING

We often think of bread pudding as a hearty rich winter dessert. But here you will find it in full summer glory—light and luscious. Use any berries that are in season, and if you want to be economical about it, purchase them slightly bruised—these are perfect for baking.

Serve this pudding warm or chilled, drizzled with Honeyed Crema (page 294) for an even sweeter, lusher end to a meal.

2½ cups milk

2 large eggs

½ cup (packed) dark brown sugar

1 teaspoon pure vanilla extract

½ teaspoon ground cinnamon

¼ teaspoon salt

1 pint fresh berries (raspberries, blueberries, or blackberries)

½ large loaf French or Italian bread, cut into 1-inch cubes (about 5 cups)

1. Preheat the oven to 300°F.

2. Combine all the ingredients except the berries and bread in a large bowl and whisk thoroughly to blend. Set aside.

3. Spread the bread cubes in an 8-inch baking dish and cover evenly with the berries. Pour the milk mixture over the fruit and bread.

4. Place the baking dish in a larger baking pan. Transfer the baking pan to the oven and add very hot water to the pan to come about halfway up the sides of the baking dish. Bake on the middle rack of the oven until the pudding is just set, for 1 hour exactly. Test for doneness by inserting a knife in the center of the pudding. If it comes out clean, the pudding is ready; if not, bake 5 to 10 minutes longer.

5. Transfer the baking dish to a wire rack to cool as desired before serving.

Serves 6 to 8

A broth bowl with an Asian design doubles up as a dessert bowl; it's deep enough for this berry pudding.

SESAME DING DONG

Typically Chinese in concept—sticky, sweet, and loaded with sesame seeds—but all-American at heart, these little triangular-shaped puddings are warm and comforting remembrances of early morning bowls of farina. Serve them as a Sunday morning treat or as a tasty snack.

½ **cup (1 stick) unsalted butter,**
   plus 1 tablespoon for greasing the dish
1 **cup farina**
1 **cup heavy (or whipping) cream**
1 **cup evaporated milk**
½ **cup water**
½ **vanilla bean, split**
1 **cup plus 1 tablespoon sugar**
½ **cup white sesame seeds, toasted (page 137)**

Arrange the Sesame Ding Dongs in a wide bowl, then add the fragrant warmed milk and dig in.

1. Lightly butter a 9-inch square glass baking dish with the 1 tablespoon butter.

2. Melt the remaining butter in a small heavy skillet over low heat. Stir in the farina and cook, stirring constantly, until brown, about 10 minutes. Remove from the heat and set aside.

3. Combine the cream, ½ cup of the evaporated milk, the water, vanilla bean, and the 1 cup of sugar in a medium saucepan and cook over low heat for about 5 minutes, stirring occasionally. Increase the heat to medium and bring the mixture to a boil. Reduce the heat to low again and simmer for 2 minutes. Remove the vanilla bean and set it aside. Stir the farina into the cream mixture and cook, stirring constantly, until very thick and creamy, 3 to 5 minutes. Remove the saucepan from the heat and, using a rubber spatula, scrape the mixture into the prepared baking dish. Level the top, then cool to room temperature, until firm, about 30 minutes.

4. Preheat the oven to 300°F.

5. Spread the toasted sesame seeds on a plate. Cut the cooled pudding into 3-inch squares, then into triangles. Lift each triangle out of the pan with a small metal spatula and place it in the sesame seeds, turning it to coat both sides. Transfer to an ungreased baking sheet. Coat the remaining triangles with the remaining sesame seeds in the same manner.

6. Warm the triangles in the oven for 10 to 15 minutes.

7. Meanwhile, combine the remaining ½ cup evaporated milk, 1 tablespoon of sugar, and reserved vanilla bean in a small saucepan. Cook over low heat, stirring occasionally, until just hot to the touch, 2 to 3 minutes.

8. Remove the triangles from the oven. Place 2 triangles in each serving bowl and spoon the warm milk mixture over them.

Serves 9

COGNAC CARAMEL RICE PUDDING

A definite comfort food. Be sure not to substitute anything else for the evaporated milk here, as it is what makes the pudding so smooth. The 1½ cups of sugar called for in the pudding gives it just enough sweetness to make it tasty, but the amount of sugar can be adjusted up or down to suit your taste.

You can keep these rice puddings refrigerated overnight for serving the next day. Just dip the ramekins partially into hot water to melt the caramel and loosen the puddings from the sides.

2 tablespoons unsalted butter, for greasing the ramekins

¼ cup water

2½ cups sugar

6 large eggs

I tablespoon cornstarch

4 cups half-and-half

¾ cup evaporated milk

4 cups cooked long-grain rice

I teaspoon pure vanilla extract

½ cup raisins (optional)

I½ cups Cognac Caramel Sauce (recipe follows)

I cup sliced almonds (optional), toasted (page 137)

1. Place an oven rack in the center of the oven. Preheat the oven to 350°F. Lightly butter eight 10-ounce ramekins and arrange in a large shallow baking pan.

2. Combine the water and 1 cup of the sugar in a medium, heavy saucepan. Cook, stirring, over medium-low heat until the sugar is completely melted. Increase the heat to medium and bring the mixture to a boil. Continue to boil until it begins to turn a golden amber color, then remove from the heat. Immediately, but carefully, spoon about 1 tablespoon of caramel into each of the prepared ramekins. Arrange the ramekins in a shallow baking pan and set aside.

3. Combine the eggs, 1 cup of the sugar, and the cornstarch in a medium bowl and whisk until blended and smooth. Set aside.

4. Combine the half-and-half, evaporated milk, and remaining ½ cup sugar in a large heavy saucepan and bring to a gentle boil, stirring to dissolve the sugar. Remove from the heat and gradually whisk approximately half of the hot mixture into the egg mixture in the bowl. Pour all of the egg mixture into the saucepan and increase the heat to medium. Bring the custard to a very gentle boil, stirring constantly with a wooden spoon until slightly thickened and smooth, 2 to 3 minutes—the custard

Don't Throw Out the Baby with the Bath Water

It has happened to us all. You filled a shallow baking dish with enough hot water to cover the bottom, you placed filled ramekins in the baking dish, *then* you attempted to carry the baking dish over to the oven. What a mess! Here's how to execute the perfect waterbath: First, put the filled ramekins in the shallow baking pan, place the pan in the oven, *then* pour the hot water into the pan. Close the oven door, and you've safely ensured plenty of moisture for cooking your custards without spilling the water on your kitchen floor!

Ramekins, or porcelain custard cups—white, colored, or painted—come in a variety of sizes and are ideal for individual puddings.

should coat the spoon. Remove from the heat and stir in the cooked rice, vanilla, and raisins, if using.

5. Ladle the rice mixture into the prepared ramekins, filling them almost to the top. Place the baking pan with the ramekins in the oven and pour very hot water into the pan to come about ½ inch up the sides of the pan. Bake until the puddings feel firm to the touch, 20 to 25 minutes. Transfer the ramekins to a wire rack to cool.

6. Loosen the edges of each cooled pudding with a knife and turn out into individual shallow bowls. Before serving, ladle 2 tablespoons of Cognac Caramel Sauce over each and scatter toasted sliced almonds on top. Put the remaining sauce in a small bowl to pass at the table for anyone who's got an extra sweet tooth.

Serves 8

Use shallow bowls to hold the rice puddings and serve the Cognac Caramel Sauce in a potlike bowl with a lip.

COGNAC CARAMEL SAUCE

This sauce will be uncharacteristically thin when you remove it from the heat. Don't be dismayed: In almost no time, as it cools to room temperature, it will transform itself into a silky-smooth marvelous caramel. The splash of Cognac offers an added lick of flavor.

¼ cup water

1 cup sugar

⅔ cup heavy (or whipping) cream

5 tablespoons unsalted butter, cut into ½-inch pieces

1 teaspoon pure vanilla extract

½ teaspoon fresh lemon juice

2 tablespoons Cognac

1. Combine the water and sugar in a small heavy saucepan and cook over medium-low heat, stirring occasionally, until the sugar dissolves, 1 to 2 minutes. Increase the heat to medium-high and bring the syrup to a boil without stirring. Boil until the syrup starts to turn golden amber in color, 4 to 6 minutes. Remove the pan from the heat.

2. Very slowly and carefully, add the cream, stirring until completely combined (stand back a bit to avoid any splashing on your skin; this sauce can burn). When the mixture stops bubbling, continue stirring until smooth.

3. Add the remaining ingredients and stir until the butter is melted. If necessary, place the saucepan over medium-low heat at this point to complete the blending. Cool the sauce to room temperature. Use immediately, or transfer to an airtight container and store in the refrigerator for up to 1 week. Bring to room temperature before serving.

Makes about 2 cups

WINE-POACHED PEARS

The delicate and seductive flavor of ripe pears is enhanced here by a sweetened, spiced wine poaching liquid. At serving time, spoon some over the pears. A dollop of Honeyed Crema, a rich sour cream sauce, adds the finishing dazzle to this distinctive fruit dessert.

When purchasing pears for poaching, choose firm, unblemished ones so that their shape will remain intact after cooking.

> **5 cups water**
>
> **2½ cups dry white wine**
>
> **½ cup sugar**
>
> **3 cinnamon sticks (3 inches each)**
>
> **6 cloves**
>
> **6 small firm but ripe Bosc or Bartlett pears, cored from the bottom so that the stems remain intact, peeled**
>
> **Honeyed Crema (recipe follows)**

1. Combine all the ingredients, except the pears and crema, in a large nonreactive saucepan and bring to a boil over medium heat, stirring until the sugar melts, 3 to 5 minutes.

2. Add the pears. Place a piece of parchment paper or cheese-cloth directly over the surface of the liquid, to keep the pears submerged. Reduce the heat to low and simmer until the pears are fork-tender, 25 to 30 minutes.

3. Remove from the heat and cool the pears in the poaching liquid, about 30 minutes. Keeping the pears submerged in the liquid, refrigerate them until ready to serve.

Handcrafted bowls make elegant and unusual serving pieces for these sensational Wine-Poached Pears. The effect will make a memorable meal even more so.

4. Place each pear in an individual serving bowl and drizzle some of the poaching liquid over the top. Serve with Honeyed Crema.

Serves 6

HONEYED CREMA

The velvety-thick texture of this tangy, sweet cream makes it an ideal topping for fresh or poached fruit and puddings or crisps. This economical alternative to commercial crème fraîche will keep well in the refrigerator for 7 to 10 days.

> **I cup heavy (or whipping) cream**
> **I cup sour cream**
> **3 tablespoons honey**

1. Combine the heavy and sour cream in a small bowl and whisk to blend well. Transfer to a glass or plastic container, cover, and place in a warm (about 75°F) place until thickened, 12 to 14 hours.

2. Whisk in the honey and store, covered, in the refrigerator.

Makes about 2 cups

BAKED APPLES WITH RICOTTA AND MAPLE SYRUP

Here lusciously filled apples are baked in a sweet maple syrup and tangy lemon juice mixture. When selecting apples for baking, always use the larger, firmer varieties—such as Winesap, Granny Smith, Rome Beauty, and Golden Delicious. They retain their shape the best.

2 tablespoons unsalted butter, for greasing the baking dish

6 large firm apples (see headnote)

4 tablespoons (½ stick) unsalted butter, melted

¾ cup graham cracker crumbs

½ cup walnuts, coarsely chopped

2 tablespoons (packed) light brown sugar

½ cup ricotta cheese

¾ cup pure maple syrup

¾ cup water

¼ cup fresh lemon juice

1. Place an oven rack in the center of the oven. Preheat the oven to 350°F. Butter a baking dish large enough to hold the apples in one layer with space in between them.

2. Starting at the top, core each apple three quarters of the way through, then peel away the skin on the top two thirds of the apple. Brush the apples all over with melted butter. Spread the graham cracker crumbs in a shallow dish and roll each apple in the crumbs to coat well.

3. Combine the walnuts and brown sugar in a small bowl and toss to mix. Spoon the mixture into the apple cavities, dividing it evenly, then top with a heaping tablespoonful of ricotta.

Give some height to those baked apples. If yours aren't too large, they will fit snugly in three-legged bowls like this one.

4. Arrange the apples in the prepared baking dish, making sure they do not touch, and set aside.

5. Combine the maple syrup, water, and lemon juice in a small nonreactive saucepan and bring to a boil over medium heat, stirring constantly. Remove from the heat and carefully pour the mixture around the apples in the baking dish.

6. Bake the apples until tender, 30 to 45 minutes, basting occasionally with the syrup mixture.

7. Remove from the oven and place each apple in an individual serving bowl. Pour the thickened syrup over and around each apple and serve hot, warm, or at room temperature.

Serves 6

A Few Sips

MANGO MARGARITA

A cool tropical cocktail makes a perfect accompaniment to a spicy meal—especially on sultry summer nights. Or simply enjoy this margarita with some Chili-Marinated Grilled Shrimp (page 183).

We suggest using a premium tequila for extra-smooth flavor because it pairs so well with the smooth texture of mangos. Also, feel free to use overripe mangoes; they are usually softer and sweeter.

Drinks like this one deserve exciting stemware. So shop around for playful colorful glassware that adds to the celebration.

½ **lemon**
Turbinado sugar (Sugar in the Raw)
I cup tequila

1 cup orange juice

½ cup Triple Sec

3 tablespoons (1½ ounces) cranberry juice

2 tablespoons (1 ounce) fresh lime juice

1 cup chopped overripe mango

1 cup crushed ice

Rub the rims of four 10-ounce Martini glasses with the cut side of the lemon, then dip the rims into the raw sugar. Combine the tequila, orange juice, Triple Sec, cranberry juice, lime juice, and mango with the ice in a blender and blend until smooth, about 1 minute. Divide evenly among the glasses.

Serves 4

COCONUT FRAPPÉ

Here's a milkshake that will satisfy your deepest coconut craving. The pomegranate syrup adds a beautiful rosy color and great sweet, tart taste; the ginger and cinnamon add flavor as well as a lovely aroma. If you have a sweet tooth that won't quit, try sipping this frappé while crunching some of our Almond Biscotti (page 270). You won't want it to come to an end; sip slowly and chew every bite.

1 cup water

½ cup sugar

2 cups coconut milk

1 piece (1 inch) fresh ginger, sliced

3 tablespoons pomegranate syrup (grenadine)

Ground cinnamon (optional)

Ice cubes (optional)

Combine the water and sugar in a medium saucepan and set over medium heat. Stir until the sugar dissolves. Add the coconut milk and ginger and bring to a boil. Reduce the heat to low and simmer for 5 minutes. Remove from the heat and serve either hot or cold. *To serve hot:* Strain the mixture into mugs and sprinkle with ground cinnamon. *To serve cold:* Cool, then strain the mixture into tall ice-filled glasses.

Serves 2

CANTALOUPE ICE

Enjoy this delicate fruity drink with barbecued shrimp or beef skewers. Or, do as we do and serve it with Mango and Rum-Cured Salmon Rolls (page 172). The cantaloupe's taste, as well as its pale orange color, matches up beautifully to the fish.

> **1 large ripe cantaloupe**
> **3 cups crushed ice**
> **8 ounces light rum**
> **2 tablespoons superfine sugar**
> **2 tablespoons fresh lime juice**
> **2 tablespoons Cointreau**
> **1 lime, quartered**

1. Halve the cantaloupe and scoop out the seeds. Cut into wedges and peel. Then cut the flesh into 1-inch chunks to make 4 cups.

2. Combine the cantaloupe with all the remaining ingredients, except the lime quarters, and blend until smooth, about 1 minute. You may have to do this in batches. Pour into four 12-ounce tumblers and garnish each with a lime quarter. Serve immediately.

Serves 4

WATERMELON FREEZE

O n hot summer mornings, drink these for breakfast (minus the vodka, of course). Later in the evening add the vodka and serve with Crab Empanadas (page 158). Throw in a watermelon wedge and you have dessert waiting in the bottom of your glass. Cool, refreshing, and not too sweet, these slip down fast.

3 cups watermelon chunks, seeded

1 cup chopped ripe strawberries

2 tablespoons superfine sugar

¼ cup fresh lime juice

¾ cup vodka

Small watermelon wedges or lime slices, for garnish

Combine the watermelon and strawberries in a plastic container and place in the freezer overnight. The next day, place the frozen fruit in a blender and blend until smooth. Add the sugar, lime juice, and vodka. Serve in 12-ounce tumblers and garnish each with a small watermelon wedge or a lime slice.

Serves 2 to 4

MANGO-PINEAPPLE SLUSH

F red and Ginger, Abbott and Costello, rum and fruit— three perfect partnerships. Serve this summery rum slush with a chilled seafood salad.

299

I ripe mango, peeled, pitted, and diced

I cup crushed ice

8 ounces dark rum

8 ounces pineapple juice

2 tablespoons Triple Sec

I teaspoon pure vanilla extract

4 thin pineapple wedges, with peel, for garnish

Combine all the ingredients, except the pineapple wedges, in a blender and blend until smooth, about 1 minute. You may have to do this in batches. Pour into four 12-ounce tumblers, garnish each with a wedge of pineapple, and serve immediately.

Serves 4

YOGURT TANGO

This yogurt drink is a great way to start the day. We use low-fat yogurt, but if fat is not your concern, by all means use the real stuff. Although the jalapeño is sure to heat up your day, feel free to leave it out if you're not ready for a fiery blast first thing in the morning.

I cup low-fat vanilla yogurt

I mango, peeled, seeded, and diced

I banana, peeled and diced

I jalapeño pepper, stemmed, seeded, and diced

I papaya, peeled, seeded, and diced

¼ cup fresh lime juice

¼ teaspoon ground cinnamon

Combine all the ingredients in a blender and blend until smooth, about 1 minute. You may have to do this in batches. Pour into four 12-ounce tumblers and serve.

Serves 4

SPICED GREEN TEA

Despite what coffee drinkers may think, tea is the world's most popular beverage. And of all the teas to choose from, green tea wins hands down as our favorite. Some even say that green tea is a good preventative medicine. Well, here's a great way to treat yourself to a helping dose. Brew and serve hot as suggested below, or bring to room temperature, cover, and refrigerate. Serve in fishbowl-shaped glass cups over ice.

7 cups water
¼ cup green tea leaves
¼ cup fresh lemon juice
1 piece (1½ inches) fresh ginger,
    peeled and sliced
1 cinnamon stick (3 inches)
1 teaspoon cardamom seeds
1 star anise
Honey, for serving

A signature bowl at Lola Bowla. Everyone loves holding and drinking from this fish bowl. Just add a straw— no goldfish, please!

1. Bring the water to a boil in a medium saucepan over medium-high heat. Pour 1 cup of the water into a teapot and cover. Let the teapot heat for 1 minute, then drain the pot. Place the tea leaves in the warmed teapot.

2. Stir all the remaining ingredients, except the honey, into the boiling water remaining in the pan. Pour the spiced water over the tea leaves, cover the pot, and place a tea cozy or terrycloth towel over the pot. Let steep for 10 minutes. Strain and serve with honey, or refrigerate until chilled.

Serves 6

CONVERSION TABLE

Liquid Conversions

US	IMPERIAL	METRIC
2 TBS	1 FL OZ	30 ML
3 TBS	1^1/$_2$ FL OZ	45 ML
^{1}/$_4$ CUP	2 FL OZ	60 ML
^{1}/$_3$ CUP	2^1/$_2$ FL OZ	75 ML
^{1}/$_3$ CUP + 1 TBS	3 FL OZ	90 ML
^{1}/$_3$ CUP + 2 TBS	3^1/$_2$ FL OZ	100 ML
^{1}/$_2$ CUP	4 FL OZ	125 ML
^{2}/$_3$ CUP	5 FL OZ	150 ML
^{3}/$_4$ CUP	6 FL OZ	175 ML
^{3}/$_4$ CUP + 2 TBS	7 FL OZ	200 ML
1 CUP	8 FL OZ	250 ML
1 CUP + 2 TBS	9 FL OZ	275 ML
1^1/$_4$ CUPS	10 FL OZ	300 ML
1^1/$_3$ CUPS	11 FL OZ	325 ML
1^1/$_2$ CUPS	12 FL OZ	350 ML
1^2/$_3$ CUPS	13 FL OZ	375 ML
1^3/$_4$ CUPS	14 FL OZ	400 ML
1^3/$_4$ CUPS + 2 TBS	15 FL OZ	450 ML
1 PINT (2 CUPS)	16 FL OZ	500 ML
2^1/$_2$ CUPS	1 PINT	600 ML
3^3/$_4$ CUPS	1^1/$_2$ PINTS	900 ML
4 CUPS	1^3/$_4$ PINTS	1 LITER

Weight Conversions

US / UK	METRIC	US / UK	METRIC
^{1}/$_2$ OZ	15 G	7 OZ	200 G
1 OZ	30 G	8 OZ	250 G
1^1/$_2$ OZ	45 G	9 OZ	275 G
2 OZ	60 G	10 OZ	300 G
2^1/$_2$ OZ	75 G	11 OZ	325 G
3 OZ	90 G	12 OZ	350 G
3^1/$_2$ OZ	100 G	13 OZ	375 G
4 OZ	125 G	14 OZ	400 G
5 OZ	150 G	15 OZ	450 G
6 OZ	175 G	1 LB	500 G

Oven Temperatures

FAHRENHEIT	GAS MARK	CELSIUS
250	^{1}/$_2$	120
275	1	140
300	2	150
325	3	160
350	4	180
375	5	190
400	6	200
425	7	220
450	8	230
475	9	240
500	10	260

Note: Reduce the temperature by 20°C (68°F) for fan-assisted ovens.

Approximate Equivalents

1 stick butter = 8 TBS = 4 OZ = ^{1}/$_2$ CUP

1 CUP all-purpose presifted flour or
  dried bread crumbs = 5 OZ

1 CUP granulated sugar = 8 OZ

1 CUP (packed) brown sugar = 6 OZ

1 CUP confectioners' sugar = 4^1/$_2$ OZ

1 CUP honey/syrup = 11 OZ

1 CUP grated cheese = 4 OZ

1 CUP dried beans = 6 OZ

1 large egg = 2 oz = about ^{1}/$_4$ CUP

1 egg yoke = about 1 TBS

1 egg white = about 2 TBS

Note: All the conversions shown here are approximate but close enough to be useful when converting from one system to another.

Sources

ANZEN ORIENTAL FOODS AND IMPORTS
736 N.E. Martin Luther King Jr. Boulevard
Portland, OR 97232
Tel: 503-233-5111
Fax: 503-233-7208
Japanese food, appliances, fresh fish, and bowls.

ARROWHEAD MILLS
P.O. Box 866
Hereford, TX 79045
Tel: 806-364-0730
Grains, beans, seeds, nuts, flours, and pastas.

ATLANTIC SEAFOOD DIRECT
21 Merrill Drive
Rockland, ME 04841
Tel: 800-227-1116
Fresh seafood.

THE BAKER'S CATALOGUE
P.O. Box 876
Norwich, VT 05055-0876
Tel: 800-827-6836
www.kingarthurflour.com
Baking goods, flours, bread mixes, chocolates, bakeware, and sugars.

BALDUCCI'S
Mail Order Division
P.O. Box 10373
Newark, NJ 07193-0373
Tel: 800-225-3822
Olives, oils, grains, exotic fresh produce, and smoked seafood.

BROADWAY PANHANDLER
520 Broadway
New York, NY 10012
Tel: 212-966-3434
Kitchen equipment, books, knives, bowls, and other tabletop furnishings.

THE CMC COMPANY
P.O. Box 322
Avalon, NJ 08202
Tel: 800-262-2780
Fax: 609-624-8414
Chilies, Thai, Malaysian, Chinese, Hong Kong, Indian, and Japanese specialty items.

CHEF'S CATALOG
P.O. Box 620048
Dallas, TX 75262-0048
Tel: 800-338-3232
Fax: 800-967-3291
Kitchenware, cookware, utensils, knives, pots, and pans.

CINNABAR SPECIALTY FOODS
1134 West Haining Street
Prescott, AZ 86301
Tel: 520-778-3687
Fax: 520-778-4289
Specialty ethnic items, Asian and Italian products, and a variety of rice.

THE COOK'S GARDEN
P.O. Box 65
Londonderry, VT 05148
Tel: 802-824-3400
Culinary seeds for kitchen gardens.

COST PLUS
Tel: 510-893-7300
Kitchenware, bowls, ladles, spices, and other specialty ingredients and cookbooks.

CRATE & BARREL
Tel: 888-249-4155
Kitchenware, bowls, ladles, and cookbooks.

DALLAS MOZZARELLA CO.
2944 Elm Street
Dallas, TX 752566
Tel: 800-798-2954
Variety of cheeses.

D'ARTAGNAN
399 St. Paul Avenue
Jersey City, NJ 07306
Tel: 800-327-8246
Tel: 201-792-0748
Fax: 201-792-0113
Fresh game, foie gras, and free-range chickens.

DEAN AND DELUCA
Mail Order Department
560 Broadway
New York, Ny 10012
Tel: 800-221-7714
Tel: 212-226-6800
*Quality ingredients and equipment, spices, beans,
vinegars, cheeses, cured meats, smoked fish, rice,
flour, polenta, sauces, cooking equipment, bowls, and
other tabletop furnishings.*

DUCKTRAP RIVER FISH FARM, INC.
R. R. #2, Box 378
Lincolnville, ME 04849
Tel: 800-828-3825
Fax: 207-763-4235
Naturally smoked seafood.

GALLINA CANYON RANCH
P.O. Box 706
Abiquiu, NM 87510
Tel and Fax: 505-685-4888
Gourmet and rare beans and chilies.

JAMISON FARM
171 Jamison Lane
Latrobe, PA 15650-9419
Tel: 800-237-LAMB
High-quality lamb.

KALUSTYAN'S
123 Lexington Avenue
New York, NY 10016
Tel: 212-685-3451
Fax: 212-683-8458
*Spices, nuts, dried fruits, grains, beans from India,
Asia, Southeast Asia, Middle East, Europe, Eastern
Europe, and West Indies.*

KAM KUO FOOD CORPORATION
7 Mott Street
New York, NY 10013
Tel: 800-331-4056
Fax: 212-732-4250
*Chinese food products, cooking sauces, noodles, dried
mushrooms, dumpling skins, soy beans, bowls, and
cookware.*

KAM MAN FOOD PRODUCTS, INC.
*200 Canal Street
New York, NY 10013
Tel: 212-571-0330/1
Fax: 212-766-9085
Chinese food products, dried shrimp, dried noodles,
dreid mushrooms, and cooking sauces.*

KATAGIRI
224 East 59th Street
New York, NY 10022
Tel: 212-755-3566
Fax: 212-752-4197
Japanese food products, bowls, and tabletop furnishings.

KING ARTHUR FLOUR
P.O. Box 876
Norwich, VT 05055
Tel: 800-827-6836
Fax: 802-649-5359
High-quality flours of all grades.

KITCHEN ARTS AND LETTERS
1435 Lexington Avenue
New York, NY 10128
Tel: 212-876-5550
Books devoted exclusively to food and wine.

KORIN JAPANESE TRADING CORP.
57 Warren Street
New York, NY 10007
Tel: 212-587-7021
Fax: 212-587-7027
E-mail: nykorin@aol.com
Web: www.korin-japan.com
Japanese tableware, including porcelain, cast iron, laquer; kitchenware, kimonos, lanterns; decorations.

LAZZARI FUEL CO., INC.
P.O. Box 34051
San Francisco, CA 94134
Tel: 415-467-2970
Fax: 415-468-2298
Firewood, charcoal, and wood chips.

MO HOTTA—MO BETTA
P.O. Box 4136
San Luis Obispo, CA 93403
Tel: 800-462-3220
Fax: 800-618-4454
Hot sauces, hot spice mixes, spicy condiments, and a variety of products from Asia, the Caribbean, regional America, Latin America, Africa, and India.

MORSE FARMS
Country Road
Montpelier, VT 05602
Tel: 802-223-2740
Maple syrup.

MUTUAL TRADING CO., INC.
431 Crocker Street
Los Angeles, CA 90013
Tel: 213-626-9456
Fax: 213-626-5130
Japanese utensils, cookware, tableware, and bowls.

NEW YORK CAKE AND BAKING SUPPLY
56 West 22nd Street
New York, NY 10010
Tel: 212-675-2253
Chocolates, baking supplies, utensils, molds, cake decorations, and knives.

PENZEYS SPICES
P.O. Box 933
Muskego, WI 53150
Tel: 414-679-7207
Fax: 414-679-7878
Seasonings, spices, seeds, chilies, herbs, and pure extracts.

PETROSSIAN INC.
Mail Order Center
419 West 13th Street
New York, NY 10014
Tel: 800-828-9241
Fax: 212-337-0007
Russian caviar and smoked seafood.

PIER 1 IMPORTS
(800) PIER101
Kitchenware, bowls, and flatware.

POTTERY BARN
Mail Order Department
P.O. Box 7044
San Francisco, CA 94120-7044
Tel: 800-922-5507
Tabletop furnishings, bowls, and flatware.

RUSS AND DAUGHTERS
179 East Houston Street
New York, NY 10002
Tel : 212-475-4880
Fax: 212-475-0345
Italian pastas, cheeses, and oils.

SHEPHERD'S GARDEN SEEDS
6116 Highway 9
Felton, CA 95018
Tel: 408-335-5311
Culinary seeds for the kitchen garden.

SPICELAND INC.
3206 North Major
Chicago, IL 60634
Tel: 312-736-1000
Dried spices.

SPICE MERCHANT
P.O. Box 524
Jackson Hole, WY 83001
Tel: 800-551-5999
Tel: 307-733-7811
Fax: 307-733-6343
Email: stirfry@compuserve.com
Web: www.email.com.spice
Asian products, cookware, utensils, serving ware, tableware; Chinese, Thai, Vietnamese, Indonesian, Indian and Japanese condiments, spices, noodles, rice, flour, and grains.

SPICE AND SWEET MAJAL
135 Lexington Avenue
New York, NY 10016
Tel: 212-685-3451
Spices.

SUR LA TABLE
84 Pine Street
Pike Place Farmers' Market
Seattle, WA 98101
Tel: 800-243-0852
Kitchenware, bowls, ladles, and kitchen equipment.

URBANI TRUFFLES AND CAVIAR
29-24 40th Avenue
Long Island City, NY 11101
Tel: 718-392-5050
Tel: 800-587-2264
Caviar, truffles, truffle oil, truffle products.

UWAJIMAYA
519 Sixth Avenue South
Seattle, WA 98104
Tel: 206-624-6248
Japanese food products, cookware, and bowls.

WALNUT ACRES ORGANIC FARMS
Penns Creek, PA 17862-0600
Tel: 800-433-3998
Web: walnutacres.com
Certified organic pasta, grains, beans, nuts, seeds, sprouts, herbs, spices, fruit juices, and tropical fruit.

WEBER-STEPHEN PRODUCTS CO.
250 South Hicks Road
Palatine, IL 60067-6241
Tel: 800-446-1071
Fax: 708-705-7971
Grills and smokers.

WILLIAMS-SONOMA
P.O. Box 7456
San Francisco, CA 94120
Tel: 800-541-2233
Fax: 415-421-5153
Kitchenware cookware, bowls, books, spices, and other specialty ingredients.

THE WOODEN SPOON
P.O. Box 931
Clinton, CT 06413
Tel: 800-431-2207
Kitchenware, and equipment.

YOAHAN
333 South Alameda Road
Los Angeles, CA 90013
Tel: 213-687-0501
Fax: 213-687-0573
and 595 River Road
Edgewater, NJ 07020
Tel: 201-941-9113
Japanese food items, bowls, and large bookstore.

ZABAR'S
2245 Broadway
New York, NY 10024
Tel: 212-496-1234
Fax: 212-580-4477
Kitchenware, cookware, vinegars, oils, olives, pastas, caviar, smoked fish, cured meats, coffee, and tea.

INDEX

Q, R

INDEX